A SHELL EYE ON ENGLAND

A SHELL EYE ON ENGLAND

THE SHELL COUNTY GUIDES 1934–1984

DAVID HEATHCOTE

LIBRI
PUBLISHING

Published in 2011 by Libri Publishing ■ Copyright © David Heathcote ■ ISBN: 978 1 907471 07 0 ■ All rights reserved. No part of this publication may be reproduced, stored in any retrieval system or transmitted in any form or by any means, electronic, mechanical, photocopying, recording or otherwise, without the prior written permission of the copyright holder for which application should be addressed in the first instance to the publishers. No liability shall be attached to the author, the copyright holder or the publishers for loss or damage of any nature suffered as a result of reliance on the reproduction of any of the contents of this publication or any errors or omissions in its contents. ■ A CIP catalogue record for this book is available from The British Library ■ Front cover photography: Sue Barr 2010. heathcotebarr.eu ■ Design by Helen Taylor ■ Printed in the UK by Ashford Colour Press ■ Libri Publishing, Brunel House, Volunteer Way, Faringdon, Oxfordshire SN7 7YR ■ Tel: +44 (0)845 873 3837 ■ www.libripublishing.co.uk

DEDICATION

*TO BRIDGET MARY FAIRWEATHER, MY WIFE, A GREAT EXPLORER
AND DISCOVERER OF BEAUTY IN UNLIKELY PLACES.*

ACKNOWLEDGEMENTS

This book owes its existence in part to Zoe Hendon of the Museum of Domestic Design and Architecture (MoDA) who first asked me to produce a talk about the Shell Guides and then supported my suggestion of an exhibition at the museum on the same subject. I would also like to thank the staff at MoDA for their great help in enabling me to curate the exhibition through their various expertise and general enthusiasm. It is to Sylvester Bone that the thanks must go for goading me to write a book on the subject and I would like to thank him for his personal support and also his family for their help in loans of pictures and rare guides that could not easily be procured elsewhere. I must also thank Nicky Balfour of the Shell Art Collection for her interest and support in finding material for the exhibition and the book and above all helping me gain support from Shell for the publication of the book. I must also thank Sue Barr, my friend and colleague, for her invaluable and unstinting support in undertaking the photography for the exhibition and the book. Equally I must thank Celia Cozens for her support of the project and the unwise decision to be my publisher; and Matt Skipper for acting as my editor. I also need to thank my friend Dorothea Strube in Berlin for finding me space to write when I needed it.

Debbie Christie was a crucial supporter who through her actions enabled me to meet people involved with the guides, among lots of other things. There are many other people to thank but John Beddington, Lady Juliet Townsend, Luke Piper, Bevis Hillier, Peter Burton, and Norman Scarfe were generous and invaluable interviewees. I would also like to thank Chris Mawson for his wonderful website, R.M. Healey for his writing about the Shell Guides and Ruth Artmonsky for her support and book about Jack Beddington.

Lastly there are the great books about the protagonists, Betjeman and Piper, by Candida Lycett Green, Frances Spalding, Bevis Hillier, Timothy Mowl and, last but not at all least, William S. Peterson.

CONTENTS

*Plaster-work ceiling in the Long Gallery, Lanhydrock House, Cornwall,
by A.F. Kersting,* Cornwall, *1964, rear end-paper*

The Shell County Guides were published for fifty years, from 1934 to1984, and in that time 35 counties were covered as well as the West Coast of Scotland and the Channel and South Coast Harbours. Many of the guides were re-written, which in total adds up to over 50 different editions; and most were revised, some several times. As well as new writing and textual revisions, the guides were regularly redesigned some three or four times: layouts and typefaces were modified; softcover bindings changed to hardback, or vice versa; or colour images were introduced, either as a frontispiece or on the cover. When the series finally ceased production there were two guides still on the stocks, Peter Burton's *Yorkshire* and David Lloyd's *Bedfordshire*. Some counties like Cheshire and West Sussex, almost all of Scotland and all of Northern Ireland had never had a guide. There are other books intimately related to the Shell Guides. In 1937 John Piper's Shell Guide *Oxon* excluded the city of Oxford because John Betjeman had published his own guide to that city, *An Oxford University Chest*. Just before the resumption of the Shell County Guide Series with the publication of *Shropshire* in 1951, John Betjeman and John Piper produced three Murray's Architectural Guides to the counties of Buckinghamshire, Berkshire and Lancashire, the first two written by Betjeman and Piper, the third by Peter Fleetwood-Hesketh. Stephen Bone's Shell Guide, *West Coast of Scotland: Skye to Oban,* was preceded by a guide written with his mother that was published in 1925 (winning a prize for its woodcut illustrations by Stephen Bone) and W.G. Hoskins' *Rutland* and *Leicestershire* were preceded by guides to Rutland and Leicestershire he'd written for Leicester City Authority Publicity Department, in 1948 and 1949. A version of his *Rutland* is still in print today, as is Peter Burton's *North Yorkshire* which remains a Shell Guide in all but name.

The Shell Guides are not only guides to 35 counties in a myriad of editions, issues and designs. More importantly, they are essays on the nature of a vast subject – 'the country', in most of its meanings, during a complex half century of change. They are the product of the reflections of many good authors and photographers, and their editors, John Betjeman and John Piper, whose work in other media is more documented despite the fact that the Shell Guides were their most complex works.

The problem is how to deal with this modest juggernaut. Luckily, others have written biographies of many of the protagonists and there are many histories of the period for context. Equally, there is no need for a detailed bibliophile history of the series as this too has been done, by Chris Mawson, and is freely available on the web. This book, then, is partly about the development of the Shell Guides into a new type of text where there is a narrative equivalence between word and image. From this point of view, the guides are a prototype of what we now call 'the media': they are a kind of static television and not really books at all. The other part of this book is an attempt to understand the vision of national identity in the Shell Guides – because despite, or because of, its limitation to rural and non-metropolitan southern Britain, the series is the largest essay on the relationship between our physical environment and British identity in the twentieth century.

HOLIDAYS

THIS IS A BOOK ABOUT THE Shell County Guides which were published between 1934 and 1984. They were sponsored by the oil company Shell and were intended as guides for motorists. They weren't the first guides to British counties, nor the first motoring guides, nor even a complete guide to the counties; but they are, with Pevsner's Buildings of England series, the best guides to the counties of England and Wales (with a brief foray to Scotland's West coast).

Their unique quality comes from the combination of literature, antiquarianism, art and design with a devotion to expressing and revealing the pleasures of driving around counties by minor roads through smaller towns. Their vision was part *Under Milk Wood,* part local historical, part modernist, part conservationist; but underlying all these was a sense of holiday. These were holidays of a kind now lost in a rush to the sun by air: the Sunday drive, the weekend away, two weeks by the sea at Easter and the long drive.

The oldest and longest-published titles of the Shell Guides included *Cornwall*, *Devon* and *Dorset*, the archetypal holiday destinations of the twentieth-century English motorist who was predominantly middle class and perversely seeking that most English of vacations, the search for the unspoilt and untouristy. What these terms meant has more to do with what had happened to England in the early phases of mass tourism, which pre-dated motor tourism. This is best summed up in the contemporary idea that a traveller is not a tourist; a traveller is a seeker of the authentic place.

For many writers on Britain there was a golden age of an authentic country. This was the period when the British traveller roamed the Lake District and the Wye Valley, a romantic seeker of the sublime or the national character. This sort of experience is often contrasted with another category, the holiday – in particular the seaside holiday.

By the early twentieth century, the British seaside was a very well-developed tourist market. Because of the nature of mass travel before the car, these holidays were a very contained and artificial experience. Seaside towns developed as tourist destinations by offering ever-more contrived diversions from the core experience of the sea; but all of these were within walking distance of a destination arrived at by train. Seaside holiday destinations became satellites of the cities they served, no matter how distant; and as holidays became more democratic, seaside resorts tried to offer popular urban pleasures in their 'healthy' environment.

The original makers of holidays by the sea, the middle class, initially sought and developed newer, more exclusive, destinations; but here too there were often experiences which were no less inauthentic than the holiday entertainments of working-class tourists. Thus at Lynmouth in north Devon, a walk along the cliffs took on a more fashionably Swiss tone with the addition of Toggenburg goats to the land around the circular cliff-top promenade, which was reached via the funicular railway. Within the middle class there was

Stephen Bone's 'Girls in an Open Car', courtesy of Sylvester Bone

a reaction to this kind of resort and it took two forms. One was the development of the idea of holidaying in a cottage. The other was the cycling or walking holiday. Both these types of middle-class holiday developed fast in the late nineteenth century and have complex motivations; but principle amongst these was the desire to find a more 'real', authentic experience of the source of middle-class identity – the solid values and history of the country – in places which were neither industrial nor metropolitan.

By the early twentieth century, the coastal districts of Cornwall and Devon were being developed piecemeal into areas rather than places of resort, packed with second homes, retirees and people seeking out sites of historical interest. Seaside resorts were for the many but the country beyond was for the few. Yet despite these developments and class differentiations, nowhere within the purview of tourism could be very far from a train station and a good road.

The railway spawned its own guidebooks based on those designed for the early-nineteenth-century boom in middle-class "travellers to the Continent": the Baedeker and Murray guides. These, though they developed before the train, embraced the railways as arteries of tourism. Railways offered the non-aristocratic travellers who were the main market for these guides a simple, predictable way of getting from A to B without having to hire horses, carriages and guides. In Britain, guidebooks emerged which were

An open-top tourer rushing past red-brick Victorian suburbs toward a day out. Stephen Bone's image conveys the new freedom that increasingly cheap motor cars offered well-off contemporaries of John Betjeman in the late 1920s.

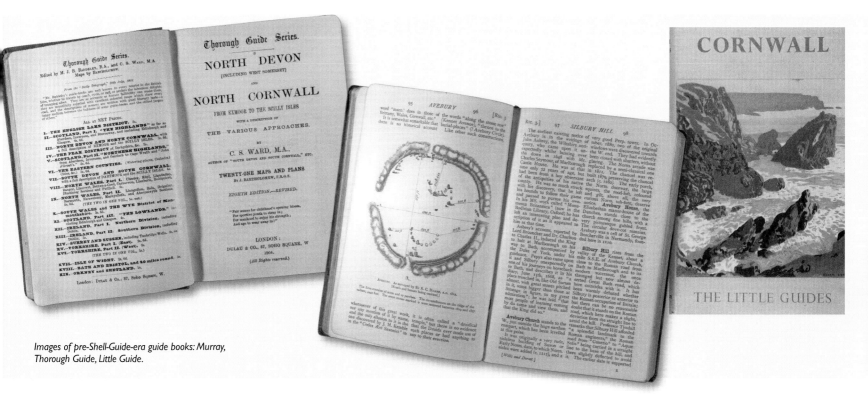

Images of pre-Shell-Guide-era guide books: Murray,
Thorough Guide, Little Guide.

based on either the railway network or destinations served by the rail network, and these guides were produced either by railway companies, tourist towns or tour companies like Thomas Cook. The guidebooks to resorts offered a description of what could be achieved on foot within the resort, along with a limited number of nearby excursions to 'places of interest'. More interesting are guides like Baddeley and Ward's 'Thorough Guides' which gave accounts of extended excursions into the country from rail stations. These guides were for the very intrepid and might involve a 17-mile walk as a day's outing or hiring a fisherman at Padstow to row you around the headland before a longish walk back to Padstow across country. These 'Thorough Guides' were aimed at the adventurous middle class in search of the real country, just as hiring a cottage a gig ride from the station put you in the middle of the country with only 'locals' as neighbours.

It was not only the middle-class tourist who sought the authentic England or was concerned at its loss to urban development and tourism. From the 1850s, Tennyson's Arthurian poem cycle *Idylls of the King* turned a sleepy and inaccessible Cornish village into a tourist town by suggesting it was Arthur's birthplace. In the 1840s, Tintagel was called Trevena and was a neglected village of medieval houses. By the 1880s it had long been renamed Tintagel (after the headland on which the ruins of the castle stood) and the

railway had arrived nearby – near enough to cause an exponential growth in tourism that led to the demolition of the old village to make way for new boarding houses, shops, pubs and hotels. One house was left, now known as the Old Post Office, and in 1903 it was saved for the nation by the new National Trust, a new part of The Establishment. The Old Post Office was almost the first National Trust property and its preservation was caused by an increasing anxiety that the forces of modernisation were destroying the deep tilth of historic Britain, considered so important to the national identity as a talisman of culture and stability. Before the preservation of the Old Post Office, the idea of Tintagel and King Arthur, with its linking of Ancient Britain and the Christian God, was considered an important part of the national identity in a way that the old village wasn't.

The preservation of the Old Post Office marked a point where national myths such as that of King Arthur came into conflict with a newer and more sophisticated set of ideas about national identity. These coalesced around the preservation of ancient structures as a way of holding onto a real, as opposed to mythic, national identity. Because objects that remain from the past are the tangible traces of that past, they are in a very literal way a part of the national identity, unlike the mythic Tintagel or King Arthur. The rise of this idea might have been expected to erode the authenticity of Tintagel in the

These guides were the precursors of the Shell Guides. Because they were based on pedestrian travel, they were packed with information on what could be achieved from various base points linked to the railway network. The essential problem facing their publishers was the combination of compactness with density of information, and this may be what led to similarities of format that amount almost to a convention: small size, snappy title and generic red cover, to make the range and type of the guide easily identifiable; plus an exhaustive description of its scope on the title page. Early Shell Guides emulated this latter feature in their ironic title pages; but by the later fifties they were simply described as "Shell Guides".

Arthurian myth. Yet what actually happened at Tintagel was not the substitution of this newer concept of national identity for an older mythic one but a simple and unquestioned creation of a compound concept in which real things and myths affirmed one another – which, after all, was the point of much archaeology in the nineteenth century. With the preservation of ancient monuments came the elision of the mythic, the ancient object, the authentic and the national identity. Tintagel as a site of national identity was actually enhanced by the preservation of ancient buildings; their authenticity shone on the myth of Arthur and vice versa, and this in turn made Tintagel a place of popular pilgrimage in an age of nationalism.

It was into this new world of middle-class aspiration and burgeoning anxiety about loss of the authentic that a young John Betjeman arrived with his father at about the time of the First World War. Betjeman's father had built an Arts and Crafts holiday house at Trebetherick, St Minver near Padstow and the family would travel by train from Paddington to Wadebridge and then to the house by horse and trap. By then Cornwall was a place known for its fishing villages through the work of the Newlyn artists and also as a place for bohemian artistic goings on. It was seen as a primitive, ancient place of myths and legends, of Arthur and Tristan but also witches and mysterious animals of the kind that inspired Conan Doyle's *The Hound of the Baskervilles*. It was a place of romantic and wicked locals, wreckers of ships and of course ghosts. To the city dweller it was also a country of warmth, early tomatoes, potatoes, daffodils and primroses. The Cornwall of Betjeman's youth was a place he could explore and as he did so, he developed his taste for old churches and chapels and also for the nineteenth-century Cornwall of tin mines, china clay, prosperous high streets and failed port schemes. All this is clear in his Shell Guide, *Cornwall*, of 1964.

It was a few years later that my mother and father transferred their Liverpudlian allegiances from North Wales and Portmeirion to a cottage in Boscastle rented from the National Trust. Later we moved on to Cadgwith on the Lizard and Cotehele on the Tamar. It was a long way to Cornwall and a fraught journey in the little cars and busy roads of the day, full of men like my father reliving the tensions of Betjeman's poem on the joys of the A30:

> A man on his own in a car
> > Is revenging himself on his wife;
> He opens the throttle and bubbles with dottle
> > and puffs at his pitiful life.
>
> "She's losing her looks very fast,
> > She loses her temper all day;
> That lorry won't let me get past,
> > This Mini is blocking my way.

> "Why can't you step on it and shift her!
> > I can't go on crawling like this!
> At breakfast she said that she wished I was dead –
> > Thank heavens we don't have to kiss.
>
> "I'd like a nice blonde on my knee
> > And one who won't argue or nag.
> Who dares to come hooting at *me*?
> > I only give way to a Jag.
>
> "You're barmy or plastered, I'll pass you, you bastard –
> > I *will* overtake you. I *will*!"
> As he clenches his pipe, his moment is ripe
> > And the corner's accepting its kill.

('Meditation on the A30', 1960)

In the late sixties and early seventies, Cornwall was very, very busy with holidaymakers – so busy in fact that new one-way systems and pedestrianisation schemes had to be developed for its old fishing villages crammed with shell shops, witch museums, tea rooms, bakeries and chippies. At that time there were more than a quarter of a million visitors to tiny village towns like Polperro and most of these came over the two-month duration of the spring and summer school holidays. Nowadays visitor numbers are more like 25,000 per year.

Mum and dad were typical middle-class tourists of the sixties and seventies, he a civil servant and she a housewife. They had done well at school and gone to university, moved south and set up home in south London. We lived in a typical modern town house surrounded by other young families. When we were young we had a Mini and then later a larger Austin 1100 estate designed, like the Mini, according to modern principles. We listened to pop music on the radio, ate off melamine. We had Scandinavian-type furniture and Beatles records. We children went to a modern mixed primary school. At Easter and for two weeks in the summer we would head west to a cottage in a small village or on its own. We sometimes stayed overnight at Shaftesbury on route and always drove past Stonehenge. Our holidays were a mixture of suitably un-touristy, though busy, beaches, and sightseeing sights that included ancient monuments, Arthurian places, stately homes and gardens, and craft shops – with a rare occurrence of fish and chips. We were taught to appreciate the real and to disdain the classic British seaside town as common. It was an age before irony.

What we children wanted were the shell shops, the ice creams, the beach shop for shrimping nets and, later, belly boards and endless hours on the beach. My parents on the other hand wanted craft shops, sub-tropical gardens, cream teas and, for my father, Dozmary Pool or a clapper bridge on Dartmoor, with an obligatory look at the prison. The beach for them mainly involved sitting on a blanket

'On the River Fowey', Edwin Smith, from *Cornwall*, 1964, p.32

'King Harry Passage, River Fal', Judges' photographs, from *Cornwall*, 1964, p.54

Cornwall was also full of pictures of mysterious and adventurous places, which was for me the essence of an ideal holiday. This may explain why I have always thought Edwin Smith's image of the River Fowey which is pregnant with possibilities of adventure was in fact the more romantic sounding Frenchman's Creek. The King Harry Ferry was full of promise to be exactly like crossing the Orinoco in a canoe.

Though I did not know it at the time the strangeness of these images represented the editors' own taste for the surreal as much as mine for the funny, odd and strange. The appeal of Betjeman and Piper's interest in the surreal was that it always retained a very accessible childlike quality often lacking in Surrealist art.

Altarnun Font, John Piper, from *Cornwall*, 1964, p.11

Roof figures St Ives Church, Studio St Ives Ltd., from *Cornwall*, 1964, p.52

Crucifixion on Celtic type cross head, St Buryan, John Piper, from *Cornwall*, 1964, p.24

eating a picnic while we disappeared into the melee of kids on the sand and in the surf. Somewhere like Tintagel was problematic for my parents since the castle was impressive, as were its vertiginous cliffs and tiny beaches promising a glimpse of seals, but the shops in the village with their arrays of child-friendly knick-knacks, sweets and snacks represented a gauntlet that had to be run at every new tourist destination we visited.

But how did my father know about Dozmary Pool, the Cornish Alps or Wesley preaching at Altarnun, or indeed the attempts to develop Padstow as a mail port? For that matter, how did we find Polzeath beach or the King Harry Ferry? They were in the Shell Guide that I think we initially borrowed from the Kidbrook Library and later Mum bought for Dad. Betjeman's *Cornwall* operated at a number of levels that were a result of the way the writing, the pictures and the layout were designed to work together. Picking up and flicking through the Shell *Cornwall*, it was full of images that were mood essays making everything seem interesting, beautiful, dramatic or mysterious. There were enticing things for adults and children alike. Beyond beaches there was a slightly sinister Frenchman's Creek, and some funny, surreal religious figures photographed against a sea view at St Ives; but equally there were close ups of seal pups on a beach. Even to a child these were intriguing views. The guide's captions would tell you where in the gazetteer the written entry on the place could be found and letters and numbers indexed the location on a Bartholomew's map in the rear of the book. The image

of the King Harry Ferry or the Helston Furry Dance would lead one to a thorough description of the thing, delivered with a light touch and an eye for anecdote and contextual observation. The entry for Polzeath which was illustrated and discussed in the introduction of the book was actually found under an entry for St Minver. This directed you not to the beach but to other interesting local features, a technique of mild misdirection that was designed to lead you deeper into the county.

Betjeman's 1964[1] *Cornwall* clearly displays another of the guides' techniques, the very personal point of view of its entries. In the Cornwall guide it is clear that Betjeman is often recalling childhood experiences, young adult impressions and then the rather elegiac feelings of a man in middle age so that the book is by turns enthusiastic, impressionistic, train-spotterish and nostalgic for a past lost to the pressures of tourism. Nothing is more redolent of Betjeman's feelings than the early images of the book, the Atlantic waves of the cover, Edwin Smith's close up of lustrous wet pebbles, a child's view, and the juxtaposition of Stanhope Forbes' *The Lighthouse, Newlyn* (1893), painted not long before Betjeman's birth, and Osbert Lancaster's cartoon 'Evening Shadows, Polzeath' – opposite which Betjeman notes "showing all-electric Cornwall today". In the introduction, a photo of Polzeath, 1916, at which time Betjeman was eight, is contrasted to Polzeath in 1964, not long before I and my sisters went to the same beach shop. Strangely, it looks pretty much today as it did in 1964.

Polzeath in North Cornwall became a popular beach from the late nineteenth century onwards, after the railway reached first Wadebridge and then Padstow. It is still popular today, though busier than when Betjeman lamented its crowds in the early sixties. It is often represented as 'empty' – the ideal of the Cornwall holidaymaker – as seen here in a postcard card from 1980.

Repro of Postcard of Polzeath, Cornwall (1980), Colourmaster Int'l PAD 203

Two images of Polzeath, in 1916 and c.1960, from Cornwall, 1964, p.8

Edwin Smith, endpapers of Cornwall

Cover of Cornwall, *1964*

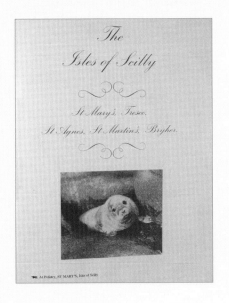

Far left: Seal, *by James Gibson,* Cornwall, *1964, p.131*

Middle left: Frontispiece, The Lighthouse, Newlyn *(1893) by Stanhope Forbes, © Manchester City Galleries*

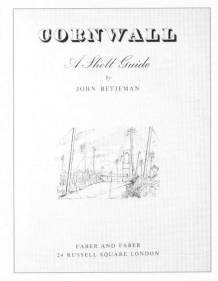

Left: Cornwall *title page with Osbert Lancaster cartoon*

Cornwall was the first Shell Guide I saw as a child. It drew me in because, in common with all the later Shell Guides, the initial images summed up the possibilities of the county and, interspersed with the more serious pictures, were always a few that were simply pleasurable – and they said beaches, boats and seals. Though Osbert Lancaster's cartoon had an adult meaning, I liked all the wires that the adults hated.

9

Betjeman's second *Cornwall*'s mix of history and description, memoir and review creates in the reader the sense that one is visiting a place that one already knows about, even down to a sense of the changes that have occurred – almost like a false memory. One effect of this is that after what is in reality a brief time (say a few weeks) of looking through the guide and visiting places described in it, one is left with a feeling that one knows Cornwall in a way that more narrowly descriptive guides like Pevsner's cannot create. This intimacy is something that the Shell Guides achieved in a format that allowed the reader to be shallow, to dip into the book rather than have to immerse themselves in a long narrative, of the form that highly personal guides usually adopt.

There was a good reason why Betjeman's *Cornwall* was so long in its vision and so personal. Not only did he re-present in his middle years his experiences as an Edwardian child, he also incorporated elements of his initial guide to Cornwall, written in the arch certainty of his late twenties as the first Shell Guide of the series, in 1933–4. The effect of this is that the 1964 *Cornwall* has elements in its writing of childish excitement, youthful irony and mature ambivalence, all lying just beneath the surface of the apparently self-denying pragmatics of a guidebook. Highly constructed yet compressed arguments are read onto the mute objects and locations that form the pretext of the guides' entries. This subversive combination of high subjectivity in the bland clothes of a guide is what characterises all of the best Shell County Guides, and it is this that made them such a powerful medium for the construction of a coherent ideology of national identity by reading highly constructed yet compressed arguments onto the mute objects and contexts that were the objects of entries in the guides.

NOTES

1 The rewrite of the guide was originally proposed in 1955; Betjeman did not want to do it and so the gazetteer was offered to G. Grigson, who turned it down. It was then offered to J.H. Willmott of the *Cornish Guardian* and Betjeman urged him to revise it freely. Some time later in 1959 the text came in and Betjeman disliked it for its antiquarianism. A new draft from Willmott came in later in 1959; John Piper said in a letter to D. Bland at Faber that it was "dull, wordy and commonplace". Betjeman rewrote it in the end and didn't like the original design. It was finally published in 1964. John Piper later said, "It is by far the best of the lot". See Peterson, 2006.

CORNWALL

IT IS HARD NOW TO IMAGINE that in the early decades of the twentieth century roads were something that had been neglected for over fifty years. The last time there had been a period of road modernisation was in the late eighteenth and early nineteenth centuries – notably Thomas Telford's London to Holyhead road, constructed to speed communications with Ireland, which survives as the A5 and the development of the macadam road by John Loudon McAdam, an effective and economical road surface and the precursor of the modern Tarmac road. After this, the development of the railways brought a neglect of roads, especially trunk roads, because rail was faster than any other form of transport. Earlier guidebooks to roads that listed the major routes to and fro across the realm gave way to Bradshaw's, while guides like Murray's used the railway as opposed to roads to create tourist itineraries across Britain. But with the invention of the motorcar the old cross-country road network became useful for more than local traffic once again. Early motor tourists were rich men with a motoring hobby. Gordon Russell describes in his autobiography *Designer's Trade* how his father's hotel, the Lygon Arms at Broadway, played host to Edward the Seventh and Henry Ford. Their cars were large, expensive and unreliable, a sport rather than a utility. The idea of the open road was also popular with the Chelsea bohemians of the late nineteenth and early twentieth centuries with as different characters as Augustus John and Alfred Munnings, Elizabeth von Arnim and (Dame) Laura Knight, not to mention D.H. Lawrence, all finding themselves part of a cult of the gypsy life. Into this growing culture of the road appeared Kenneth Grahame's Mr Toad[1] who, it is worth remembering, progressed from a faddish interest in bohemian caravanning to an obsession with motors and the open road. The manic glee of Toad's cry of "Poop poop!" as a fast car receded into the distance stood for the visceral love the car inspired in many, from the 1910s to the fifties.

In fact, the British love affair with cars developed quite quickly. In 1899, Lord Montagu's motorcar was banned from entering the precincts of Parliament but by 1933 there were two-million licensed motor vehicles on British roads, as well as 6,600 deaths in 1937 and 226,402 injuries.[2] Tarmacking of roads began in 1904, classification followed in 1909 and, in 1913, the numbering rather than naming of roads began, using the categories A, B and unclassified. In 1919, the Ministry of Transport was created. Petrol and car tax date back to 1909. Between 1928 and 1938 the number of vehicles on the road went from 1.5 million to 3 million. Between 1928 and 1935 traffic on the A13 went up 76 per cent and in the 1920s the construction of fast arterial roads (designed to have few gradients or curves) began, the A27 being opened in 1925.

Coincident to the numbering of roads was the belated recognition of cycle and motor tourists by the old rail-determined guidebooks, which began to include sections for first cyclists and then motorists. More important was the increasingly active

Ordnance Survey, Quarter Inch Map of South Wales, fourth edition, 1934, illustration by Ellis Martin

"Map memories and the Lure of the Road", publicity for O.S. Maps, Edgar Rowan, image Ellis Martin, after 1919

Charles Close revolutionised the maps of the Ordnance Survey after the First World War by using a new survey and new printing methods to produce a very accurate, informative and highly coloured map. This came at a time of increased map usage by the general public, largely due to an increased familiarity with map reading as a result of war service.

As this publicity sheet for the 'One Inch' map notes: "In the Army we busied ourselves with 'map reading'. It was a useful thing to know, by examining a map of unknown country, whether you could see the point A from the point B, or whether your stealthy progress along a certain road would be overlooked by men with machine-guns at the edge of the wood that lay a thousand yards to the east." During the war, the O.S. produced over 30-million maps. Close also used advertising in the form of illustrations by Ellis Martin to market the maps to a new generation of leisure traveller, hikers, cyclists and early motor tourists that emerged after 1918.

marketing by the Ordnance Survey under Colonel Sir Charles Close. His newly surveyed, accurate and beautifully coloured one-inch-to-the-mile tourist maps had to compete with the increasingly popular half-inch coloured tourist maps created by another entrepreneurial cartographer, J.G. Bartholomew. In fact, in the twenties the Ordnance Survey started featuring wistful images by the artist Ellis Martin.[3] Ruggedly attired gentlemen of the Richard Hannay kind stood next to their cars and gazed out across rural scenes, whilst an equally manly copy suggested that the trusty maps which got you through "no man's land" would also get you across the Cotswolds.

By the late twenties, the state of both the roads and the tools of navigation required to make sense of them had been transformed – as were the vehicles and drivers. Although motoring remained an expensive hobby, cars were available in smaller and cheaper types. Moreover, large numbers of people had become familiar with motor vehicles and their operation in the First World War, and this created both a market of would-be drivers and agricultural engineers who could fix cars. Like Mr Toad, many of the new motorists were young pleasure seekers. The age of the caravan was gone and in its place was a cloud of dust.

Bearing all this in mind, it's not surprising that the idea of a new kind of guidebook for motorists would occur to someone. That it occurred to John Betjeman is not surprising either: in his time at Oxford, Betjeman took to touring the Oxfordshire countryside by car and actively considered writing guidebooks with his friend Frederick Etchells; moreover, he sent picky correspondence to the publishers Ward, Lock & Co suggesting improvements to their Red Guides.[4] However, in the late twenties, he was not interested in motor guides so much as writing about neglected eighteenth- and nineteenth-century buildings. What was it that made Betjeman come up with the idea of a new guidebook to the counties specifically for motorists?

By 1933, John Betjeman was a not very successful aspirant ex-Marlborough and Magdalen man with a taste for the rich and well connected. Since October 1930, he been working as an assistant editor at the Architectural Review,[5] a gentlemanly journal that was becoming much more provocative under the direction of Hubert de Cronin Hastings.[6] Surprisingly by 1933, given his later career, after only a few years at the Architectural Review Betjeman was complaining despairingly of the number of times he had to write the word 'architecture'.[7] Yet the genesis of the guides wasn't simply a desire to escape the Architectural Review; and it certainly wasn't, as some have said, the need to supplement his salary at the A.R. in order to marry Penelope Chetwode[8] – though he did want to do this and did need more money.[9] Betjeman's interest in the guidebook and its subject matter went much deeper. He had from his youth been a self-confessed "Church Crawler" – a visitor of

ancient churches much like a train buff (which later he also became). He was also an amateur architectural historian who had become enthusiastic about the Regency and Victoriana with other fellow recherché aesthetes at Oxford and had, inter alia, developed a conservationist interest in ordinary Georgian and Victorian architecture at a time when these were generally held in no regard at all. Almost as a result of his long-term interest in the history of architecture he had also become a keen critic of guidebooks, as his letter of 1928 to the publishers Ward, Lock & Co about the writing of their guide to Leamington Spa shows.[10] Thus it is clear that Betjeman's interest in the subject matter and style of guidebooks was well-established by the time he joined the Architectural Review.[11] Here he met like-minded souls, but more importantly, he learned how to produce a magazine and picked up a knowledge of contemporary design and photography.

At Oxford Betjeman had got his first car, a Morris Cowley, and according to his daughter became an enthusiastic motorist[12] who toured around the Oxford and Home Counties countryside.

> Oxford May mornings! When the prunus bloomed
> We'd drive to Sunday lunch at Sezincote:
> First steps in learning how to be a guest,
> First wood-smoke-scented luxury of life
> In the large ambience of a country House.[13]

How else but by car would he have developed a love for Essex, where he spent his honeymoon in a small rural pub at Braxted?

> Like streams the little by-roads run
> Through oats and barley round a hill
> To where blue willows catch the sun
> By some white weather-boarded mill.
>
> …
>
> The deepest Essex few explore
> Where steepest thatch is sunk in flowers
> And out of elm and sycamore
> Rise flinty fifteenth-century towers.[14]

Betjeman was a man who was good at spotting new trends despite his own antiquarian leanings. He liked new stuff like motors, modern photography and design, and later the new media of radio and television. He was also good at storing up good ideas for a rainy day.

Moreover, Betjeman was living through a time when advertising

A Pictorial and Descriptive Guide to Warwick, Royal Leamington Spa, Stratford Upon Avon, Coventry & The George Eliot Country, 14th edn, 'Red Guide', London: Ward, Lock and Co. Ltd, 1926

was developing rapidly in new ways. By the early thirties, the motoring market was expanding fast and the Shell Oil Company and its competitors used billboard adverts to promote their products. Shell campaigns of the twenties operated in two ways. The first was simply to say that Shell petrol and oil were of high quality, sometimes using some Shell-fuelled sporting victory on land, sea or in the air as endorsement. Its other campaign was to suggest visiting some place in the country, usually a well-known spot or resort, using Shell products to get you there. But in 1929, a Shell employee, Jack Beddington, persuaded the company to let him revamp its advertising in order to reach out to the new motorists who were often young and wanted some kind of adventure. Beddington's idea was to use young artists to create modern art posters advertising the idea of using Shell petrol to drive to some off-the-beaten-track rural location that wasn't on the rail network. This campaign instantly changed Shell from a product into a lifestyle. Though the adverts Beddington created are well known, he is not. Beddington was a personable, dynamic, sociable and generous man who, after ten years working for Shell in Shanghai, was invalided back to Britain. In the following year, 1929, he became Publicity Manager and by 1932 he was Publicity Director and Assistant General Manager of Shell-Mex and BP Ltd. Later he became Director of the Films Division of the Ministry of Information. What was remarkable about Beddington was that, though he was powerful and successful, he was also genuinely enthusiastic about using young artists to draw in young people. Astutely, he had the foresight to put it about that he would pay young artists £50 for a poster design that could be used by Shell. Beddington instantly became a patron of the most promising young artists and he understood that these large adverts, appearing on the side of Shell delivery lorries and in other prominent places, were a fast-moving, fast-changing art gallery. They were an immediate hit and were so popular that the V&A gave them an exhibition, subsequently ordering multiple copies of the adverts that were framed and available for loan to schools on request.

Betjeman would have known about Beddington through his contacts at the *Architectural Review*. Beddington knew Lord Berners and Robert Byron and it was probably through them that Betjeman met him, just as he had met his future wife, Penelope Chetwode. He contacted Beddington and suggested that Shell might sponsor a series of guides to Britain that would be specifically aimed at the motoring 'bright young things', highly illustrated, shallow but informative and able to fit into a glove compartment. Beddington was supportive of the idea, which would be published by the Architectural Press that also published the *Architectural Review*. Beddington only wanted one dummy prepared and Betjeman unsurprisingly offered up a guide to Cornwall: his fee was £20. Later, after its preparation, Betjeman canvassed Beddington to help him turn the guides into a full-time job at Shell and thus get him away

'These Men Use Shell: Farmers', John Armstrong, 1939

from the *Architectural Review*. Beddington did not think this a good idea initially, but Betjeman did later alter his working arrangements to spend three days per week on the guides, before the war stopped their production.

The dummy Betjeman produced was innovative, stepping outside the conventions of the guidebook as they had hitherto existed. This was in itself remarkable because at this time there was little evidence that Betjeman was gifted as a writer, let alone as a book designer and editor. Traditional guidebooks had been designed to be small and compendious which meant they were usually sized to fit a pocket, a size much smaller than a paperback, and printed in small serif type, for legibility, on bible paper, which was thin. They often ran to between 300 and 600 pages and so were bound in strong bible-type semi-hard covers. Most were red in colour or some other strong colour like blue (the Blue Guides) or green (Blackie's Guides). The strong cover colour made them easy to locate on trips. The content of guides varied greatly in quality and often suffered from being based on local legend or on ill-prepared local histories.

Betjeman loved these guides and used certain of their features ironically in his *Cornwall*, most obviously his pastiche of the very elaborate title pages of old Victorian guides with their steel engravings, elaborately chaotic type designs and inordinately long titles. In fact, this was not a pastiche at all but an exact copy of the top half of the title page of a guide to Cornwall published by Fisher

Also a portrait of Jack Beddington, who was by all accounts very suave in real life.

and son of London in 1831, about the time of the first Murray guide.[15] On the other hand, what Betjeman didn't like about existing guides was their stuffiness, their neglect of the historically everyday and unworthy, particularly Georgian and Victorian architecture – and their lack of pictures.

Betjeman's *Cornwall* was 63-pages long, printed on glossy paper that would take images well and over twice the size of a conventional guidebook. It was spiral bound using a new cheap system (Spirax) that enabled the book to be opened onto itself without breaking. Half of the book was taken up with black-and-white photographs and reproductions of old prints. Elsewhere the map of the region had photographs of local types photo-montaged onto it and there were whole-page reproductions of images and photographs on coloured paper (as was the style at the *Architectural Review* but which had the effect of conveying a vaguely late-Victorian décor feel). The front and rear covers were full-bleed black-and-white photographs, the front showing an old Cornish 'type', printed on shiny card and featuring reversed-out, sans-serif titles in a fashionable Gill or Gill-type font. It was called *Cornwall – Shell Guide*. In fact, the cover showed Betjeman's great talent for absorbing fashion in its use of Maurice Beck, who was an experienced and modish photographer for the *Architectural Review* but had also worked on Vogue and designed posters for London Transport.[16]

The faux nineteenth-century title page was also used in the early Shell Guides like *Wiltshire*, *Derbyshire* and *Kent* and modified for other guides like *Devon*. This device represents the fondness for Victorian ephemera that Betjeman had developed at Oxford.

Title page of Cornwall, 1934

Below left: The cover of *Cornwall* combined very modern style, sans-serif lettering, a full-bleed photo and spiral binding with a portrait of the Cornish 'type' that reveals a very metropolitan humour. Betjeman abandoned this them-and-us approach in his next guide for *Devon*.

Below right: Like the cover, this montage of map with local types reflected Betjeman's concern in the initial guides to be modern, witty and self-consciously shallow.

Front cover of Cornwall, 1934

'The Road to Cornwall', Cornwall, 1934

Cornwall was small and flexible enough to be rolled up like a half-size magazine. It was also relatively pricey at 2/6d and obviously wouldn't last. It was reassuringly expensive and fashionable. It sold well, going into a second edition by 1936. Being the first of the series and therefore a kind of manifesto, the inside cover was devoted to what kind of guide it would be – or rather, wouldn't be.

> There are two sorts of guide book, the antiquarian and the popular, and with a few notable exceptions most English guide books fall heavily into one or other of these classes. …This book about Cornwall does not try and compete with either type. It is more of an anthology. The pioneer service it performs is that it draws attention within its confined limits to the many buildings of the eighteenth and nineteenth centuries that have architectural merit.[17]

He criticises the earlier antiquarian guides for their obsession with the ancient, and popular guides for their lack of concern with culture. He makes only two observations about his *Cornwall*: the first that it is unique in its interest in the architecture of the eighteenth and nineteenth centuries, which he knew was untrue in view of his own comments about Ward, Lock & Co's Leamington guide; and that it was an anthology, that is to say not unlike the popular guides he describes in the previous paragraph. Another thing he criticises in old guides is their devotion to church-crawling but, paradoxically, much of the guide is devoted to accounts of Cornish saints, Cornish crosses and detailed accounts of out-of-the-way churches.

In retrospect, *Cornwall* is not very good as a guide. Not so much an anthology as a serendipitous collection of topics from golf to saints, to fishing and sailing, and a lurid account of the Scilly Islands Ferry: "there are grisly tales of men who sailed seven times round the Horn, yet lost their appetite for the rolling deep after the apparently minor business of a trip to St Mary's."[18] *Cornwall* has very little space to describe places in Cornwall. In fact, where in the later guides the text is dominated by a gazetteer of places, in this guide there is no gazetteer, only a chapter listing towns and another listing churches. 'Towns' is seven-pages long and 'Churches' nine. The places in the 'Towns' section consist mainly of villages and the entries are bizarre in their relative lengths and what they describe. The entry for Boscastle is three times the length of that for Penzance, whose description is laughable for its lack of information:

> **Penzance.** Situation – Penzance is in a magnificent situation commanding an extensive view of Mount's Bay. There is excellent bathing and boating. While the country around is full of cliff scenery and prehistoric remains. Buildings – The finest building in Penzance is the market-house built in 1836 by William Harris of Bristol. Some of the lesser streets have good Georgian buildings, but the town has not the beauty of Falmouth, to which it bears a certain resemblance.

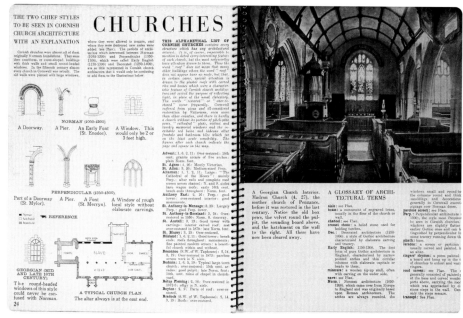

Section on church architecture, Cornwall, 1934

This could have been written by a character in an Evelyn Waugh novel. However, the entry for Wadebridge (which he liked) has some of the poetic compression that became the hallmark of later guides:

> **Wadebridge.** Situation – Wadebridge is on the River Camel. and [sic] as Arthur H. Norway has said in *Highways and Byways of Cornwall*, "when the tide is out it is almost as if the town had lost its soul". Up the Camel Valley there are pleasant journeys to Grogley Halt on the Southern Railway – a good place for blackberries – while the downs toward St Column, which are above the town, are full of prehistoric remains. Buildings – The chief beauty of Wadebridge is its mediaeval bridge of seventeen arches across the Camel. Along the river at Egloshayle – that is to say, the Northern bank – there are some delightful Georgian houses reminiscent of the architecture of the Isles of Scilly.

Though even this has a slight air of pastiche. Pastiche and funniness are in fact the guide's most obvious failing. In a smart urban way it mocks its subject, poking fun at everyone and everything from "artistic" orange-coloured curtains of second homers in Polperro to the "lumpen" appearance of the locals, notably in the caption to the image of a very Victorian lady: "Methodism is a great bulwark of Cornwall. This is a blind Primitive Methodist Woman preacher of a type that is fast dying out". The guide is very clearly aimed at the metropolitan visitor to Cornwall, with whom Betjeman seems at this time to have identified himself.

Against his own declared aim, much of the first Shell Guide had strong echoes of the church-crawler 'antiquarian' guides Betjeman wished to challenge.

The strength of the guide lies in its serendipitous view and fascination with the local rather than well-established 'sights'. There is, for instance, a full-page image of a back alley in Polperro that is purely about the picturesqueness of the juxtaposition of stone walls. The wide range of subjects covered in the guide is experimental and many were gradually dropped from the guides; but in *Cornwall*, Betjeman was trying to appeal to what he supposed were the interests of his upper-middle-class audience. There are sections on hunting, fishing and sailing as well as prehistoric Cornwall, bird and plant life, and food. Some work: the section on fishing by Betjeman's father is something one could use today, whereas the hunting section is a gesture. But there were other elements to *Cornwall* that were very innovative and became a feature of the guides for many years. What remained throughout the series from 1934 right through to the late sixties was the use of abstracted images for the endpapers, in this case a close up of an open mussel shell on rippling sand. A feature that gradually slipped away were the references to Victorian imagery and book conventions, here best illustrated by the contents page with its grandiloquence and its many typefaces. Other regular

Sinking Ship, Cornwall, 1934

Above: This double-spread image sits by his father's entries on fishing in Cornwall and represents the distinctly undergraduate humour of the early guides.

Below: The Shell Guides always used every inch of the available paper as a way of saying something. In particular, the endpapers of the early guides used designs in which an everyday item that typified some aspect of the county in question was repeated to form an almost abstract pattern. The 1964 *Cornwall* featured endpapers of pebbles on a beach.

Left: A real innovation in the first Shell Guide was its use of the 'townscape' detail of an everyday back-street as a way of pushing Betjeman's agenda for the appreciation of the ordinary loveliness of English towns.

Polperro back alley, Cornwall, 1934

Endpapers of mussels, Cornwall, 1934

features introduced were punning cartoons about Shell, here by Edward Bawden – "Lanteglos-by-Fowey but Motorists buy Shell" – and discursive footnotes in the text that appeared right until the last page of the last guide, *Nottinghamshire*, in 1984 which concludes with "a note on Nottinghamshire pronunciation".[19]

The guide must have been a success because Beddington offered Shell's support for more guides, and during the 1930s a total of 13 were produced under three publishers. *Cornwall*'s magazine styling, its visual modernity and its equally modish irreverence for its subject did their job of making a splash. One suspects that Betjeman understood that making a splash was more important than writing for posterity, for having secured the editorship and sponsorship of a series under the patronage of Shell and Beddington, Betjeman set about making better more serious guides almost straightaway.

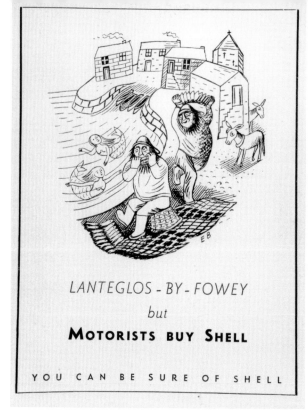

Lanteglos-by-Fowey, Edward Bawden, Cornwall, *1934*

Garden with sculpture bust, title page for section on the Scilly Isles, Cornwall, 1934

Tresco Abbey Gardens
(4, Inset).

Combining Bawden's graphic style and a humorous punning by-line, these cartoons were a feature of the Shell Guides until 1939 and then again from the publication of *Herefordshire* in 1955 until John Piper dropped them on becoming editor in the late sixties.

Perhaps because of the generation of their editors and the period in which the Shell Guides first appeared, from the beginning the guides displayed an eye for the surreal image, such as this De Chirico-esque photograph. These were often included only because of their surrealism and, over the years, added subtle new expectations to Britain's sense of its own countryside.

Notes

1. Toad appeared in *The Wind in the Willows* in 1908, the same year as the first Ford *Model T* rolled off the production line in Detroit.
2. Marriot, 1941
3. Hauser, 2008
4. About some inaccurate details in their guide to Leamington Spa.
5. Thanks to Maurice Bowra – see Hillier, 1988, p.348
6. Managing editor, 1927–1973, of the Architectural Press, *Architectural Review* and the *Architects' Journal*
7. See Hillier, 1988, p.274, quoting Betjeman's piece called 'Architecture' in the *London Mercury*, November 1933
8. Daughter of Field Marshall Philip Chetwode, Commander in Chief of the Army in India
9. By 1933/4 Betjeman was on £400 a year at the *A.R.* but this was both for editing it *and* creating Shell Guides. (See Lycett Green, 1994, p.124, letter from J.B. to Jack Beddington, 17 August 1933)
10. Quote from letter; see Lycett Green, 1994, pp.39–40
11. Betjeman began work at the *A.R.* in October 1930, a post he obtained through the influence of a friend of Maurice Bowra, Dean of Wadham College. Betjeman was a member of his circle both at Oxford and afterwards.
12. See Lycett Green, 1994, pp.19 and 21
13. Betjeman, *Summoned by Bells*, 1960 quoted in Lycett Green, 1994, p.21
14. Betjeman, 'Essex', *A Few Late Chrysanthemums*, 1954 quoted in Scarfe, 1968, p.8
15. Mentioned in Peterson, 2006, p.15
16. Maurice Beck worked on a lot of the thirties Shell Guides. He had been a fashionable 'society' photographer and knew Beddington from Shanghai. Later, when he had fallen on harder times, it was Beddington who gave him work for Shell. Beck brought stylish modern photographs to the new Shell Guides that rescued them from Betjeman's early ironic tendencies. See Artmonsky, 2006, p.30
17. *Cornwall*, 1934, p.6
18. *Cornwall*, 1934, p.56
19. *Nottinghamshire*, 1984, p.188

WILTSHIRE, KENT AND DEVON

AFTER THE SUCCESS OF *Cornwall*, Betjeman was faced with the strategic problem of the series' development and the logistics of its production. Looking at the titles produced in the thirties, it's clear they were aimed at a primarily metropolitan audience and covered counties that were popular holiday destinations for nearby cities. Cornwall was a place Betjeman knew well and so was an obvious first choice; and the West Country was a well-loved tourist destination for the cities of the Midlands and the South so, again, it isn't surprising that guides were commissioned for Wiltshire, Dorset, Devon and Somerset. Equally, the Cotswolds were a popular Midlands destination and the Peak District was popular with more Northerly cities, so guides to Gloucestershire, Oxfordshire and Derbyshire were commissioned. The guide to Northumbria and Durham covered the tourist North East and *West Coast of Scotland* gave Glasgow and Edinburgh a guide. Londoners travelled to all these places, but Betjeman also commissioned guides to more local touring areas for the capital – Kent and Buckinghamshire, the Chiltern county. The only really surprising choice given the strategic proximity of the counties of these first Shell Guides to large urban populations was Hampshire; but this may have been a reflection of Betjeman's bigger idea for the series to cover every county.

Betjeman's biggest logistical problem was finding authors or compilers of the guides. In the thirties, both terms were used since the job combined writing, research and choosing or taking suitable photographs. The fee for writing a Shell Guide was in the beginning £50, which was the same fee as given for producing a poster. It must have been clear that only the very committed or those of independent means would consider producing a guide.

For the first of the Shell Guides, Betjeman used authors from his social circle which in retrospect, while conventional for a man of his education and ambitions, was not very successful. For the Shell Guide to Wiltshire he approached Robert Byron and for Kent he chose Lord Clonmore. Both men were at Oxford with him. Robert Byron was hardly older than Betjeman but had much more experience, being a confident and well-known travel writer and also a very sharp critic. According to Bevis Hillier, Betjeman admired and emulated his style of rather arch criticism. Lord Clonmore, by contrast, was a rather straightforward religious person with an honest outlook. According to Hillier, Clonmore was the first Lord that Betjeman knew. All of them shared an interest in religion – though not the same religion – as well as architecture and Victoriana, which at that time was a subversive taste. By 1934, all of them had written for the *Architectural Review* too.

Betjeman chose authors for the guides based on his approval of their attitudes. In the early guides this seems to have meant that they shared his preoccupations as these had developed at Oxford, where Betjeman had fallen in with the aesthetically inclined crowd patronised alternately by the mutually hostile dons George

Clonmore's Morecambe, Architectural Review, 1933

(Colonel) Kolkhorst and Maurice Bowra, later the Master of Wadham College. Bowra and Kolkhorst were homosexuals who gathered around them students that were either interesting to them or attractive. Betjeman, who seems at this time to have been the kind of man who needed others to give him intellectual direction, was attracted to the combination of mild religiosity, aestheticism and campness of Bowra's and Kolkhorst's circles. In contrast, he didn't like his assigned tutor at Magdalen College, C.S. Lewis, and Lewis didn't like him. Lewis thought Betjeman shallow and Betjeman disliked his tutor's straightness. Betjeman, leaving aside a certain opportunist bisexuality that may have drawn him to the Bowra–Kolkhorst coterie, seems to have embraced their churchiness. This was of a kind that was interested in the ceremony and forms of the church rather than spirituality, and seems to have gone hand in hand with a delight in Victoriana.

Robert Byron didn't work for the *Review* but he did contribute photographs and articles based on his travels to Eastern Europe and Asia, as well as influential architectural polemics. He was also a keen Victorianist at Oxford, even building a collection of artificial flowers in glass domes, and was sufficiently interested in religion to write a book about Mount Athos and visit monasteries in Tibet. Byron was also a friend of Betjeman's wife, Penelope Chetwode – in fact, he had suggested she take her article on Indian cave temples at Ellora to the *Review* where Betjeman went through her photographs; it was their first meeting. Byron's adopted county was Wiltshire, where his family had a house in the Savernake forest.

Though Betjeman admired Byron's writing, Byron didn't take to the idea of the Shell Guides and had to be persuaded by Jack Beddington. Even then there were ongoing differences between the

In the early days of the *Architectural Review* under Hubert de Cronin Hastings and of the Shell Guides, the standard of writing fell below the far more modern standard of the imagery and typography.

two men over the contents of the guide, with Betjeman urging Georgian and Victorian architecture be given prominence while Byron resisted this idea in favour of including Saxon and medieval architecture and prehistoric sights, much to the annoyance of Betjeman. They had particular disagreements over the Saxon church at Bradford on Avon which Byron insisted on including against the wishes of Betjeman. Byron also insisted on the absence of good Georgian and Victorian architecture in Wiltshire despite later being instrumental in the founding of the conservationist lobby the Georgian Group, in 1937, and penning a very influential plea for the conservation of Georgian and Regency buildings in London – titled with typical irony 'How We Celebrate the Coronation – A Word to London's Visitors'.[1] Betjeman disliked the gazetteer of Byron's *Wiltshire*, dropping it in favour of a version by a mutual acquaintance of theirs, Edith Olivier, without telling Byron.[2] It was an inauspicious start to the series.

Byron had another mutual friend with Betjeman and Beddington, Lord Berners, who he used for some of the photographs in the Wiltshire guide. Berners was also a diplomat, knew Futurists and Surrealists, was a talented librettist, musician, painter and satiric, salacious novelist. He lived at Faringdon in Oxfordshire where he kept a flock of brightly dyed doves to decorate the garden. Unusually for the time he lived in an openly gay relationship. He was the kind of eccentric aristocrat Betjeman found irresistible.

Lord Clonmore was simply a friend of Betjeman's and, although he married an architect and wrote for the *Architectural Review*, it is fair to say he was not a talented writer. In 1933 he wrote a piece for the September *Architectural Review* on the Midland Hotel at Morecambe by Oliver Hill.[3] In the same issue is a piece by Betjeman where he begins his long campaign for the Euston Arch, 'Dictating to the Railways'. Interestingly Betjeman's title page, taken from a series of prints about Euston Station, presages the revived Victorian stylings of the thirties Shell Guides. Clonmore's 'London, Morecambe and Elsewhere' reads as if it were a piece of inept journalism by one of Wodehouse's fictional characters. It begins by damning the Gothic Revival in passing: "on the whole it was a failure, with bad results second only to the industrial revolution. One might perhaps call St Pancras its climax". Of Oliver Hill's hotel, he begins by admiring its "simplicity of design, which has done so much to beautify Germany and Austria", countries he would have seen on a visit he made while a student in the company of a cicerone and new friend, John Betjeman. In a very unjournalistic moment he writes, "the photographs give a better description than any amount of writing". The *Architectural Review* at that time didn't credit its photographers: the one in question here was Sidney Newburgh and his photographs were stylishly modern in their use of wide oblique angles and high-contrast lighting. In fact, what is striking about the design of 'London, Morecambe and Elsewhere' is that it is very modern, one layout featuring a double spread of empty glossy paper with a single image taking only a half page – a bravura use of graphic space in sharp contrast to the out-of-its-depth prose. The *Architectural Review* at this time looked modern but read like an amateur gentleman's club paper. Where the architecture and graphic design occupied the same contemporary space, the writing was left somewhere between Ruskin and the Golf Club:

> [The Midland Hotel] rises from the sea like a great white ship, gracefully curved, and when I say this I am not giving any rhetoric, nor do I mean that the building suffers from the crowning defect of so much English architecture, trying to look like what it is not. There are no show funnels or masts, or nonsense of that kind, nevertheless it looks like a great white ship rising out of the sea, like a venus anadyomene in white cement.

Concluding in Wildean mode, Clonmore adds "Good railway hotels are as fitting to an ending to a good railway journey as a well attended funeral and a well-worded inscription to a respectable life". After writing like this, it comes as no surprise that his *Kent* essay on Canterbury Cathedral begins, "To travel in Kent without visiting Canterbury is rather like eating plum pudding without brandy butter" and continues:

> The Cathedral gives you a shock the first time you see it, which is, I think, rather more acute than the effect of any other building in England. I do not intend to embark on a purple patch at this point, but I think that everybody who has seen the upward sweep of the piers of the nave, and the bold curves of the apse leading to the mysterious chair of St Augustine, will agree with me.

The surprising thing is that Betjeman was so tolerant of Clonmore's text when he ruthlessly edited Byron's *Wiltshire*; but that is friendship.

Both Clonmore's *Kent* and Byron's *Wiltshire* are in their own ways very eccentric guides. High among *Kent's* eccentricities is the first essay by fellow Catholic convert and 'earthy' novelist, Sheila Kaye-Smith on the Kent and Sussex Borders which describes Sussex but not Kent. Clonmore made some fairly eccentric gazetteer entries describing Tunbridge Wells rivalling Tennessee as a centre of the Low Church and featuring an image of an ancient royal railway carriage which he noted as a feature of the railway branch line that served Tenterden. Clonmore included in his introductory parts of the guide an essay on hop pickers, 'The Invasion of Kent', by Miles Sargeant (another fellow Anglo-Catholic), which describes the progress of the holidaying working class through south-east London en route to the Kent hop fields. Actually the essay reads rather well and has something of the quality of someone recording a folk dance or other folkloric custom, as was the fashion before the more urban anthropological documentarists of the 1930s. But 'The Invasion of Kent' was more reportage than guidebook entry and *Kent* has the feel of something put together on the theme of Kent rather than being a guide in the conventional sense. The most obvious evidence of this is Evelyn Waugh's father, Arthur's charming essay on Dickens and Kent, placed after the gazetteer and before the index. Evelyn Waugh was another mutual friend and this essay seems to be here because it is a good read (better certainly than the accounts of Rochester and Canterbury by the Dean of Rochester and the devout Clonmore) and beautifully illustrated with old prints; but most of it adds Kentish bulk to a book that didn't actually have much about Kent in it. The gazetteer has only ten sides of text and an introductory section on country mostly not in Kent at all.

That said, *Kent* is eccentrically entertaining, giving atmosphere and making the county vivid. Its images are instrumental in this. The cover shows an apple tree covered in blossom and is an intense, almost abstract image suggestive of the county in an allusive manner that later became a mainstay of the Shell Guide illustrative arsenal. Inside, a full-page image shows a lane turning a corner around a flint wall near Reculver. This is an example of another type of image that would become key to later guides – metaphoric and rich in atmosphere, though so general as to be almost an abstract, essential image of the minor pleasures of walks along lanes. Through its very marginality, this kind of image is almost like someone pointing out a hitherto-ignored element of the view and making the point that it is lovely. As Richard Mabey said of East Anglia, its beauty lies in its small incidents.

Where *Kent* is in the end as enthusiastic as it is eccentric, *Wiltshire* is rather worldly and dark, and Byron's voice more unsettling and ironic than that of Betjeman's *Cornwall*. The front cover of *Wiltshire* is not a photograph of a single place but rather a dense photomontage of elements of the county, people, buildings and animals in a higgledy-piggledy arrangement reminiscent of a child's scrapbook. This image, compiled by Lord Berners, is a more exaggerated and surreal version of many of the images in Betjeman's *Cornwall* in that it objectifies the county as a series of quaintnesses and oddities. These early expeditions into surrealism, which are in their way very literary – being narratives – soon gave way to the elegiac evocations of mood found in the later guides by the Nashs and Piper.

Wiltshire begins with a typical piece of Betjemanism: the frontispiece sports a print of William Beckford's Fonthill and the caption below reads "Fonthill Abbey Before Its Collapse". Fonthill was much more modishly Georgian than Byron would have liked in this guide and the contest between Betjeman's interest in the eighteenth and nineteenth centuries and Byron's resistance to it runs through the text. Taken as a whole, Byron's natural writing talent seems to be overwhelmed by the task of writing a guidebook making his parts of the *Wiltshire* guide simultaneously well-written

Roman wall, Reculver, Kent, 1935, pp.46–7

Hop Pickers, Kent, 1935, p.13

Queen Victoria's Carriage, K&ESR, Kent, 1935, p.10

Two Regency crescents — one at Ramsgate (left), and the other at Tunbridge Wells (Calverley Crescent, right). The architect of Calverley Crescent was Decimus Burton, who also designed the Athenaeum Club, the Hyde Park Corner screens, and the font at St. Leonards-on-Sea.

Ramsgate and St Leonard's, double-page montage, Kent, 1935

Tunbridge Wells, Kent, 1935, pp.26–7

Though more conventional than Byron's *Wiltshire*, *Kent* had several innovations to make to the form of the Shell Guide. The first was an interest in trains that continued in these motor guides to the end. The second, which soon disappeared, was to feature people in the guides. This became very unusual indeed soon after, with Betjeman feeling that the aim of the guide was to focus on the country and the built environment. More successful for later guides was the inclusion of Regency terraces at Ramsgate, St Leonard's and Tunbridge Wells. Betjeman liked their repetition of forms and their feeling of provincial imitation of metropolitan 'betters'. Equally, with the reproduction of an old panoramic print of Gravesend, *Kent* represented Betjeman's taste for old topographic prints, which appeared in the guides until the late 1960s. The most innovative image is that of the Roman wall at Reculver as it represents the first of many carefully reproduced, almost abstract and highly textured images of details – one of the ways in which the guides subtly taught its readers how to see.

The Pantiles, Tunbridge Wells.

Gravesend, double-page spread, Kent, 1935, pp.36–7

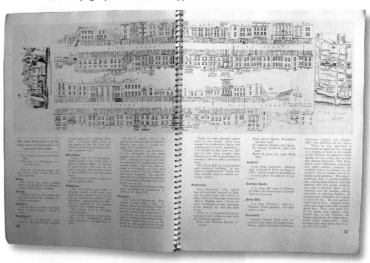

and badly conceptualised and structured. The main problem is a desire to relate the past to the present which he is unable to do and a strangely tract-like structure which has section headings that include 'War and Moral'.

Byron begins by quoting Camden describing Wiltshire as a Mediterranean county, which is funnier than Betjeman could be at that time; but then he rounds on his audience: "to them [the young] it is a new discovery, a beauty spot fragrant to the soul, which fulfils the twin conditions of such a title: convenient access to London, and an appearance of reposeful good taste. This discovery, though still only in its early stages, threatens to overwhelm the eastern part of the county with the fate of Sussex and the Cotswolds". It is the last paragraph of 'The Face of Wiltshire' which best shows Byron's edgy, uncomfortable style:

> The uplands are deserted, save by sheep, race-horses and tanks – seasonal occupants. Thus there is an air of mystery about them. Their outline is always visible, provoking a perpetual curiosity as to what goes on up there, atop these harmonious domestic Pamirs. Across Salisbury plain which measures 20 miles by 12, there is no railway. Some villages are seven miles from a station and isolated farms further still. The outstanding beauty of the county is the landscape of the uplands, an ocean of rolling grass, over which the cloud shadows

play like a cinematograph – an ocean suddenly frozen. ...a few industries complete the scene. The latter are chiefly at Swindon, a place whose existence is regretted by those who seek the beautiful without reference to human development. This sentiment may be shared by the tourist. To the resident it is unacceptable. We cannot live only in the past, and Wiltshire, as this book will show, is not such an Austria among counties as most people think.

Byron desired to validate the now as a continuity with the past, seen in his reference to the cinematograph, at times making his writing very tortured. This is most present in his section on the antiquities of Wiltshire:

> if we gaze with interest on a bronze cooking-pot disinterred from a barrow, let us gaze with awe and thankfulness upon the daily sausage despatched from the factory at Colne and frizzling upon the stove. A guide-book is not usually the repository of philosophical maxims. And this is the end of them. But they will explain the form of this guide-book, and contribute, if read, to its usefulness.

One problem of Byron's essayist approach is that the sections he writes do work that should be done in the gazetteer, although the truth of this was probably only beginning to dawn on Betjeman who

These covers show the constant state of flux in the design of the early guides as Betjeman veered between the stylishness of Beck's *Kent*, the tourist-friendly cover of his own *Devon*, a style the guides were never very happy with, and Lord Berners' surreal photomontage that has something of the scrapbook collage about it that went well with Byron's often arch text. Experimentation with Shell Guide covers carried on well into the 1950s before Piper introduced a succession of standardised approaches at the end of the decade.

Cover of Devon, 1935

Cover of Wiltshire, 1935

Cover of Kent, 1935

was developing the gazetteer in his new guide to *Devon*. In his section on pre-Christian antiquities there are two potential gazetteer entries buried in the text, dragging unnecessary lumps of prose around with them. Of Avebury he says:

> The Avebury circle is megalithic, and older than Stonehenge. It consisted, originally, of about 600 unworked boulders, of which some 20 are still standing, while a few more are buried in the ground. The rest have gone to construct the village of Avebury, a derelict little place, which now occupies the centre of the circle and obscures any general view of it.

Of Stonehenge he is more lyrical:

> Today Stonehenge lies at the fork of two asphalt roads, is fenced round to preserve it from souvenir-hunters, and is approached, on payment of a fee, by a turnstile. In the distance can be seen Larkhill Camp, and closer at hand are the vestiges of another military rubbish heap. The great stones transcend their sordid environment. … Late on a winter's afternoon is the time to see the place at its best, when the huge, weathered monoliths loom out of the murk while their modern accessories are swallowed up.

Elsewhere referring to Swindon he writes, "The main bulk of Swindon must be almost unique among English towns for its negative, characterless ugliness". Byron's remarks about places make him look good but don't encourage the visitor and this may have been why Betjeman decided not to use his gazetteer but one written by Edith Olivier, an experienced writer and friend of Lord Berners. In her version:

> Avebury is a ghost: the great earthwork which once enclosed the huge prehistoric Temple now contains a large part of the modern village, the cottages jumbled about among the few remaining monoliths, the rest of which are dispersed into fragments and built into the walls of farms, barns and cottages all around. The long avenues of stones which led to the Temple had also almost disappeared, but one is being reconstructed and its stones unearthed by Mr. Keiller. Some of these stone were still in situ, some were buried and one stood upside down: the traditional Beckhampton avenue has not yet been recovered, though it was seen standing, some twenty years ago by a clairvoyante.

This is a much more enticing description than Byron's and stands alone, unburied in prose. Of Stonehenge she writes, "Preserves its air of intrinsic utter loneliness"; and though she like Byron then goes on to criticise the site, she concludes optimistically: "The National Trust has bought the skyline, and swept away the aerodrome, so

Double Cube Room, Wilton House, Wiltshire

perhaps their broom may some day sweep even nearer to this magnificent monument".

Betjeman and Olivier knew that the point of a guide was to encourage the visitor, but Byron seems to have been unable to see this, perhaps because he didn't agree with Betjeman. The result was a guide full of strange inclusions like the section on war where Byron begins, "The philosopher will reflect that on Salisbury plain, where bronze age man once exercised his primitive weapons and slew his hundreds, our modern warriors learn to slay their millions: an interesting example of the progress civilisation has made since those barbarous days of paganism". He gibes at Betjeman's injunction to refer to the architecture of the eighteenth and nineteenth centuries where possible, resulting in the entry beginning "Wiltshire is comparatively poor in monuments of the eighteenth century" followed with a listing but no description of Bowood, Stourhead, Wilton, Fonthill and Hardenhuish. The first four should have received more attention or at least illustration – though there are images, probably edited in by Betjeman, of the Nymph of the Grot at Stourhead and the earlier Double Cube Room at Wilton. Byron's illustrations are of a tobacco and snuff label, "still used by Anstie's of Devizes", and a photo of some eighteenth-century ecclesiastical joinery.

Both *Wiltshire* and *Kent* seem to come from the same place as Betjeman's *Cornwall* despite being in many ways very different. *Kent* has the same interest in folklore and social tradition and perhaps more interest in the Victorian because of the seaside resorts there. It contains themes later recurrent throughout the Shell Guides – popular architecture, railways and the incidental pleasures of the rural. *Wiltshire* on the other hand shares *Cornwall*'s sense that the author looks upon the county as Other, a place to be looked at and viewed in a mildly alienated way by a sophisticated city dweller. In

Byron didn't really consider Wiltshire to be rich in eighteenth-century gems as Betjeman had hoped he would, hence Byron's inclusion of a double-page spread of the earlier Double Cube Room at Wilton house, designed by Inigo Jones. Interiors are a very rare feature of the Shell Guides since, for obscure reasons, they concentrated on exteriors.

fact, *Wiltshire* seems the blackest of ironic views in its mourning the changes brought on by the modern world – a theme that was always an undercurrent in the guides.

In 1935 Betjeman published his guide to Devon, no doubt under the influence of responses to *Cornwall* from people whom he respected, like Byron. In addition, his experience of producing *Kent* and *Wiltshire* had given him a clear understanding of what was needed in a guide. Gone are the montages, the shotgun approach of small chapters on a wide range of subjects, the very brief, uninformative gazetteer entries and the jokey images. In their place, a much more sober, simpler guide. In the acknowledgements, the final credit reads "For mental inspiration the Editor had only to think of Mr C.S. Lewis, tweed-clad and jolly, to get busy with his pen". Although he hated Lewis, he probably disliked Lewis's view that he was a fraud most; and so for *Devon* he determined to do a better job than with *Cornwall*.

Certainly he had learnt a lot in a short time. The greatest innovation of *Devon* is the larger role given to the gazetteer. In the previous guides, the gazetteer sat unhappily alongside essaylets on various subjects and, as in the case of *Wiltshire*, entries in the gazetteer were duplicated and even subverted by descriptions of the same places in the narrative. What Betjeman – and possibly Hubert de Cronin Hastings, who alongside Betjeman worked on the layouts of the early guides – seems to have realised is that the short essays had a tendency to have an internal structure that suited the essayist, not the guide, and also reduced the amount of space given to describing the places of the relevant county; whereas a gazetteer had a minimal structure – an alphabetical list of places relevant to the county – and so could describe in detail a whole county in short unrelated sections with few narrative devices since no big themes or links were needed. In addition, Betjeman seems to have begun to realise that the object of the guide was to write up places, to make the reader want to visit them and that long entries in narratives encouraged equivocation whereas short entries by their nature emphasised the positive and didn't bother with the negative.

A good example of the new Betjeman approach is the following extract, the sequential entries for Bideford and Bigbury:

Bideford: 11, A Port. May once have been thought not so genteel as Barnstaple, but certainly its medieval bridge over the Torridge, of twenty-four arches, is impressive. Some of the houses on the bank opposite the town are in the worst Plymouth suburban style. Bideford is a dimmer place than Barnstaple, but it beats Barnstaple in possessing Bridgeland Street, which is full of beautiful houses. The best is number 28, which was built in 1691–3. The interior of the Royal Hotel by the bridge should be seen for the renaissance ceiling (c. 17th century) in the drawing room and for the staircase. They say Kingsley wrote part of *Westward Ho!* here. The trade of Bideford is largely cuffs and collars.

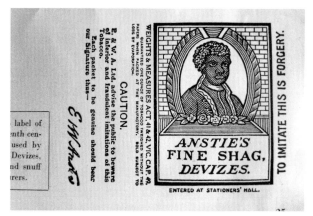

Anstie's Shag, Wiltshire

Pigs, Wiltshire

In common with Betjeman and others at Oxford, Byron had a strong attraction to flamboyant printed ephemera of the eighteenth and nineteenth centuries. This kind of trade plate was also a feature of Piper's art in the early thirties where it acted as an objet trouvé, but for Byron and Betjeman such things were simply a source of fun – although later, popular imagery became a staple of the guides with the development of a widespread interest in English popular culture in the 1940s.

Bigbury-on-Sea: 8. Is a bungaloid paradise not far from the mouth of the Avon; and Kingsbridge is near, but not near enough to be infected. The scenery around is good, especially inland. Hingeston and Houghton, two farms were once manors.

Betjeman here very neatly encourages a visit to Barnstaple while still recommending Bideford, gives a general impression of the place and some very specific and accessible detail and finishes on a splendid bit of useless and possibly vulgar humorous information.

Wiltshire was the earliest of the surreal Shell Guides drawing on Byron's taste for the absurd and possibly some hostility toward Betjeman's idea of a guide. Pigs are seen as endearing in the image but as bacon in the text. However, Byron's *Wiltshire* was the first guide to really link image and text in a meaningful rather than illustrative manner.

Barnfield Crescent, Exeter, by Maurice Beck, Devon, 1955, p.46

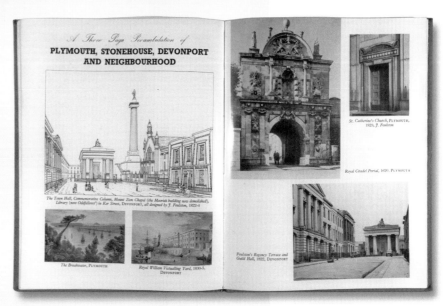

Betjeman's Perambulation of Plymouth in Brian Watson's Devon, 1955, pp.72–3

Primroses in a drain by Paul Fripp, Devon, 1935 (p.106 in Devon, 1955)

'Face of Devon', Devon, 1935, p.7

Betjeman's second Guide, *Devon*, of 1935 tried quite hard to be a motor guide compared to *Cornwall* and was particularly good at using images to suggest the qualities of travel and arriving. For the 'Face of Devon' a lane is seen from the driver's point of view as is the A30 near Honiton, both photographed by Maurice Beck. Together they suggest travel on the open road and arrival in a secluded village. Equally the tiny detail of a primrose in a drain is another attempt by Betjeman, a keen botanist in his youth, to make us see the beautiful quotidian detail. In *Devon* much more than *Cornwall*, Betjeman actually promotes the qualities of Georgian and Regency architecture in his perambulation of Plymouth (long before Pevsner did his perambulations) and the slide-lecture-style picture of formal fenestral harmonies at Barnfield Terrace, Exeter, again by Maurice Beck.

Avenue of trees on an A-road by Maurice Beck, Devon, 1935, pp.16–17

27

Moving on, he damns Bigbury and then rescues it by suggesting the country is good, there are some interesting old farms and encouraging a visit to nearby Kingsbridge. Here is distilled the best feature of the Shell Guide which is the use of entries to encourage the reader to go to even the worst place while at the same time suggesting a further hunt through the gazetteer.

At the bottom of the page was a less successful idea that was also gradually dropped from the guides: a picture of "Bideford as it once was. A Georgian china shop now destroyed." But Betjeman could not resist campaigning. On page 25, under the entry for Exeter, was an image of a newer type that became more common in the guides, here showing Ash Grove in Exeter, to the North of the High Street. It is an example of what was to become known in the *Architectural Review* as 'a townscape', or a tiny moment of architectural loveliness. A small Regency terrace sits below a higher-level gas-lit path by a slightly grander and contemporary Gothick house. This type of found beauty in ordinariness is what the Shell Guides became very able at pointing to and gradually made into a 'desirable' residential ideal for the majority of the middle class of the past 60 years.

Two other types of image used in *Devon* were to become staples of later guides. On the rear cover is a photomontage of a tumbling stream and beach rocks created by the editor from images by Muir Wiseman and Paul Fripp. Though the photomontaging disappeared as the series progressed, the use of elemental details of rocks and water remained a decorative feature of the guides, particularly the 1964 *Cornwall* whose endpapers are close ups of pebbles on a beach. Elsewhere the gazetteer is concluded under Zeal, South (see South Tawton) – a very Betjeman joke – below which is a close up of primroses flowering by a roadside culvert into which water enters from a pipe, almost like a tiny formal garden. These type of 'essence' images were used throughout the guides to recreate in the reader the sense of being a child. This was another of Betjeman's skills: remembering pleasures from his childhood[4] and making the reader reach back into their own – both real and imagined. These types of Shell Guide image were used to create a sense of holiday, childhood and memory which was one of their biggest hooks for the reader.

As editor, Betjeman would have seen the best of the earlier gazetteer entries and realised their inherent advantage. Equally, short entries listed purely in alphabetical order made images easier to integrate into the text and made pages easier to lay out as each of the elements involved was small. That said, some of Betjeman's entries in *Devon* are very long – 'Plymouth' runs over five pages with all its images and the perambulation of the city it describes. Mostly though, entries are short and numerous – a further great advantage of the gazetteer being that it allowed more places to be covered in more depth, providing the entries were telegraphic or poetic but not descriptive.

However, Betjeman was a natural digresser and even his little piece titled 'Gazetteer' deals with the subject briefly and seemingly dismissively: "A gazetteer has been described as an alphabetical arrangement of unrelated facts. I have put down the fruit of my experience in alphabetical order – and very dull it looks". It quickly moves on to mention the unique point of his guide – "the listing of the Georgian period" – and encourage the visiting of remote houses and the use of the one-inch Ordnance Survey map to get away from well-worn tourist routes. This reads almost like an advert for these relatively new maps marketed at the leisure user, containing a steadily growing amount of information on historical sites.

The most Betjemanian elements of the guide, things that became staples of the series, are: the entries about the Georgian terraces of Exeter accompanied by very modern images which really force upon the viewer the virtues of what was then an ignored architectural icon of Britain; and the perambulation of Plymouth celebrating the idiosyncrasies of eighteenth- and nineteenth-century provincial architecture. Though the perambulation never really developed as a section in the Shell Guides, the architecture celebrated in *Devon*'s 'Plymouth' did; and the perambulation became a regular feature of that other guide, Pevsner's Buildings of England series. John Piper described Betjeman's *Devon* as "the model Shell Guide for all time"[5] and it certainly is a confident and assured celebration of place – though some of the places he described he did not visit, relying rather on trusted local informants in the time-tested manner of guidebooks. *Devon* also shows the genesis of the elegiac and warm-hearted image of Betjeman that was to become famous. In the guide, the section on the face of Devon is prefaced by a lane entering a village; and elsewhere an avenue of trees on the A30 near Honiton (that still exists) symbolises travel west. These images with their eloquent and small everyday pleasures are a visual celebration of ordinariness, something that Betjeman would later became so famous for. Equally, the erudite combination of history and interpretation delivered lightly was also a hint of things to come.

But Betjeman was still experimenting and developing his new guides and he began to turn to artists to compile them, perhaps thinking that they would handle images more fluently than himself and Byron. The artists he chose were much less personally eccentric, coming from solid middle-class London and Home Counties backgrounds similar to his own, and like him their experience of and feeling for the country had its root in childhood escape from either an urban or suburban milieu. Something that may have pushed Betjeman toward artists as compilers of guides is the problems he had with his authors, who in general were unable to rise to the challenge of combining informative, brief text with images. The guides for Somerset, Hampshire and Derbyshire were each, in their own way, object lessons in how not to write a Shell Guide – though that didn't mean they were necessarily badly written.

NOTES

1   Which appeared in the *Architectural Review* of May 1937.

2   In point of fact, the Olivier version is a good gazetteer.

3   Lord Clonmore, September 1933

4   According to Bevis Hillier, Betjeman would spend hours on the beach looking for stuff in rock pools. Before his love of architecture emerged, "he loved the taxonomic world of plant identification and the flowers of Cornwall – the early Primrose and even earlier Daffodil." (Hillier, 1988, p.84)

5   *Oxon*, 1938, p.4

SOMERSET, HAMPSHIRE AND DERBYSHIRE

A GUIDE TO SOMERSET was a logical step for the Shell Guides in the early phase of the series. Guides were also being written for the surrounding counties Wiltshire, Devon and Dorset and it was also a popular part of the West Country, probably better known then and more popular than today (leaving aside Glastonbury). Betjeman asked Peter Quennell to write it. Quennell, a mutual friend of Betjemen and Harold Acton and already known for poetry and his work on Lord Byron, wrote *Somerset* with his father who died in 1936 the year the guide was published. C.H.B. Quennell was an Arts and Crafts architect and designer who worked on Hampstead Garden Suburb and helped develop the wealthy south London suburb of Bickley, where his son was born in 1905. Like many of the Shell Guide authors, Peter Quennell was in his late twenties when he wrote *Somerset*. It is probably the weakest of the early Shell Guides for several reasons but mainly for its dullness – a quality that Evelyn Waugh, with whom Quennell shared a mutual dislike, pinpointed in his pithy comment calling Quennell a "fuddy-duddy fish-face".[1] The guide comes from the period when Betjeman chose young writers from his wide social circle as authors and then used the design skills of the Architectural Press for the rest of the guide. At the time *Somerset* was produced, Betjeman had begun to look towards artists to produce the guides perhaps because they might be better at unifying text and image. This had certainly been a problem with *Kent* and *Wiltshire*, but was even more so with *Somerset*.

The early guides used a cover design that, though uncredited, looks like the work of Maurice Beck. When authors were offered a contract to prepare a guide they were usually offered his services as photographer and to all intents and purposes he was the 'in house' photographer for the guides until the war.[2] Their designs now seem a peculiarly corporate and English kind of Art Deco with their use of strong black-and-white photographs titled in a sans-serif type in two weights and cases; clear, modern and attractive. *Kent* and *Somerset* are very successful covers despite their subsequent contents and this lack of continuity was something that Betjeman was aware of and corrected in later guides. He was quick to spot problems and quick to learn and with the next generation of artist–writer guides the series hit its stride. The awkwardness and disjointed design of *Somerset* is very clear if the front cover is compared to the rear cover, which uses a device that could work in the hands of John Nash but not the Quennells. The rear cover is two images placed one above the other to create a crude dialectic: in this case, a thatched cottage with a garden is juxtaposed with a Weston Super Mare beach full of umbrellas and deckchairs. Where the cover has a carefully composed image of a remote and untouristy site (which became a typical cover device in many later Shell Guides), rich in textures and taken from a typical modernist photographer's viewpoint, the rear cover amounts to two very

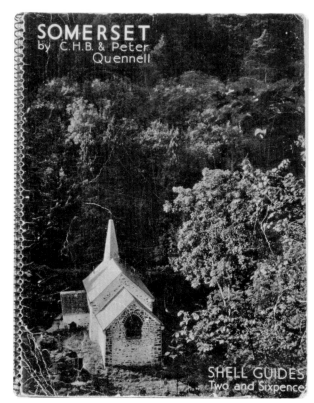

Somerset, 1936, cover

One of Beck's best, crispest pictures, this would have pleased the authors in its conjuring up a sense of the remote ancient Somerset of Arthur and Alfred without resorting to a picture of Glastonbury Tor.

conventional views of 'leisure' taken from a conventional viewpoint. It is hard to know how much influence over the design of the guide the Quennells had; but from the widely varying use and quality of the images in the guide – in contrast with the front cover – it may be guessed that they had quite a measure of control over the choice of images and that they hardly used Maurice Beck at all.

As a result, the images in *Somerset* have many of the faults that occur when a writer chooses images for a book – they tend to be token denotative illustrations of an aspect of the text. A case in point is the image above the brief section 'Somerset Hills'. This part of the guide, an arcane section common in guides before the development of the powerful motorcars available in the 1930s, gives a list of all the difficult hills in the county from the 1-in-4 Porlock Hill, "length 3,960 yards; two acute hairpin bends" to that on the Bath to Stroud road, an anodyne "1-in-11 Length 3 miles; several bends". The picture above it is simply there to fill a space and its caption reads, "J. Wyatt's Column at Ammerdown, Frome (Eighteenth Century). Many of the hills of Somerset are adorned with folly towers and columns." Leaving aside the tenuous link to what is listed below it – dangerous hills for vehicles – the image itself shows trees in the foreground on apparently flat land, with Wyatt's column tiny in the far distance.

Barns, Somerset, 1936

Wyatt's Column,
Somerset, *1936*

Combwich, Somerset,
1936

*Bath, Lansdowne
Crescent,* Somerset,
1936

Above: More typical of *Somerset* are dull, unimaginative photographs like these three barns chosen by the authors to do no more than illustrate their words. If the Shell Guides were to succeed they needed more assertive, allusive images.

Right: Somerset contenders for the worst Shell Guide photographs: Wyatt's Column disappears into the background almost to the vanishing point; Combwich is given second place to the muddy Parrett at low tide; and the Lansdowne Terrace at Bath is reproduced unintentionally out of focus.

Elsewhere, a half page image of "Combwich, near the mouth of the river Parrett" appears in the gazetteer section under T while "Somerset Barns: 1. Glastonbury (fourteenth century) 2. Pilton 3. Doulting" appears alongside the S section of the gazetteer. In later guides it was the practice to illustrate places before they occurred in the text in order to make the reader look forward rather than backward from text to image; but even the captions here are badly laid, with clumsy spacing and the odd inclusion of some dates but not others. The pictures themselves are stock shots clumsily cropped to fit the page. The main problem with these images is dullness and, at best, they illustrate rather than evoke. All this may seem very picky but in the vast majority of later guides the standards of design were much higher and the lacklustre images, captions and layout form a subtly dulling environment for the text.

C.H.B. Quennell was an architect, his wife was a social historian and Peter Quennell was amongst other things a literary historian, so it is not surprising that the centrepiece of their *Somerset* was an exhaustive essay on 'Bath and its Associations', despite the presence of a full entry for Bath in the gazetteer. Where Clonmore's essay on Canterbury in *Kent* is personal and full of a naive goshness, the Quennells' Bath is almost the opposite: wordy, worldly and pompous, and seemingly very long. It begins as it means to go on: "In a world that has never quite recovered from The Dark Ages – when the mathematical genius of the Roman Empire dwindled and decayed, the tiled roofs of her villas collapsed onto the mosaic floors beneath, and the breached aqueducts poured their waters into the fields – few cities have developed according to plan." The text then races through history to Palladio's Vicenza and finally reaches "Bath, as we know it" at the bottom of the page – but soon we are off again on a long journey to an earlier Bath.

> But, whenever [hot springs] were discovered – and, no doubt, it was at a very remote period – the Roman colonists were quick to take advantage of them; and between the first and fifth centuries A.D. there existed – probably at the foot of the Lansdown – one of their neat quadrangular settlements that had sprung up all over the Empire from the banks of the Tigris and Euphrates to the green misty regions of the furthest west.

The prose in *Somerset* is all written in this style, which recalls that of the Victorian guidebooks Betjeman was trying to get away from. One sentence – the second in the section on the seventeenth- and eighteenth-century architecture of Somerset – is ten-lines long and contains nine bits of punctuation, commas, semi colons, brackets and dashes before the full-stop. In its concluding clause, Quennell declaims that Bath is "where the elegance and classical reserve of the eighteenth century still protest against the spreading squalor of the Industrial Age". The wordiness of the essays in the guide might have

been mitigated by a good gazetteer; but where the reader was regaled with too many of Bath's associations, the gazetteer is by turns briefly uninformative – "Blue Anchor: 2: A popular resort of holiday campers. Cliffs with curious alabaster veining" – or lengthily downbeat:

> **Axbridge**: 13: A small town with an extremely long history. The church, though partially restored at the end of the last century, is still worth a visit. There is an interesting roof of the 17th century. Fragments of 14th century fresco have been spoiled by repainting. On the west side of the tower is a figure thought to be that of Henry VIII.

Of Exmoor they write:

> Most people think of Exmoor as a second Dartmoor: but, though equally wild it is nothing of the sort. On Exmoor we find no granite tors; the hills are very rounded, the valleys comparatively fertile, overgrown here or there with twisted oak scrub, relics of primeval forest. Wild red deer are not so numerous as is supposed, but a stag hunt can generally be viewed in the hunting season.

There are some good entries as in the case of Glastonbury but far from celebrating Somerset and enthusing the reader with thoughts of the county, the Quennell guide is underwhelming in all its parts – even its sections on fishing and shooting which begin respectively, "Compared with some other counties Somerset is not too well-off for salmon and trout fishing, and what does exist is often in private hands" and "The shooting in Somerset is rather like the fishing, not very distinguished".

Somerset was the worst of the early Shell Guides, lacking even eccentricity and it was never attempted again; but in the following year another one-off guide appeared that was an attempt to do something far more innovative. While John Rayner's *Hampshire* was like *Somerset* never revisited (a later edition by John Arlott was never finished), it is a gem of design, conceptualisation and writing and is only let down by its poor use of imagery.

John Rayner is a bit of a mystery at the edge of many well-known characters. Betjeman knew Rayner through his wife, Joan Eyres-Monsell, whom he met when he travelled with his wife, Penelope, to the Rome house of Gerald Berners in 1936. Betjeman used a couple of her photographs in his *Oxford University Chest* (1938). Rayner later divorced from Eyres-Monsell but both remained friends with Betjeman. She was another woman Betjeman found very sexually attractive, as he told her in a letter sent when she was later married to Patrick Leigh Fermor. As well as, unusually, being the unknown husband of a well-known wife, Rayner was, according to Wikipedia, a typographer, journalist and member of SOE, which makes him seem very glamorous for a typographer.

Apart from the Shell Guide to Hampshire he didn't write much; but he did write about Thomas Bewick, who was being rediscovered in the thirties and forties, both in the *A.R.* and in a famous King Penguin about him too. The fact that like Bewick he was a typographer is evident in his *Hampshire* as its sections are headed with reproductions of wooden display type; and his future in the SOE may be inferred from his very breezy, sharp writing that makes the guide a great read. Rayner's guide is organised entirely as a gazetteer and, as much as the saving graces of Edith Olivier's *Wiltshire* gazetteer, Rayner's *Hampshire* may have shown how flexible and useful to the aims of the guide this form was.

Hampshire begins robustly under A with "ABC order is the plan of this guide so that you can find what you want easily. You will be able to look up a particular thing, person or place you want to know about and also dip into the book for random reading." This last point is the real strength of the gazetteer form and explains why it was so useful to Betjeman – it asks nothing of the reader in terms of attention, promises instant gratification and has the serendipitous quality of wandering along shelves of books. Rayner continues, "The facts are representative and not meant to be all-inclusive: and have been more or less arbitrarily chosen, partly according to whim and partly on the generally overlooked principle that guide-book readers are all sorts." Unlike the Quennells, Rayner welcomes the reader as an equal and even better says, "Of specialists two things are asked, that they should do what specialists and experts don't do, and allow for the translation into inexact everyday idiom of facts often unfairly isolated about their high hobbyhorse: and that they should look up the section Errors. If you want to know about the birds of Hampshire, don't look up ornithology – look up BIRDS." Rayner seems to have been the authorial equivalent of Betjeman's target audience: direct, curious, wearing his knowledge lightly – and witty. The next heading is 'Aborigines' and has the quality of informal speech rather than the rhetoric of the Quennells. Some way in he says in parenthesis, "(near Droxford; go and see it, it's one of the best in the country, though Danebury is something again)". Insignificant though this seems now, the use of such demotics then was asking for trouble as was his later aside, delivered as if in a clubhouse or saloon bar, "Invaders from the Continent were Iron age peoples, Bronze Age, Neolithic and the Belgae: I have had a fact-packed Belgian in a little village in the Ardennes claim relationship on the last account". Of Hampshire he says, "And for the third class of people, those who already fancy another county, this book is out to seduce; in favour of Hampshire, a blue-eyed, bubble breasted blonde of a placid age". He is scathing about Bournemouth as might be expected, describing it as a "mother-borough", which sounds bad. But he could also make it sound fascinating between insults: "It is a place where people spend money rather than make it, where there are twenty thousand more women than men, where R.L. Stevenson

wrote *Kidnapped* and *Dr Jekyll and Mr Hyde*, and where there is every sort of seaside amenity", concluding with the parting shot, "there is no real need to go there unless you have a weak chest and you think the air would do you good". Part of Rayner's style is to make places good and bad so as to show you how to behave properly. Thus he writes of the New Forest, which he loved, "Many people have discovered this [that the New Forest had no visitor restrictions], and motor perhaps a hundred miles from London, to draw up on the grass beside the petrol-fume-blue main road which throbs across the heath: there, with windows wound up so as to avoid actual contact with nature, they eat their sandwiches and watch the cars go by. A little snooze, and they drive home again." That could be my parents in the 1970s, let alone the thirties. What Rayner liked was exploring and finding the unusual and this really was the tone of all the good Shell Guides. Under F, he describes how Hampshire should be done:

> **Farley Monument is a strange manifestation of the English spirit, combining hippomania and the almost invariably successful grandeur of follies. If you follow the Roman road from Winchester to Salisbury (you can find it on the one-inch Ordnance map: it is mostly flints and holes, with sometimes grass growing between the wheel tracks, but passable) you will see, when you come abreast of Pitt Down, on your left, nearly four miles along the road, a strange sight. A sort of metronome box with little doors, which crowns the high down in front. It is a monument to a horse which is buried underneath.**

The great weakness of *Hampshire* is its images which are either simply illustrative photos, old prints and one old child's drawing. Though they are interesting adjuncts to the text, they don't show you anything of Hampshire – even the image of Bournemouth, though highly symbolic in its proximity to Rayner's comment, "Whoever made the country, man certainly made the town of Bournemouth"[3], is in the end just a picture of steps. The old prints are just that and make weak shadows of the text. In later guides the use of old prints to illustrate would become scarcer and more relevant to the experience of the county. But with *Hampshire*, the very strength and dominance and drive of the text is what makes it untypical and a one-off; even in the experimental beginnings of the Shell Guides the role of images was equal to that of the text. In fact, though the images in the body of *Hampshire*'s text aren't memorable, the title page and in particular the cover are. Rayner's cover design moves away from the safe commercial Deco of *Cornwall*, *Kent*, *Somerset* and *Derbyshire* toward something much more surreal. A photo of a river glassily moving past trees and reeds is superimposed on the silhouette of the county, which includes the Isle of Wight. The silhouette of the county is laid onto white and so the river of Hampshire appears to flow into the channel. Most Shell

Cover image by Will F. Taylor, Hampshire, 1937

Municipal Horticulture at BOURNEMOUTH
n front of the Pavilion. Bournemouth plants

Bournemouth by Will F. Taylor, Hampshire, 1937, p.15

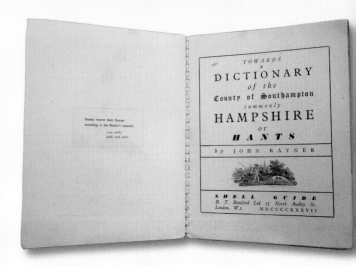

Title page of Hampshire, 1937, woodcut by T. Bewick

covers were tonally dark where this is light, and literal where this is surreal. Rayner's typography was no less ahead of the other guides: where they use sans serif he uses a face that became synonymous with the Festival of Britain of 1951. Inside, the frontispiece eschews Betjeman's Victorian style for a pastiche of an eighteenth- or early-nineteenth-century book as befitted his fascination with Bewick; and below his name he portrays himself perhaps, using a Bewick image of a man happily out walking his pig and his dog.

Rayner's *Hampshire* is unique amongst the early guides being better written and more modern than any of the others; but like the original *Cornwall* it was not obviously part of a series and Betjeman was, through his tendency to repeat ideas and impose forms on authors, clearly desirous of the corporate feel that goes with a series. Along with the Nashes and later Piper, Rayner was an artist–writer and Betjeman's move towards artists away from writers paid off, taking the Shell Guides away from old textual strategies into forms that were, as he wanted, more intertextual, more modern.

Derbyshire was one of the first tranche of Shell Guides and is as experimental as *Kent* or *Wiltshire*. Like Betjeman, Clonmore and Byron, its editor Christopher Hobhouse was in his twenties when he wrote his guide, 25 in fact. Like Byron, he was killed early in the war. In 1935 when *Derbyshire* came out Hobhouse had already written a successful biography of Charles James Fox published in 1934 and in 1937 wrote what was to be another success, *1851 and the Crystal Palace*, illustrated by Osbert Lancaster, published to

celebrate this talisman of Victorian ingenuity after it was burnt in December 1936. He also wrote a guide to Oxford. Hobhouse was remembered by Betjeman's daughter as "tall, conceited and brilliant and lots of people of both sexes were in love with him".[4] He was, like Byron, a good writer, interested in Victoriana and possessed of strong opinions; he was a conservative anti-appeaser. However, as with other early guides, *Derbyshire* is a bit of a curate's egg precisely because of the author's virtues; certainly Betjeman seems to have been entirely steamrollered by Hobhouse as there is little evidence that the former exercised much control in respect of either form or content. The guide has the shortest gazetteer of the series and is written in a hybrid style, part old-fashioned narrative guide of the Victorian type and part a more modern type of guide that you might get today aimed at walkers with cars. *Derbyshire* was the first Shell Guide that really took the motorist seriously, positively recommending the virtues of the car over the train and suggesting itineraries based on car use; though the suggestion of itineraries was slightly against the emerging ethos of the guides.

Derbyshire begins with images of roads stretching across wide open spaces or descending gorges to make the point that the sublime natural landscape of the dales is best reached by car, a point reinforced immediately by the text. The first line states, "The motorist has an advantage that the railway traveller lacks", by which he means the driver can go over the hilly landscape rather than through it as the train must. As he says, "The railway works all over Derbyshire

Together with *Dorset* and *Wiltshire*, *Hampshire* has the most imaginative of the early Shell Guide covers. For *Hampshire*, Rayner modified an image of a Hampshire river by overlaying a white silhouette of the county over it so that the image becomes 'Hampshire' and its subject, the river, appears to flow out of Southampton Water. This simple montage, with its bold type looking forward to the style of the fifties, is the most fully synthesised design of the three, combining clarity, surrealism and modernity. Inside the picture is less clear as the text overwhelms the imagery; but throughout, the latter is still adventurous, with the title page avoiding the Victorian in favour of a seemingly more modern type of pastiche, this time of late-eighteenth-century design, inspired by Thomas Bewick's man, dog and pig, which are incorporated. Rayner's entry on Bournemouth illustrates the primacy of design and writing in *Hampshire*: the photograph becomes a fall guy for the joke created by the framing text.

Winnats Pass, Derbyshire, 1935, pp.44–5

Derbyshire was the first of the Shell Guides to really celebrate driving as a way of seeing a county and this message was predominantly carried by images suggesting empty landscapes traversed by open roads. In the case of the title page, the road is barely suggested by the telegraph poles and stone walls traversing the photograph of Thorpe Cloud.

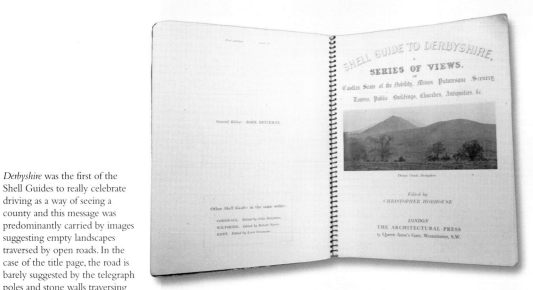

Derbyshire, 1935, title page

Derbyshire, 1935, cover

are undeniably bold: everywhere huge viaducts, precipitous cuttings, and sweeping curves of line add their enhancement to the landscape. But you might travel about on them, Bradshaw in hand, for a month without finding as much of the essence and spirit of the county as a discriminating motorist will discover in a week." But after this bold and appropriate beginning we find that Hobhouse has a particular view of Derbyshire: there are places worth attention and others that are not. "Duffield, Ilkeston, Clay Cross, Hucknal, Staveley, Bolsover – it is like a goods train passing by. Admirable as are many of these little towns, they are not holiday resorts, and the reader of this Guide will be shepherded away from their vicinity." This is a guide to parts of Derbyshire that, quoting Byron, he notes are "'as noble as Greece or

Switzerland'. Why, one feels, motoring over the Snake Road, less than two hundred miles from London, why go further afield." It is clear that the reader is to be guided to the wild and sublime parts of the county as if it were the lakes and though shortly after he concludes 'How to see Derbyshire', "So you will return to Derby, having seen in a week, or more probably a month, more wonderful country than you thought that England held" it is by his own reckoning only a small part of the county and one dominated by the wild country of the peaks rather than its industrial or agricultural areas. The concluding images of the introduction make Hobhouse's views plain, as does the caption, "You can look two ways in Derbyshire. This is the Castleton Valley looking west [empty fields, stone walls, trees, distant

Derbyshire was unusual for the Shell Guides because it was openly against the idea of towns, villages and the commercial effluvia of tourism, instead presenting a view of Derbyshire that favoured empty wild landscapes free of any building.

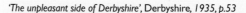
'You can look two ways in Derbyshire', Derbyshire, 1935, p.11

You can look two ways in Derbyshire.   This is the Castleton Valley looking west (above)—

—and here is the same scene looking east.

'The unpleasant side of Derbyshire', Derbyshire, 1935, p.53

The rather more unpleasant side of Derbyshire to be seen in the otherwise pleasant town of Castleton.

ridge, big sky] and here is the same scene looking east" – a bungalow snack stall crudely advertising hot water and teas. So from the start the guide isn't really about the county but about part of it, and that a part from which all vulgar commercialism is absent.

The next section is one that occurs in all the very earliest guides, a description of the monuments of Derbyshire by period, dully delivered and straight; but shortly we come to sections that really interest Hobhouse: 'Great Families and Great Houses', pages 18–32, and 'The rivers of Derbyshire and Dovedale', pages 32–6. In fact the chapters roll on though descriptions of the High and Low Peak and 'Derbyshire Industries' until page 52 where the gazetteer 'Derbyshire Places' finally begins, running to page 57. The book is in fact an old-fashioned, slow-reading narrative guide and this is its great failing. The reader cannot dip in and out, the advantage of a gazetteer structure, but is rather dragged through the concerns of the author, in this case great families and the legal virtues of the Wirksworth Barmoot Court, which administered the lead mines of the county. Luckily Hobhouse is an attractive writer and one barely notices that one hardly knows a place before the sections on the two Peaks. Hobhouse shares a modern fascination with the lives and homes of the rich and devotes pages to Bess of Hardwick, though her main house, Hardwick Hall, lies outside his prescribed area of interest. He is nearly as scathing about the modern Chatsworth of her descendants as he is of Curzon's Kedleston of which he says, "it is a singularly appropriate monument to a man whose pride and love went deeper than his taste in interior decoration". Of the Duke of Rutland's home at Haddon Hall, however, he is at his best and most jingoistic:

> It is the most enigmatic of buildings. It is difficult to say whether it is large or small, close to you or far away. Its detail is small, yet its scale is vast: its proportions are light and elegant, yet its construction is massive. You come closer and its mystery grows. It is a fortress made of gossamer, a castle as welcoming as a cottage. …it has grown to be more English than any house in England. …There are no Haddon Halls along the banks of the Rhine or among the passes of the South Tyrol, and a man who could see Haddon Hall unmoved must himself have the spirit of a Hun.

Yet at the time of writing, as he critically notes, "There are no more tourists now; permission even to take photographs is refused". In fact Hobhouse, though obsessed with the great and bad, is also a firm believer in open access to the England that he loved. His liberal love of the country is the thing that comes shining through this guide, which is mainly about driving to remote places, walking and fishing in an unenclosed landscape. Uniquely in the Shell Guides he describes some walks in detail. The guide was written not long after the Great Trespass on Kinder Scout and the first government

enquiry into the idea of National Parks, and was contemporary with the creation of the Pennine Way. It is clear on where we should stand on this issue: "a very large proportion of the forty miles of open country between Manchester and Sheffield is denied to the teeming population of those towns for the benefit of ten or twelve sportsmen. There is, of course, nothing whatever to be said in defence of this state of affairs."

Hobhouse is equally unequivocal on walkers, about whom there was a lot of snobbery, and bungalows, of which there are still a lot:

> There is one more point to make. The Peak in summer is extremely popular with the young men and women of the industrial towns; it is positively yellow with their undergarments. If you dislike these people, you had better spend your week-end in the mud-bath at Smedley's than on Kinder Scout. Aesthetically, the Peak is grand enough to stand any number of them and any amount of litter. What it will not stand is bad building and commercialism. A single brick bungalow, a single asbestos roof, will lay waste to a valley of twenty square miles: and the growth of charabancs, advertisements and touts is threatening to spoil the pleasure of the whole thing.

As with the rest of *Derbyshire*, the very short gazetteer is really not about actual places but attitudes and what's on offer to the fisherman and walker. Thus in Ashbourne he writes, "It was on the road to Derby that Johnson observed that if he had no duties, and reference to futurity, he would spend his life driving briskly in a post chaise with a pretty woman: it is still a charming road". Of the church he only notes the sad monument to Penelope Boothby where other Shell Guides would have noticed everything else. Of Bakewell he says, "Today the main attraction of Bakewell is the Duke of Rutland's fishing" and of Edale, "It is much the best place for those who want to explore on foot. The Church Hotel is a great place of resort for walkers, and the proprietor is a fountain of good advice". And of Rowsley, "There is, in fact, only one snag about Rowsley – it is noisy. Large numbers of milk trains make the night hideous, so get a bedroom on the side away from the station".

Reading *Derbyshire*, the longueurs of noble history and paeans to fishing cannot detract from Hobhouse's vitality and breezy modernity. His love of the land, his fellow-feeling with the working classes enjoying the cheap leisure of walking, his dislike of the mean shops that exploited them and the privilege that kept them from the hills, are attractive. One cannot help but feel that better use could have been made of his talents and prejudices had he been made to write a guide as they later became, with a brief introduction to the county followed by a detailed gazetteer. The Shell Guides were a new form of guide and Hobhouse did himself no service by, perhaps unconsciously, reprising many of the faults of the guides that Betjeman sought to replace with his series.

Opencast mines, Derbyshire, 1935, p.60

New Mills, Derbyshire, 1935, rear cover

NOTES

1   Lambert, 31 October 1993
2   Ruth Artmonsky notes in her
    book *Jack Beddington: The Footnote
    Man*, "When Maurice Beck, the
    society photographer, found his
    business declining, Beddington,
    who had originally met Beck in
    Shanghai, commissioned him to
    provide work not only for Shell
    advertising but also for the
    County Guides." (Artmonsky,
    2006, p.30)
3   *Hampshire*, 1937, p.15
4   Lycett Green, 1994, p.163 –
    footnote by the editor to a letter
    from J.B. to Wilhelmine Cresswell
    of 10 December 1936

One aspect of the Derbyshire guide that worked very well, and was used ably by Hobhouse as a shorthand critique, was its images; for though they showed little of towns beyond Buxton's Crescent, they did show the abstract beauty of the Peak with its minimal landscapes of fields, roads and walls while elsewhere critiquing the retail hangers-on of its tourism. Perhaps most prescient of all of our modern attitudes to landscape was his admiration of the industrial for its ruined spectacle. At the end of the gazetteer is an image of open-cast mining with the caption, "There is hardly any part of Derbyshire without signs of some industry or another, and such scenes as the above, in Chee Dale, are as typical as are any of the 'beauty spots', and tend to improve rather than detract from, their surroundings." On the rear cover is a roofless mill below a viaduct; workers' terraces lead the eye to a distant horizon. This is not an image of despair but a Piraneseian wonder at the scale and transience of the works of man.

Derbyshire was the first of the Shell Guides to the North and before 1939 two more followed: *Northumberland and Durham* and *West Coast of Scotland*. Both, like *Derbyshire*, were far more political in their view than the guides to the South.

Though against the commercialisation of the Derbyshire Dales and Peak, Hobhouse was an early appreciator of its industrial heritage which he romantically lumped together with the grand landscapes as all being in their own way sublime.

DORSET, BUCKINGHAMSHIRE, NORTHUMBERLAND AND DURHAM, AND THE WEST COAST OF SCOTLAND

THE EARLY PUBLISHING HISTORY of the Shell Guides is dense with change and consequently their publication dates are not necessarily a guide to similarity of design. Nevertheless, it's fair to say that the earlier guides, up to *Somerset*, had similar cover designs with reversed-out white sans-serif titles and full-bled (borderless) monochrome photographic images, which gradually moved away from *Cornwall*'s figurative image and Berner's complex photomontage for *Wiltshire* toward a simpler use of landscapes. As always with the Shell Guides, however, there were exceptions, like *Dorset* and *Hampshire*, both using photomontage front covers, and one version of the *Gloucestershire* cover which employed a violet reproduction of a Victorian engraving.

Though *Somerset* and *Dorset* were published in the same month – April 1936 – *Dorset* marked the beginning of another style that used a larger title in a black serif face. The guides were spiral bound with wire up to 1937, when they moved publisher from the Architectural Press to B.T. Batsford and gained a new plastic spiral binding. This ultra-modern binding allowed the title to appear on the spine, stamped in a small serif face, and offered a number of colours for both spine and title. These spines added a new level of modernity to the titles (though some were published by Batsford with wire spines). This level of detail may seem arcane but one feature of the Shell Guides that differentiates them from all the others is the level of design detail applied to every aspect of the book. More importantly it is also indicative of the rapid evolution of the guides, which by 1937 were moving away from the abrupt combination of Victorian homages with modern covers and photography toward a subtler interplay between historical references and modern layouts. Throughout this period the Shell Guides were developing their style in tandem with the *Architectural Review*, even after the move to Batsford, as it progressively modernised its design. These design changes went hand in hand with important changes in content, notably the development of the gazetteer as the central structure of the guides and the gradual but distinct increase in importance of the introductory section over other sections, particularly those on sports, which slowly withered.

The most pronounced change to the guides involved their authors. Prior to 1936, Betjeman had used writers as 'editors of' the guides, though this was much nearer to authorship. These had proved eccentric and with the possible exception of Robert Byron, also a photographer, rather detached from the visual content of the guides. This latter was largely handled by Betjeman, Hubert de Cronin Hastings, managing editor of the *Architectural Review*, and others at the Architectural Press, with inputs from other interested parties like Maurice Beck who certainly influenced the early Deco style of the covers.

Dorset proved to be a new direction as the guides entered a period where they were 'compiled' or 'by' artists. *Dorset* was compiled by Paul Nash and the next guide, *Bucks*, was by his younger brother John. In fact, until the war all the new guides were by artists with the exception of *Gloucestershire* by the journalist and author Anthony West. Both Nashs credit Jack Beddington with their guide commissions; but whether it was Betjeman or Beddington that decided to give artists a try at the guides rather than writers, it brought about

The early Shell Guides were bound with wire; but with the move to Batsford they gained a new plastic binding system that allowed for the title to be printed on the spine, usually in a contrastingly very un-modern face. In 1939 the guides moved to Faber and Faber and they rebound the existing titles in a hard back. Amongst other profound changes to the design of the guides, Faber and Faber introduced the embossed spine titles against a coloured cover that remained a constant feature of the hardback guides until 1984.

a real advance in the quality of the series in every respect.

In retrospect it seems that the early authors were not as aware as Betjeman and others at the Architectural Press that the guides were a new kind of medium, being in effect magazines. Looking back at the magazine culture of the thirties, *Vogue*, *Life*, *Picture Post* and the *Architectural Review* were as much about images as words: the fast-developing art of the graphic designer meant that magazines no longer looked like illustrated texts but were increasingly a total medium where image, text and layout existed symbiotically. In the early guides and intermittently throughout the series prior to the war, there was an imbalance between these parts created by the structures that authors imposed on the guides through their writing. When the guides began to be created by artists, they leapt forward to become total works, each element informing the whole.

The reasons for this are probably to do with the contrasting relationships to books and magazines of the idea of the modern artist and the idea of the author. The Shell Guides were tourist guides generated out of a milieu of architectural appreciation and criticism. The place of this kind of writing in the thirties was hardly at the apex of modern literature. However, though magazines and guides were likewise not the height of the ambitions of the modern artist, neither were they insignificant: contemporary art practice was very interested in the new media of magazines, graphics and photography and artists themselves were drawn to the idea of a kind of new Renaissance man, an artist whose gifts were as expressible in one visual medium as another. By the same token, the practice of the artist was suited to the medium of the guidebook specifically because their training was dominated by the idea of the sketchbook. For British artists, the sketchbook was a basic tool of the trade and its nature was parallel in many ways to the idea of the Shell Guide. Sketchbooks were not simply collections of sketches of things in the world that interested the artist; they were also a place where brief contextual notes were written, including descriptions of mood and colour, and also places where small interesting objects could be stuck in. Artists' sketchbooks were part sketchpad, part diary, part scrapbook. Arguably many writers' notebooks were the same; but unlike writers, artists did not see these books as simply a source for their art. Many artists saw and still see the sketchbook *as* the art. Fortunately for Shell, all the artists who created guides in the thirties saw the sketchbook in this way. Under their influence, the Shell Guides found a surer voice through the form of the sketchbook.

To return briefly to the drawbacks of writers, one of the main problems with them was that they liked to write. For artists and perhaps poets like Betjeman, writing could be a short thing and the guides as they were developing – with an increasing reliance on the gazetteer form as the main element – favoured the written sketch which was easily reconfigured as a short gazetteer entry. Writers also almost always used pictures as rather literal illustrations to the text, where the picture is simply a neutral image of the thing described – and preferably a picture of the *whole* thing described. By contrast, artists trained in life drawing with its emphasis on significant detail saw illustration in a different way, prioritising poetic meaning over descriptive completeness.

When Nash received his commission for the Dorset guide he already had a relationship with Beddington, for whom he had earlier produced a poster of Rye Marshes where he had lived for health reasons. Nash had served as a soldier and a war artist in the First World War and, perhaps as a result, sought out remote and peaceful places to live which he seems to have found therapeutic. To undertake the Dorset project he moved to Swanage in Dorset where he lived for about a year, for part of the time in a small terraced house on the seafront. As well as touring the county he made sketches and paintings of what he saw and this led to another poster for Shell, of Kimmeridge. He also took a great number of photographs and thus was innovative among the guides' authors to date in undertaking so much work for his guide; but from an artist's position this was a normal response to such a project. His production of text, sketches, paintings and photographs all for the guide gave *Dorset* a unity of voice that no earlier guide could match and set a standard for others to follow.

But without a doubt the most important feature of Nash's contribution to the Shell Guides was his introduction of a particularly English version of surrealism that remained with them from then on. Actually, *Dorset* allowed Nash to develop his own surrealism free from the dominance of the continental variety that he had earlier tried to work through in his art-world career. Nash had been a founder member of Unit One in 1933. This was a group of artists committed to European modernism including Ben Nicholson, Henry Moore and Barbara Hepworth as well as the writer Herbert Read. As surrealism flourished on the Continent, Nash became an adherent of the movement and was particularly interested in its Freudian possibilities. However, like other British artists sympathetic to the movement, he felt oppressed by its doctrinaire tendencies and the contempt of the contemporary art world for British traditions in art, specifically landscape, in contrast to a reverence for continental modernism, whether in the form of abstraction or surrealism.

Paul Nash's problem with the surrealism of the London art world was that it didn't correspond to his experience of the surreal. For Nash, surrealism was not after all something to do with Freud or automatic writing and the other intellectualisations of international surrealism. Nash was not an intellectual. Nash's idea of the surreal was rooted in something more subliminal, more incoherent and more experiential. Nash was originally attracted to surrealism because he felt it related to his experience of nature as a child and his need for it as an adult. In his unfinished autobiography, *Outline* (1949), he relates how he and his brother would explore the Buckinghamshire country around their house. There, he explained, there were landscape features like groups of trees from which he felt a sort of spirit or resonance, sometimes sinister, sometimes benevolent. Later in life he became interested in ancient sites and the idea that these had traces of the lives that were bound up in them through history that could be sensed in the present – a sort of Jungian notion but also very traditionally British, like Pope's spirit of place. It was this sense of the spirits and traces of former people emanating from the land that he wanted to link to surrealism, which he saw as a cognate concept. However, this idea that the landscape is inherently surreal and pregnant with the experiences of history didn't go well with the more urbane sensibilities of continental surrealism. To this frustration should be added Nash's personal instability: he is thought to have been shell-shocked, and this led him to need peace and isolation and above all solace from the land. In view of all this, *Dorset* was not only a chance to develop his own surrealism but an 'out' from the pressures of the contemporary art world. It was therapy. For all these reasons, his *Dorset* is a sort of cry from the heart, a statement of his Englishness, but an Englishness that many shared and share.

Paul Nash was quite a lot older than Betjeman and his preface gives a clear sense that they didn't share similar views. He lightly pushes Betjeman's *Cornwall* aside to plough his own furrow:

> I have based the guide throughout upon the first, and to my mind, best of the series – *Cornwall*, by John Betjeman. That is to say, I have, in the main, examined and admired the way he has treated each section, and then done something as different as possible. This is because I recognise Mr Betjeman as highly ingenious but inimitable: even so to him must go my first acknowledgement.[1]

It would be hard to write a better dismissal and this passage is unusually adroit for Nash, who could be very blustery – as is shown in the dedication and end note which bracket the book. The former concludes, "To all those courageous enemies of 'Development' to whom we owe what is left of England"[2]; the latter fulminates, "When you go into an inn, ask for English food. If you are given badly cooked so-called French food kick up a row".[3]

To judge Nash by these comments would be unfair. They show the pain he felt at what had happened to Buckinghamshire, the county of his youth, and reflect generally a fear that appears again and again in the guides that the unfettered modern world is destroying England, to the extent that it was becoming unfamiliar. A more telling sense of Nash's spirit comes from a quote from Hardy:

The introductory images for *Dorset* were intended to startle the reader into a new consideration of the ancientness of the county, something very far from its more popular association with the works of Hardy. Nash's *Dorset* was a land of creatures and fossilised beings, some on the cover acting as *object personages*.

Dorset, 1936, title page

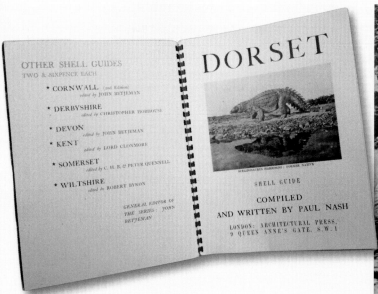

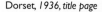

Endpapers by M. Beck, Dorset, 1936

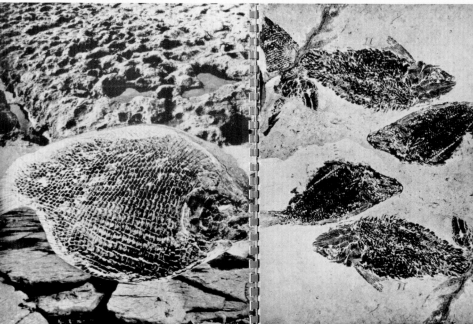

An August Midnight

A shaded lamp and a waving blind,
And the beat of a clock from a distant floor:
On this scene enter – winged, horned and spined –
A longlegs, a moth, and a dumbledore;
While 'mid my page there idly stands
A sleepy fly, that rubs its hands…

Thus meet we five, in this still place,
At this point of time, at this point in space…[4]

This seems to sum up Nash's feeling that in some places it is possible to see and touch a different and parallel world. In his own words he described photography thus: "the peculiar power of the camera to discover formal beauty which ordinarily is hidden from the human eye";[5] and called his subject, things in nature, the "object personage".[6] However, his choice of Hardy's words at once describes the scene more gracefully whilst somehow being pregnant with more than the reality those words depict. This is, in essence, Nash's surrealism and a view that, after *Dorset*, would in one way or another inform all the guides. Over half the images in *Dorset* are by Nash while the rostrum work was by Maurice Beck, whom Nash

Cerne Abbas, Shell Poster by F. Dobson, 1931

Cover of Dorset, *1936*

acknowledges in his preface for his "perfect photographs". It is for these images, either by or overseen by Nash, that the guide is chiefly remembered; but his writing is also very good. His long introduction, 'The Face of Dorset', is – far more than either Hobhouse's *Derbyshire* or the account of Wiltshire's plateau by Robert Byron – a fantastic and seductive evocation of an England full of meaning below the earth, at once surreal, mythic and Arthurian. Two passages stand out:

> To pass through Chalbury at twilight, shut in by the ridged hills, seeing the long tombs cut against the afterglow, is to experience an almost unnerving feeling of the latent force of the past…[7]

> I have read of enchanted places, and at rare times come upon them, but I remember nothing so beautifully haunted as the wood in Badbury Rings. Long afterward I read of the tradition that King Arthur's soul inhabited a raven's body which nested there – indeed it is one of the last nesting-places of the wild raven in England – but I needed no artificial stimulus to be impressed. Beyond the rings heave up and round in waves 40 feet high. A magic bird in a haunted wood, an ancient cliff washed by a sea changed into earth. There is scarcely anything lacking…[8]

The strength of Nash's writing is to make the reader sense the magic of these ancient places and thus to make us want to go there, though he was censored in the case of the Cerne Abbas Giant and

The Cerne Abbas Giant was a natural subject for Beddington's Shell poster campaigns since it was notorious and a long way from a train station; but the reason for its notoriety, the erect penis of the giant, made it impossible to illustrate uncensored. Nash therefore didn't bother, preferring only to say gnomically, "on a hill high above the town the huge ancient design of the naked Giant, 180ft high, tends to diminish the importance of mediaevalism"; whereas for his poster, Dobson came up with the idea of a shadow acting as a handy fig leaf.

can only mutter about "meddling fools" and "officious prudes" and his "unfortunately suppressed" image. This evocative skill is repeated in his account of the landscapes of the county and he achieves what Hobhouse was unable to do in his *Derbyshire*: to convey a sense of the particular beauty of landscapes. This was a new feature of the Shell Guides and in a way the unique selling point of motor tourism – the ability of the motor to reach the out-of-the-way sights previously only available to the heroic cyclist and walker. Nash found a language to tempt the tourist to a grassy mound by evoking the poetic.

Unsurprisingly given that Nash evidently preferred the hills, heaths and valleys of Dorset to its towns, his gazetteer is another relative failure of few pages. Not only is it short, running to less than seven pages of text, but it is bizarrely arranged in alphabetical order relating to each big settlement and then subdivided after that entry into an alphabetical order of places nearby. Yet within this very arbitrary list there are some good entries and Cerne Abbas in particular is rescued:

> Remote and unspoilt village in the valley of the Cerne, 8m N. of Dorchester. Romantic association of an ancient Benedictine Abbey dominates still. The gatehouse must be seen, and also the church. Look up at the curious carving of the Virgin and Child and the beautiful golden vane. Powerful haunt of legends; the healing spring of St Augustine at the end of a dark grove, and so on. But on the hill above the town the huge ancient design of the naked Giant, 180ft high, tends to diminish the importance of mediaevalism.[9]

In Dorset, Nash goes way beyond what in retrospect seem Betjeman's very modest aims for the guides to re-evaluate the ordinary eighteenth- and nineteenth-century architecture of the counties. In their place, Nash begins to look at, to evoke a much wider range of material, something which again became a hallmark of the series. Elsewhere he also manages to attack the great bête noire of the guides, suburbanisation and 'development', be it in Bridport, Lyme Regis or, most scathingly, in Swanage: "Perhaps the most beautiful natural site on the South Coast, ruined by two generations of 'development' prosecuted without discrimination or scruple".[10]

But Nash's best work in the guide is the combination of images and text which moves the whole into the realm of a discreet surrealist artwork, more subtly than his rather overt 'Monster Field' essay in the *Architectural Review* of 1940.[11] The images set up a visibly surreal world surrounding the text, thus skewing the frame of reference. His cover designs combine real elements of the coast into a sinister world of textures, rock, flora and fauna somewhere between De Chirico and Max Ernst, whereby Devon becomes a Jurassic Martian coast. Inside, Maurice Beck's montage images of

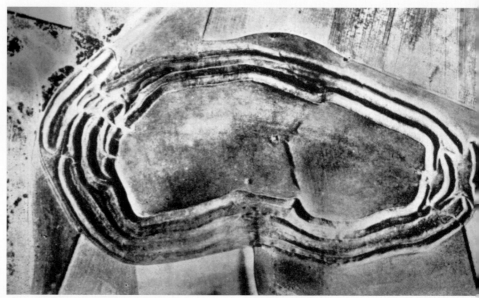

Maiden castle, Dorset, 1936, p.8

Stair Hole, Dorset, 1936, p.13

Quarry hut, Dorset, 1936, p.12

Nash's images could make links between the forms of objects that were suggestive of greater closeness than mere facts would suggest.

Grass steps, Dorset, 1936, p.30

Sheep, p.38, and Adder, Dorset, 1936, p.39

Toller Fratrum, Dorset, 1936, p.25

fossilised fish develop the sense of a strange ancient and alien world, defused only slightly by the humour of the title-page image of Scelidosaurus Harrisoni captioned 'Former Native ambling menacingly along a model beach'. Then comes a second, unaltered but by implication surreal, aerial image of Maiden Castle looking like a Neolithic eye, on pink paper, next to the section title 'The Face of Dorset'. In this introductory section, the text is illustrated with similarly 'real' images that make the familiar strange: an old quarry hut seems as old as the dinosaurs while Stair Hole's strata writhe struggling to leave the sea, radio shacks perched on their backs. After page 20, a whole series of images abstract the countryside into geometricised landscapes and tourist destinations free of modern

Nash's imagery also had a tendency toward suggesting the sinisterly comic as if there were things going on that were not quite explainable.

45

humanity – all rendered timeless and almost classical. In the gazetteer, full advantage is taken of black-and-white photography to make oriental the alabaster tomb at Athelhampton Chapel and deeply sinister the font at Toller Fratrum (this, by the way, is the first John Piper image in a Shell Guide, taken from the *Architectural Review*). Elsewhere the grass steps of Milton Abbas again recall De Chirico while the flora and fauna section of the guide is full of terrifyingly Freudian moths, phallic adders and sheep resembling eighteenth-century statesmen. While many non-surreal images are in the guide, the number that are very surreal tips the book and Dorset into a place that seems entirely plausible but alien. This was Nash's purpose, to make the motorist see Dorset through the both old and new eye of the avant-garde.

A year later, his younger brother's guide to Bucks came out under the Batsford imprint. Buckinghamshire was an interesting county for the Shell Guides as it represented within its long, thin, north-to-south boundaries all the pressures on a modernising Britain, tradition and agriculture giving way to suburbs and 'light industry'. Its southern boundary is the Thames between Staines and Henley which had long been a 'Three Men in a Boat' playground suburb for Londoners. Along its eastern boundary were the rapidly developing London end of the A4 and A41 roads that brought with them industry and more suburbs. In the south-east corner of the county lay Uxbridge and the industrialised town of Slough. From the eastern edge of the county came the Metropolitan railway that turned Chalfont, Latimer and Amersham into Metroland, the archetypical comfy, ruralised suburb. Incidentally, it was also home to some of the British film industry and its stars, and one of London's best known 'country walks', Burnham Beeches. Yet the north west of the county was quiet and agricultural, bordering Bedfordshire, Northamptonshire and Oxfordshire. It is the very model of a Home County and all that means. John Nash and Paul were raised in the county at its London side near Iver Heath and at the time the guide was written John lived there, near Aylesbury. By then he had also rented a house at Wormington in Essex near the home of Edward Bawden, finally moving there permanently in 1943, Essex being in the forties as Bucks was to his father in the 1890s.

It is a commonplace to note that many people in the thirties were hostile to suburbanisation and all it brought with it; but what should also be remembered is the special flavour of their horror, owing to the complicity of the aesthetic middle class in the process. For they pioneered the suburb and defined its form through the works of Shaw, Voysey, Baillie Scott and minor architects like Quennell, author of the Shell *Somerset* and developer of Bickley, Kent. The Nashs' father's home at Iver Heath was such a pioneering effort, as was that of John Piper's father in Epsom in similar Surrey. Though in Betjeman's *Cornwall* and Paul Nash's *Dorset* there is disparaging mention of development, it is in *Bucks* that the subject

really had meaning. John Nash disliked the despoliation of his county and deals with the matter in two ways: mainly, *Bucks* is about the rural parts of the county; but here and there he goes to town. Whilst Buckingham "is fortunate that its situation has saved it from the results of progress",[12] Chalfont St Peter:

> has suffered even more severely from the age we live in. The main road from Aylesbury to London has crashed right along the valley and down the hill into the village, sweeping away houses, trees and hedges. On the banks of the Misbourne, at the point where the road crosses it, is the Old Greyhound Inn, whose floodlit sign tells us it is, "genuine fifteenth century".[13]

Yet Nash is quite subtle in his approach to the subject, railing at the unknown horrors in small places but quietly understating the well known so that in the introduction he briefly notes that,

> During the past thirty years, London has reached out its tentacles into this part of the country and many of the lanes and villages have become ruthlessly suburbanised. Here also lie the two largest towns, Slough and High Wycombe, where prosperous industrial conditions have led to a sacrifice of the countryside.[14]

About Slough, Nash's gazetteer entry is an attack by froideur and inference:

> A modern manufacturing town on the Bath road, Slough is the largest town in the county. A hundred years ago the population was less than 1,000: to-day it is 34,000, and is still growing. Its prettiest feature, a Georgian coaching inn on the corner of the road to Eton, has recently been demolished, and a neo-Georgian inn erected in its place.[15]

He then lists without comment 45 different industries in the town, from brushes to watercress via ointment. But his real attack on Slough is the double-page photomontage, 'Slough Then and Now', contrasting its agricultural roots with the present where, as the caption notes, mannequins are 'An Industry'. This image is one of three by Cecil H. Greville, the others being a montage called 'River Activity and Rest' and the last, 'Canal People'. Greville was a local photographer who has an archive now in the Slough museum. His work shows that the political uses of modern photography techniques like montage and documentary were not just practised by London's cultural lions but were widely understood. Nash uses Greville's work because it is local and a bit crude, not deprecatingly but because it says what he needs to say. Betjeman was undoubtedly affected by 'Slough Then and Now' for the content of his poem 'Slough' written in the year of *Bucks*' publication, 1937:

Slough

Come, friendly bombs, and fall on Slough
It isn't fit for humans now,
There isn't grass to graze a cow
Swarm over, Death!

Come, bombs, and blow to smithereens
Those air-conditioned, bright canteens,
Tinned fruit, tinned meat, tinned milk, tinned beans
Tinned minds, tinned breath.

Mess up the mess they call a town –
A house for ninety-seven down
And once a week a half-a-crown
For twenty years,

And get that man with double chin
Who'll always cheat and always win,
Who washes his repulsive skin
In women's tears,

And smash his desk of polished oak
And smash his hands so used to stroke
And stop his boring dirty joke
And make him yell.

But spare the bald young clerks who add
The profits of the stinking cad;
It's not their fault that they are mad,
They've tasted Hell.

It's not their fault they do not know
The birdsong from the radio,
It's not their fault they often go
To Maidenhead

And talk of sports and makes of cars
In various bogus Tudor bars
And daren't look up and see the stars
But belch instead.

In labour-saving homes, with care
Their wives frizz out peroxide hair
And dry it in synthetic air
And paint their nails.

Come, friendly bombs, and fall on Slough
To get it ready for the plough.
The cabbages are coming now;
The earth exhales.[16]

'Slough Then and Now', Bucks, 1937, pp.36–7

Portrait of Cecil H. Greville, Slough Museum archive

'River Activity and Rest', Bucks, 1937, p.41

John Nash found a local photographer, Cecil H. Greville, who had an eye for making small 'picture essays' of the type that was then emerging in photo magazines. The image of 'Slough Then and Now' evoked the disappearance of the old Buckinghamshire so eloquently that it has been mistakenly accredited to Betjeman, who later wrote his famous poem about Slough. It is more likely that he was influenced by the photograph.

Cover, by
Maurice Beck, of
Bucks, 1937

Beech trees by Humphrey Jennings, Bucks, 1937, title page

John Nash, like his brother Paul, had a talent for the comic. Whether it be Buckingham Town Hall's swan or Burnham Beeches viewed from a familiar but rarely photographed angle, he made familiar Bucks unfamiliar.

Like Greville, John Nash uses the potential of modern art practice to achieve effects in a different register. Unlike his brother Paul, John was what might be termed a part-time surrealist for, by his own observation, he was primarily a realist painter. However, in his Shell Guide he uses realism to create surreal effects or, as in the case of Greville's work, used the surrealism of others. Notably, his title page uses a Humphrey Jennings photograph looking up a beech tree. On the one hand, Nash seems to be saying this is the most characteristic view of Bucks whilst, on the other, Jennings' surrealism has given the tree a disturbing, feminine anthropomorphism, as if seen from a child's height. So as with 'Slough Then and Now', the image has a gentle double meaning, real and funny, yet surreal and disturbing too. Similarly the cover image, made by Maurice Beck with Nash, shows a close up or cropped detail of Buckingham Town Hall with an outsize sculpture of a swan on the roof. The proximity of the title, Bucks, to the swan, which dominates the image, makes an obscure joke of the idea of the Aylesbury Duck — one that many Shell readers would have picked up on, and felt reassuringly in the know. Likewise Beck's image of chairs, in the industry section, which is also taken with an awareness of the objet trouvé potential that would make a photograph of chairs interesting in to a young, culturally aware audience. Elsewhere in the gazetteer, images of signage at Stony Stratford are used to make the reader see the objet trouvé in situ — the surrealism of the street. But Nash also turned very realist images to mildly surrealist purposes and this lightens the mood of what is after all a guide. Just before the gazetteer begins there is a photo of a funerary sculpture by Roubillac at Quainton captioned 'A man who wasted away young'. Coming as it does at the end of a worthy but overly informative account of the history of sculpture in England as found in Buckinghamshire church

monuments by Katharine Esdaile — who also annotated the gazetteer entries, adding churches with good monuments — this is bound to make you laugh.

Like Paul's *Dorset*, *Bucks* uses the full range of imagery from sketches to photomontage to illustrate its text. The weakest part of this is the printing of black-and-white images on coloured paper, which in both books is used to show the country free of the trappings of the contemporary, to make the reader see the place anew through a slightly distanced-from-reality image. This never really works: the tinted paper and the extracted colour make the pictures seen anaemic and clumsy compared to photographic reproductions or etchings; whereas the sketches of leaves made by Nash for the endpapers to *Bucks* work well.

Unlike *Dorset*, *Bucks* was a very understated guide in many ways; but this is also more apparent than real for its plainness comes from its simple structure. *Bucks* was the first Shell Guide where the introductory section and concluding parts were very brief and the gazetteer correspondingly large, running from page 15 to page 41. Eventually a large gazetteer became the norm because the form, which demanded brevity of its entries and their copious illustration, allowed the guides to construct experience of each county under the umbrella of the very ordinariness that the gazetteer form seems to imply to its contents. John Nash's entries were also typical of the direction that the guides would take in that he tends to give long entries to odd small places alongside short entries to larger, duller settlements: Bledlow, "a large village", is given the same length entry as Aylesbury and Beaconsfield. He has a typically double-handed comment on New Beaconsfield describing it as "a suburb of the very best quality... destroying a great deal of beautiful South Chiltern woodland scenery".[17]

'At the chairmaker's', Bucks, 1937, p.43

ORDINARY THINGS are often well worth looking at. Up to one hundred years ago craftsmanship in England was rarely skimped. This ironwork support for the sign of the Bull Inn, STONY STRATFORD (with modern accretions) is a fine bit of blacksmith's ironwork of the late 18th century. On the right is a pretty, early 19th century shop-front in the same town.

Ordinary things at Stony Stratford, Bucks, 1937, p.35

'A man who wasted away young. Part of the Dormer Monument. Quainton. Sculpted by L.F. Roubiliac (Died 1762)', Bucks, 1937, p.15

Both Nashs could write very vividly and beautifully. Of beech woods, John Nash writes:

> Winter is by no means the least beautiful of the seasons in the woods. The sun turns the carpet of dead leaves to pale red and orange, over which the intricate shadows of the tree trunks and branches curve and dip with every rise and fall of the ground. Or on a dull day after rain a blue mist hangs in the woods, changing the leaves to a dark red, through which the wet soil shows through in black rifts…[18]

And this was the surprise: that the artists with their eye for colour could conjure up the land in words where the writers got carried off by their own virtuosity. What seems to have been Beddington's innovation moved the guides on to a new level, both in the use of imagery but also through the idea that the gazetteer entry could be a sketch rather than an essay or a report.

Published at the same time as *Bucks*, *Northumberland and Durham* was by contrast an ill-starred project. Its author Thomas Sharp was later a very influential town planner. Born in Bishop Auckland, County Durham he had worked as a planner for the County Surveyor and then moved to South Lancashire where he wrote an extensive report for the county, which was not credited to him but rather to a superior. In anger he resigned and then spent two years unemployed, during which he wrote *Town and Countryside* published in 1932. He believed that there should be an absolute separation between town and country, abhorring the garden-suburb idea believing rather in well-designed towns and carefully managed villages. He believed the English village to be the perfect village form and admired the planning of cities like Newcastle and Edinburgh. In short, on the face of it he was a fellow traveller of Betjeman and like-minded souls at the *A.R.*; but he was a new kind of guide author, being a local expert and also an academic (for by 1936 he had employment in the Architecture School of Durham University at Newcastle).

Northumberland and Durham was novel for the guides in that not only does it cover two counties – because "Industrially and economically the two counties are interdependent and inseparable"[19] – it also had separate gazetteers for both, a form later used for the Welsh Shell Guides. These are perhaps the least of its peculiarities for Sharp chose a style which is at once

John Nash was not a surrealist but he liked the surreal – particularly the surreal *objet trouvé*.

bumptious, deprecating and defensive: "How fully to describe the industrial parts was the chief problem to be resolved at the very outset. There was never any intention of attempting to avoid them. The guide who, with his head in the air and his nose in a pocket handkerchief, takes you to see a battered bit of church, and never so much as hints at the filthy village that surrounds it, is a maddening creature".[20] He goes on: "So whether the reader likes it or not, I declare here and now that it is my intention not to let him pass, if I can help it, through these two counties without showing him something at least of the shameful ugliness and social decay of some of its parts, as well as the delight and beauty of others".[21] A politicised guide could be refreshing but Sharp had a talent for talking down to everyone and everything. 'The Face of Northumberland' section begins, "Geology and the inclosure [sic] movements are rather frightening subjects, especially to him who wishes to both run and read, as you, dear average motoring public reader, probably like to do."[22] He also was a führer rather than a cicerone, as is clear from a footnote about the best way to see Hadrian's Wall:

> Let the arrangements be quite clear, or there will be frayed tempers and some extra miles of uncertain walking. Here one driver, A, will get out to begin his five-mile walk, going through the field-gate on the right of the road. The other driver, B, will drive on till he comes, at the scattered hamlet called TWICE BREWED, to the first road leading North (to the right, by the Youth Hostel, *not* the gated farm road which he will first see). Taking this side road for about half a mile, he will come to the Wall, right on top of the hill. Here he will leave the car on the roadside, lock it and begin walking the Wall eastwards. He will meet A about half way (or say at Housesteads, where they can inspect the fort together), and will hand over the key of the car. A will continue westwards, B eastwards, and A will eventually come to the car and drive it eastwards, to where B will be waiting for him at the place where they originally parted company.[23]

The gazetteer, whose job it is to tempt the visitor, does not respond well to Sharp's alternately sparse, dry and hectoring style. Any number of entries show the first two characteristics, not least the first page of the gazetteer:

Alnmouth, Quiet seaside village. Excellent sands, coast walks, fishing, two golf courses, a few huts and tents, but no promenades. No attempt to rival Blackpool.

Amble. Busy, and grimy, little port and ship-building village at the mouth of the Coquet.

Ashington, Pop 40,000. Mining town, mostly built in the early part of this century. Dreary rows a mile long. Ashpits and mines down the middle of still un-made streets.

Cover, by L.T. Parke, of Northumberland and Durham, 1937

"Shops closed, an air of death and decay over everything."
A scene in JARROW

Jarrow, Northumberland and Durham, 1937, p.43

Two sorts of North Country scenery, Northumberland and Durham, 1937, pp.46–7

Colliery town, County Durham, Northumberland and Durham, 1937, p.39

Thomas Sharp was a passionate advocate of the North and the puffin on the cover of his guide to Northumbria and Durham was a wild counterpoint to the common view of the area as all industry and mines. Equally, many of the images in the guide make political points about the North East of the Depression. This was not what was expected of a motor-tourist guidebook.

Beadnell. A scatter of bungalows, villas, huts and shacks, but good sands.

Belford. A rather hard-looking little town on the Great North Road. A good centre.

But where Sharp really gets into his stride is in the Durham gazetteer, with entries full of suppressed emotion:

Gateshead. Pop 125,000. With contiguous Felling, is an unhappy urban area. Defoe wrote Robinson Crusoe here, about 1719.

Hetton-le-Hole. Pop 17,500. Pit village multiplied by ten: matchless lack of "amenities" also a considerable lack of employment – one of a score of similar places in the county.

Horden. Post-war mushroom mining town: result of a similar kind of energy to that which created the industrial towns of the last century.

Page Bank. A typical pit village wedged on the river-side between the woods of two private parks. Once the pit employed 750 men; now it is a vast heap of bricks and rubbish, and the population has been about 80 per cent unemployed for six years and more, with no hope for the future.

Shildon. Drab, straggling railway and colliery town; associated with railways from their beginning. The first train ran from here on the "Darlington and Stockton" Railway in 1825. Now partially derelict. Pits dismantled ten years ago. Population 50 per cent or more unemployed – some for 15 years.

His anger is most clear in his entry for Jarrow:

Once famous for shipbuilding, now the best-known derelict town in England. Built almost entirely to house the workers of one firm; when that went "bust" so did the workers. A great mass of streets, almost deserted by traffic; shops closed, an air of death and decay over everything. All MPs, all prosperous southerners and smug optimists should be made to spend a month here.[24]

While one can admire Sharp's aim in these entries, the combination in the two gazetteers of anodyne descriptions of apparently nice places with intense visions of dereliction, decay and human waste – plus the school-mastery introductory sections – makes the written sections of the guide seem inept when compared to its contemporary Shell Guides of 1937. For anyone who knew the area there are also some strange omissions. Take Holy Island for instance:

if written by, say, Betjeman, the entry would describe the castle, modified by Lutyens for the editor of *Country Life*, but Sharp makes no mention of this. However, though many of the images are often simply stock shots of gazetteer entries, there are others which are far more eloquent than Sharp's text. Above Jarrow appears an image of a forlorn and shut fish-and-chip shop, and there are equally evocative full-bleed photographs printed on grey paper where medium and image reinforce the desolation of a colliery in the centre of Newcastle; or the dour grandeur of that city's centre seen from the Tyne Bridge; or the image of washing blowing in the smoky wind of a colliery town.

Northumberland and Durham was, generously, a missed opportunity like the earlier *Kent* and *Somerset*. Maybe, as with *Wiltshire*, the author had no regard for Betjeman since unlike most guides there is no acknowledgement of Betjeman, Beddington or Beck in Sharp's text. Luckily for Betjeman, his other northern Shell Guide, Stephen Bone's *West Coast of Scotland: Skye to Oban*, was a much happier experience: political, evocative and a best seller. It was, like *Dorset*, *Bucks* and *Hampshire*, the work of an artist – though Betjeman rated it as his best job of editing to date. Both guides shared some similar design features – reproductions of Victorian paintings for the title page, a Gothic type face and a missing contents page – but their main similarity is that they see themselves as separate from the South, foreign even, and this sets them apart from the other guides. This may explain why *West Coast of Scotland* begins with an essay on Highland clans.

Stephen Bone was not a Scot but he certainly wanted to be. His father Sir Muirhead Bone was, being Scotland's equivalent to Sir William Nicholson, the innovative graphic artist (and father of Ben Nicholson); but Stephen Bone was a Londoner with Scottish sympathies. Like Paul Nash, he was trained at the Slade, and later acted as art critic for the *Manchester Guardian* and was a member of the BBC Brains Trust. His mother was a well-known author and in 1925, when he was 21, they collaborated on the hand-printed and privately published *Of the Western Isles* that won a prize at the 1925 Paris Exhibition. He produced the woodcuts and she the text. It may have been this book that led to his Shell Guide, which during the fifties was a best-seller. He was a keen explorer of Scotland and made several sketching expeditions to the Highlands and Islands including a camping tour of the Cairngorms. He was a typical product of the Slade and his method – travelling, sketching in oils outdoors and taking notes – was really his art. Like Constable he was fascinated by weather, producing *British Weather* for Collins' Britain in Pictures series in 1946. He revised his guide in 1952 and died in 1958.

In some ways Bone's *West Coast of Scotland* is a very old-fashioned guide with its sections on Gaelic, clans, pipes, harps and all the other paraphernalia of romantic Scottishness – legends, complex

51

feuds, and the '45 rebellion. Add to these details of rainfall, midges and temperature, train services and ferries to the isles and there is the basis of a very complete guide even before the entries for places; but what it is not is a motorist's guide. The cover shows a view of Rum from the deck of a sailing boat leaving Mallaig, the title page an old painting of the approach to the Shiant Isles, so it is clear that the guide is more of an island guide than anything else. Elsewhere, the rail journeys to the coast are rated for their scenery and there are descriptions of the best ascents of mountains. But this doesn't matter because the guide is so dense with information and imagery that its pretext is immaterial. In 44 pages there are 57 images, some double page, and near the front a whole section of 17 images, one to a page in violet monochrome on heavy cream paper like a late-nineteenth-century album. Another deviation from the Shell Guide format is the absence of architecture. When it is mentioned, buildings are used to give scale to a view or terminate it or are the scenes of events. Primarily, the images are landscapes where man and his works are rendered small, as in the view of Ben Nevis from Corpach on page 11.

Betjeman was right to be pleased at the unique editing which was a really compact solution to a short book full of various types

Cover of West Coast of Scotland, *1938, by Cyril Arapoff*

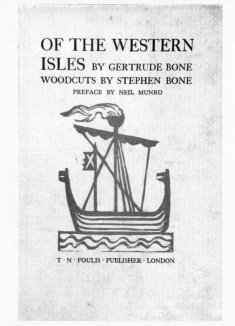

Cover of Of the Western Isles, *1925*

The only influence that Stephen and Gertrude Bone's hand-printed book *Of the Western Isles* (1925) had on his later, more modern *West Coast of Scotland* was its subject and choice of typeface; for where the former was simply romantic, the later was political and romantic, thus reflecting the mood of the thirties as opposed to the dated, Edwardian feel of its predecessor.

Ben Nevis from Corpach, by Will F. Taylor, West Coast of Scotland, *1938, p.11*

Moran Fisherman, by Cyril Arapoff, from 'Large Photographs' section of West Coast of Scotland, *1938*

Bone's innovation was his ability to combine political commentary with beauty so that the *West Coast of Scotland* presents an intelligent, un-complacent, youthful guide to a famously beautiful area.

of text and image. The key to the structure is given in the page marked 'Gazetteer', written partly in Bone's hand, with Betjeman's note "and, incidentally, a specimen of Stephen Bone's handwriting given below". Bone's is a beautiful italic script and matches the meticulous ingenuity with which he has laid out his gazetteer. One column is the gazetteer of places and across the other column, of twice the width, runs the other gazetteer, of contexts. Occasionally, unnoticed by the reader, the places gazetteer widens to three columns leavened by in-text images across two or three columns, as in the gazetteer of Skye.[25] The images themselves are a mixture of reproductions of drawings, paintings, old etchings and photographs that almost without exception have a good range of tones and good resolution, something that cannot be said for all the guides (*Derbyshire*, for example). In short, by using small well-chosen images, short context entries and longer place entries, each page covers three different subjects, making the guide three-times longer than at first glance. Betjeman tried something similar with *Devon* with its side remarks on pixies and so on, but in *West Coast of Scotland* it really comes off because the context comments, whether about fairy eggs or foxes, are short and witty:

> Foxes, are shot. They are technically "vermin". Sometimes instead of being shot, they are packed carefully in a hygienic box and sent to a hunting county. It is not known which the foxes prefer…[26]

Where they are about history and politics they are full and clear, the entry on the clearances running across three pages. It concludes:

> The loss of population from the highland counties has been placed at 200,000. The highlands have never really recovered from the clearances. Sheep later gave place to deer and the decay of the country progressed one stage further…[27]

The argument is ingeniously continued below on the same page and onto the next under 'Crofters', which concludes: "Complaints have been made that the Scottish Board of Agriculture has not always been as energetic as it might have been. Between 1911 and 1927, for instance, it received 20,000 applications for land and granted only 4,000."[28] Below this comes 'Deer' in which the extended argument concludes: "Shortly before the war a Royal commission found that of three and a half million acres of deer forest, one and a half million acres were fit for cultivation."[29] Taken as a whole, Bone manages to make a clear political argument out of three apparently disassociated subjects and contexts without resorting to more than a statement of facts and so not scaring the horses. But Bone does not disguise the political nature of the guide as can be seen in the handwritten initial gazetteer entry:

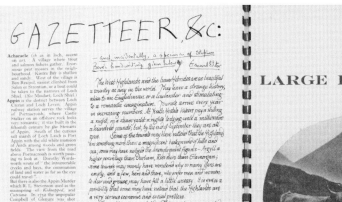

Gazetteer, West Coast of Scotland, *1938, p.6 and large photographs of highland life and scenery (Violet Banks Photo)*

> The problem is soon stated: This country once supported a considerable population. Today, outside a few small areas it is practically uninhabited. Soon unless a change occurs, it will be quite uninhabited: The highlander will be extinct. That is the problem. This is no place to discuss possible solutions, but a book on the Highlands cannot leave out all mention of it.[30]

West Coast of Scotland is in its own way a very gentlemanly book, wearing its knowledge and politics clearly but lightly, leaving enough space for the reader to make up their own mind, and enough space for some avuncular and full entries and beautifully balanced landscapes. The entries share a non-sequitur style that are a feature of the best of the guides. A good example is the beginning of the entry for Tobermory:

> The only town in Mull – about 800 inhabitants – was built in 1788 for the herring fishery, but the herring went and the town declined. It is crowded round an almost landlocked little bay. Pleasant wooded walk to the lighthouse. Above the town is a semi-baronial hotel and below the town – at the bottom of the harbour – is the Spanish galleon *Florida* (or *Florencia*).[31]

Betjeman's layout for *West Coast of Scotland* was his favourite and demonstrates his ability to build up dense layers of meaning in a small area. This was a significant design innovation of the new magazine-style layouts of the Shell Guides and the *Architectural Review*, where he'd learnt his trade.

53

After the war, and perhaps in a spirit of healing consensus, *West Coast of Scotland* was filleted of most of its political content; and a couple of years later, *Northumberland and Durham* became simply *Northumberland* and rather less radical than its predecessor. The forthright comment of the youthful thirties guides gave way, not to a total absence of the political, but to a different idea of politics: issue politics, and in particular the ideas of conservation for which the opposite is 'development'. Interestingly, the guide to Derbyshire was not rewritten until 1972 and *Durham* was not written until 1980. Both were by Henry Thorold and contain little that would have been recognised in the thirties as 'politics'; but both are rich with concern for 'issues'. These ideas were certainly present throughout the thirties, however, and they received a particularly clear exposition in a guide that cast as long a shadow as those of Betjeman over later additions to the series: John Piper's *Oxon*.

NOTES

1   *Dorset*, 1936, p.7
2   *Dorset*, 1936, p.6
3   *Dorset*, 1936, p.44
4   *Dorset*, 1936, p.8
5   Quoted in Nash, 1951, p.5
6   Nash, 1951, p.13
7   *Dorset*, 1936, p.10
8   *Dorset*, 1936, p.10
9   *Dorset*, 1936, p.24
10 *Dorset*, 1936, p.31
11 'Monster Field' appeared in *A.R.* No. 527, October 1940, pp.121–2
12 *Bucks*, 1937, p.19
13 *Bucks*, 1937, p.20
14 *Bucks*, 1937, p.11
15 *Bucks*, 1937, p.34
16 'Slough', *Continual Dew* (Betjeman, 1937)
17 *Bucks*, 1937, p.16
18 *Bucks*, 1937, p.12
19 *Northumberland and Durham*, 1937, p.5
20 *Northumberland and Durham*, 1937, p.6
21 *Northumberland and Durham*, 1937, p.6
22 *Northumberland and Durham*, 1937, p.9
23 *Northumberland and Durham*, 1937, p.14
24 *Northumberland and Durham*, 1937, p.43
25 *West Coast of Scotland*, 1938, pp.31–5
26 *West Coast of Scotland*, 1938, p.19
27 *West Coast of Scotland*, 1938, p.15
28 *West Coast of Scotland*, 1938, p.16
29 *West Coast of Scotland*, 1938, p.16
30 *West Coast of Scotland*, 1938, p.6
31 *West Coast of Scotland*, 1938, p.27

OXON TO GLOUCESTERSHIRE

IT WAS ALMOST INEVITABLE THAT John Betjeman and John Piper would meet since they shared so many friends and contacts in the relatively small culturati of 1930s London. In the end it was J.M. Richards, the new editor of the *Architectural Review*, who introduced Betjeman to Piper. Richards and his wife Peggy Angus were friends with Piper and his wife, Myfanwy Evans; Richards and Piper shared an interest in the popular architecture of Britain. Piper had begun producing work for the *A.R.* in 1936 at a time when his own work was in a state of transition. Like Paul Nash, with whom he and Myfanwy were also friends, Piper was growing uncomfortable with European modernism. Though Piper was not as interested in surrealism as Nash, he had believed that the way forward in art lay in the direction that European avant-garde artists had taken, toward essentialism and abstraction. By 1936 Piper was using his appreciation of abstract art to reassess his much earlier interest in the art in English churches. In particular he was beginning to see similarities between modern sculpture and early church sculpture in Britain, a link that others like Epstein, Moore and Nash also made. In fact in Oxfordshire, where he had chosen to live and about which he was shortly to write a guide, there was an eleventh-century crucifix at Langford which had become an established place of pilgrimage for young British artists because of its influence on Eric Gill. The link between the essentialist abstractions of contemporary art and the primitivism of Saxon sculpture, for instance, led him toward a more trans-historical sense of the continuum of abstraction in art than that offered by the modern art world – which was at that time fundamentally hostile to the past, believing that art must strive to be always a part of the future here in the present or, in other words, avant-garde.

In short, like Nash, Piper was looking for a way to be English and new. The contiguities between contemporary concerns for purity and a more ancient simplicity in the grand art of sculpture were a link between modern artistic concerns and a continuity in British art. Piper wanted a way out of having to be a doctrinaire modernist artist, as he felt this was a Bond Street straightjacket; in its place, he wanted to be able to relate to the aspects of Englishness that attracted him, to make his practice include reference to old buildings, sculptures and landscapes. To do this, he had to change his way of working by moving away from 'making modern art', instead using modern ideas of the artist as tools to explore his national identity.

These ideas of the artist emphasised continual work in a variety of media, including new media like photography; the modern artist was a person of process and continual production rather than the developer of 'major works'. The *A.R.* thus presented an opportunity for Piper to escape the world of Fine Art into one where his art – including writing – could be a vehicle for describing the buildings, their environment and history. He used his time at the *A.R.* to create work that analysed the everyday built environment of provincial Britain: from the pub to roads, 'Nautical Style' (appearing in the *A.R.* in January 1938) and church towers. This work moved him away from the techniques of the Fine Artist toward those of the more modern multimedia artist, using photography, typography, illustration and layout. It was this combination of creative skills and intellectual concerns that made Richards recommend Piper to Betjeman: in many ways they were trying to do the same thing, to find a means of expression that was novel or modern for both their interest in the old, quotidian and authentic, and the national identity.

Though the Shell Guides were by now published by Batsford, there was still a very strong design direction coming from the *A.R.* This was partly because of the continued links between Betjeman and the *A.R.* but also because the *A.R.* was where many of the ideas about graphic design and architectural design were thrashed out on a monthly basis by a wide and changing circle of participants, most of whom were or would become Shell Guide contributors too. As important was Hubert de Cronin Hastings' desire to modernise the magazine and make it a pole of culture debate in Architecture and Design; for, over the years he had been in charge, he had made every effort to continue the development of an *A.R.* house style that was the most modern possible. By 1938 the *A.R.* was a very different

High street pub

High Street was one of several rather wistful evocations of popular culture published by the Architectural Press. Hubert de Cronin Hastings and others at the *Architectural Review* including J.M. Richards, Betjeman and Piper were all united in their anxiety that with the post First World War modernising of the high street in most towns and cities came the destruction of 'authentic' popular culture in favour of a more ersatz and Americanised consumer culture.

animal from the *A.R.* of 1930 or even 1936. In fact, the reputation for design that stayed with the magazine through to the 1970s really found its stride in the years just before the Second World War and this coincided with the coming of age of the Shell Guides. The link between the series and the *A.R.* changed from a simple emulation in the guides of the *A.R.*'s photographic styles to a more complex relationship between content and design, the *Review* and the Shell Guides. By 1937 the *Architectural Review* had an interest in reclaiming for architecture the popular buildings and industrial architecture of the eighteenth and nineteenth centuries, and with this came an interest in vernacular traditions of architecture and townscape. The champion of this reassessment of the popular past and examiner of its present was J.M. Richards. After he became editor, features on popular heritage appeared in most issues ranging from articles about gravestones and funerary sculpture to an account of the black-and-white tradition in British vernacular architecture[1] that was the occasion of Richards and Piper's first collaboration. In 1938 Richards also published *High Street*, a small book about the design of old shops illustrated with colour lithographs by Eric Ravilious.[2] While *High Street* is a nostalgic evocation of old shop fronts, Piper's pieces for the *A.R.* treat similar material in a different way. Though the images are often whimsical and could easily become nostalgic they are rescued by a rather dry and modern layout – a technique that Piper later used to leaven the content of the Shell Guides. However, in 1938 the design of the guides lagged behind that of the *A.R.*

Betjeman and Piper got on well. They recognised their similarities: they were both church crawlers and had a long-term interest in topographic books; and both were opinionated. For Piper, the main attractions were that Betjeman's offer that he should do a guide provided him with a new kind of project and some money. He was commissioned to compile a guide to Oxfordshire in April 1937, which was not to include Oxford as Betjeman was already preparing a guide to the city. Both guides were published in 1938. Betjeman's was called *An Oxford University Chest*[3] and Piper's simply *Oxon*.[4] To prepare the guide, Piper toured Oxfordshire with his wife and, incidentally, read Betjeman's *Devon*, given to him by Richards while on a tour of the West Country in June.[5] Like Paul Nash, he intended to take many photographs and make many sketches but he also had the assistance of Maurice Beck, the photographic éminence gris of the Shell Guides in the 1930s.

Oxon is an important guide because of Piper's continued involvement with the series from then until its end in 1984. But had that not happened and were it the only Piper contribution, the book might be judged differently. In its form if not its text it very closely follows the lead set by John Nash's *Bucks* with which it shares a short, almost identical form of preface, an introduction to the landscapes of the county, a long and full gazetteer, an essay on monuments by K. Esdaile as well as a minor gazetteer of them (albeit

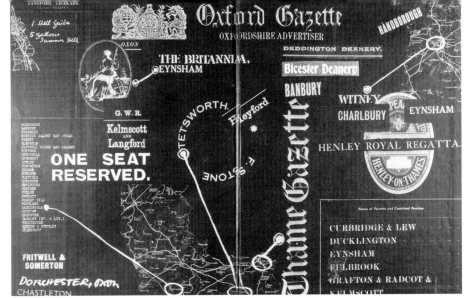

Oxon, 1938, endpapers

These endpapers to *Oxon* provide the key to understanding much of Piper's approach to guide writing, which was a development of the sketchbook notes he kept on the tours of Britain he'd been making for some time before becoming involved in the guides.

Group of scarecrow pictures from West, 1979

17 Rycote (photo J.P.), 1937

18 Scarecrows (photos J.P.), 1938–77

Title page of Oxon, 1938

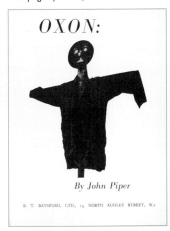

OXON:

By John Piper

B. T. BATSFORD, LTD., 15, NORTH AUDLEY STREET, W.1

Piper photographed scarecrows over many years – the examples shown here date from 1938–1977. The image top right was used as the basis for the title page of his *Oxon*, 1938 where it acts as a surreal self-portrait of the author.

both rather brief compared to her effort in *Bucks*) and a double-page montage-cum-visual-essay – on Oxon rather than Slough, of course, but really in the same style as Cecil H. Greville. In *Oxon* there is an essay on deserted places by Myfanwy Evans (Mrs Piper) but no sections on industry or flora and fauna, though there is a list of 29 Oxfordshire notables. The most striking initial difference is in *Oxon*'s endpapers which are a reversed out collage of maps, found typography and notes made by Piper, the whole looking a bit like an artist's notebook-cum-scrapbook. Following this comes an equally striking title page showing a photo of a scarecrow between the title, "Oxon", and the words "by John Piper". The inference is that the scarecrow is a surreal John Piper. [6] In fact *Oxon* is the first guide where there is the simple statement that it is "by" the author; and to make the point, it is said twice: on the cover and the title page. Returning to the cover, its unassuming image of a gable end of two rough stone houses, one shrouded in elderflowers, with the reversed-out signature of Piper in the corner is a sort of leitmotif for the whole aesthetic of the book. This itself perfectly expresses the taste not only of the Pipers but of all of those like them such as Jim Ede, famous for Kettle's Yard, for what *Oxon* celebrates as the very English taste for the invisible, the disguised, under-the-radar place where the personality can flourish unnoticed and undisturbed, save by those with the code.

An important part of that code is a love of the distressed and forgotten gem, an aesthetic perfectly expressed in the other introduction to this book, Myfanwy Piper's 'Deserted Places'. Myfanwy's essay celebrates dereliction because it represents discovery of beauty neglected by others; and the beauty she really finds in Oxon are houses that closely resemble their own home at Fawley Bottom, just over the border in Bucks, into which they had only recently moved and were rescuing from its own neglect. The deserted places in Myfanwy's Oxon are hidden but not remote farmhouses, small, and set in their original environment of big protecting trees, horse and cattle ponds, outbuildings, cart barns, stone walls, tiled roofs, crows, patches of grass on dusty unmade lanes leading to unmade farmyards littered with the detritus of old farm life: barrels, cloches, patent containers, moleskins and dead crows hung in rows, old carts hidden in barns and worn paint on an old plank back door. Beginning with the cover, most of the images in *Oxon* are essays in this taste. "A dovecot to be seen from the hidden churchyard at Kiddington"[7] perfectly expresses the Pipers' tastes for the discreet charms of the rural petit bourgeois.

In another book, this might grate as a kind of smug, down-from-London, cliquey fantasy; but *Oxon* is just on the right side of this, being more a celebration of something a new couple have discovered for themselves and made their own. In 'Deserted Places', Myfanwy makes their actual Oxon ideal plain:

Holwell, Oxon, 1938, p.16

Dovecot seen from the hidden churchyard at Kiddington, Oxon, 1938, p.23

Of all the places in Oxfordshire Great Tew is the place for atmosphere. What has vanished has vanished completely, behind high walls and rich evergreens. And then it is only a few garden alleys and old trees – unless you count the village itself, a relic of former splendour and domestic content. The insistent absence of all the things that once flourished there makes it shadier and closer, like the most impenetrable of 'unkempt gardens' even in the sight of the spruce Oxfordshire stone vicarage or the handsome eighteenth-century mansion overlooking the lower end of the village.

As important as the love of the neglected is the idea that it is within sight of the obvious, well-maintained loveliness of less-imaginative others. In this respect the Pipers were in the avant-garde of a very English taste in rurality – the hunt for the authentic gem – and their *Oxon* is almost a how-to manual for the similarly minded, cultured middle class. *Oxon* more than any of the other earlier guides reflects the aspirations of the audience Shell and Betjeman were looking for. Piper sums up the view he shared with Myfanwy succinctly: "Though I like churches to be special I like country to be ordinary".[8]

The whole guide is devoted to the special things in apparently ordinary places, which themselves are naturally made special by the discovery of the hidden in them. For the Pipers, the special is a surreal parallel universe of neglected small manors surrounded by objects pregnant with a sense of recently departed human agency,

Oxon was written as John and Myfanwy Piper were settling down together and their partnership had found architectural expression in the love of small but substantial and decrepit farmhouses like their recently found Fawley Bottom. Their choice of domestic environment is subconsciously laid out many times over in the kind of places praised in *Oxon*.

a surreal countryside that exists alongside, almost within, the smart Cotswoldsiness that was already well established in the thirties.

This obverse of what is special is no less clearly described in the Pipers', as it should really be accredited, *Oxon*. Inverted snobbery is perhaps the guide's greatest weakness, though this is the vice of taste.

The entries for Claydon and Cowley represent the Pipers' thesis and antithesis:

Claydon: extreme north of Oxon on a hill. "Bi-weekly red Midland bus from Banbury." You do not know Oxon until you have seen isolated villages like Claydon. *Clattercote* is a farm in the fields near, once a priory. [9]

Cowley: Oxford has been called "Cowley's Latin Quarter". Battalions of Morris cars are assembled here. Battalions of villas ditto. [10]

Where one can sense the silent ticking of boxes in the first, one can almost hear inverted commas around "assembled" in the latter – a word chosen to exclude the possibility that either cars or villas of the Cowley type are 'made', that is to say crafted.

On the preceding page, the 20 lines and a photograph (of its most 'deserted place' dovecot standing in a field) accorded Chastleton contrast with the tiny, damned-with-faint-praise entry for Checkendon: "Week-endy. Secluded. Paintings in the church. Cherry country."[11] The implication: discovered; don't expect surprises. Whereas Chinnor, "under the Chilterns, Limeworks a good feature. Nice to look at, and they give the village a non-agricultural, non-arty point. (see absence of To Let notices, busy pubs). Fourteenth century glass (fine) in restored church of same date. Single line railway (Risborough to Watlington)": we like – undiscovered. Kelmscott is not really liked: "it has become the prototype for arty country places everywhere. The village is firmly guarded against development",[12] nor is Kidlington, which merits a photo of its suburban horrors and is introduced as, "Worst Oxfordshire example of building atrocities. The Banbury road is hideous for miles on each side of it."[13]

But many places receive a similar treatment: Milton "has a red-tiled church. Local authorities who veto flat roofs and concrete in rural surroundings should be shown it as an example of how to ruin a landscape with their own taste for simplicity and convention"[14]; and both Draytons, one, "near Banbury and rather suburban"[15] while the other, St Leonard's, "is getting council-housey".[16] At the other end of the scale, "**Westwell**: is so snug and so Cotswold and so dinky that it ought to be put in a glass case. Altogether a nice packet of postcards".[17]

But against all this snobbery can be set the majority of *Oxon* which celebrates and elegises the small beauties of "one of the most

Great Tew, Oxon, *1938*

Until a decade or so ago, Great Tew was an oasis of total undevelopment in Oxfordshire, having hardly changed since it was built. Even in the 1930s, its unreconstructed nature was remarkable.

Oxon, 1938, pp. 8–9

The Pipers liked the idea of the ordinary countryside but this was really a code meaning ordinary country filled with very beautiful and special backwaters that no-one else has found – an early example of the idea of under-the-radar taste of the kind the Pipers shared with others like Jim Ede and even Pevsner.

Kidlington, Oxon, 1938, p.26

Langford, Oxon, 1938

ordinary of the English counties".[18] In its own way, this celebration became the chief virtue of the Shell Guides. In addition, it is worth noting that in the 1953 revision of the guide, John Piper made a point of apologising, implicitly, for their earlier smartnesses, tacitly in revisions and directly in the preface.

> In fourteen years the county has changed a good deal; the man has changed more. ....I like a guide book to be to some extent a diary, with a diary's prejudices and superficialities, and perhaps some of its vividness, and I would apologise beforehand to residents in some country towns and villages where in my rapid comments the first two of these qualities are too prominent, and are not outweighed by the third.[19]

The Pipers were very good at attractive, atmospheric, thumbnail sketches. At the end of the entry on Enstone, itself very entertaining, comes "*Cleveley*, nearby, is a lovely hamlet in a bottom by the Glyme with an old stone farmhouse, and cows in steep fields".[20] Epwell follows: "for remoteness and beauty, in a landscape of lumpy hills,"[21] and Little Faringdon "in the land of small parks".[22] In fact, entry after entry makes almost everything seem as if it must be visited with only a few places, for contrast, to be reviled. And as a leaven to all this positivity is the Pipers' rather Gothick elegiac love for ruin: "Hampton Gay: is now forlorn. The overgrown ruins of a Jacobean manor house neighbour a lonely church with thin eighteenth and nineteenth century features near the Oxford Canal and the railway. Water rushes over a sluice from the dam of a destroyed mill."[23] For every Kidlington there are many Langfords: "Off main road in flat country. On the branch line to Fairford, with a station by itself in the fields, where an old GWR engine usually puffs about idly with a few trucks. Church has Saxon and Norman work including the famous carving of the Crucifixion that has so much influenced Eric Gill and other sculptors. Other carvings and excellent later details."[24]

This last entry gives the clue to why the Oxon guide stands out from others produced in the thirties and also why the Pipers brought so much to the guides. *Oxon* in its modern, arty and literate combination of text and image not only told the reader what to see but how to see it; like Ruskin, Piper gives the reader a sense of how things are good and this is an important quality of all the subsequent Shell Guides.

Oxon is particularly good at using images to add an extra dimension to meaning rather than simply reinforcing it: directly below the Langford entry is a small enigmatic image of the Crucifixion; and a picture adds to the entry for Great Tew, taking care to show why 'Tewland'"is favoured by artists".[25] This allows the entry to say much more about its history without having to describe its beauty:

> John Claudius Loudon, early nineteenth-century landscape gardener, transformed Great Tew by planting evergreens all around it. It is no ordinary village, but looks a little like a rural inland watering-place. It would not be much of a shock to find a Grand Pump Room in the valley. Lucius Carey, Lord Falkland, lived here (see people). His manor house has been replaced by a later one. His church is fine and spacious (tombs and elaborate brasses) hidden behind Falkland's high walled garden. Rich country. *Little Tew* is favoured by artists and gentry. The district is known affectionately as 'Tewland'.

Another great skill shown in *Oxon* is the placing of images in a way that draws you into the gazetteer. There's not only an image of the surprisingly un-"watering place" cottageyness of Great Tew on the pages where the Tews appear but also two very enigmatic images, one of a turf maze at Somerton and the other a full-page image of pumpkins on the floor of Charlbury church. Both these incidental images positively urge you to turn to the gazetteer entries for each, on pages elsewhere.

Oxon sucks in the reader. The combination of its visual artiness, its by turns critical and hagiographic entries, and its images that favour atmosphere over description, does what the Shell Guides were supposed to do all along: make the reader want to go there. Where Piper differed from Betjeman is that he didn't make Oxon seem worthy and quirky in the way that Betjeman's *Devon* does, alternately lecturing about Georgian terraces and joking about pixies. Oxon is made beautiful, temptingly undiscovered, artily, modernisticly primitive and available to the taste-rich, money-poor, cultured young. In short, Oxon was made cool.

Leaving aside any questions about writing, the contrast between *Oxon* and Betjeman's *An Oxford University Chest* gives a clear idea of what Piper could bring to Betjeman's Shell Guides project. Betjeman's Oxford guidebook had been in preparation since 1934 and Betjeman intended it to be his "sophisticated guide book";[26] but by its publication in 1938 it looked more dated than his poetry books, like *Continual Dew* (1937), or the Shell Guides; and similarly, the text was in his younger style. It was laid out in a pastiche of high Victorian middle-brow style, with mixed Gothic and classical faces and a centred layout on the title page, and was filled with cartoons by Osbert Lancaster and photographs by the Bauhausler, Moholy Nagy. Betjeman's structure and writing was also in his earlier mocking style, leaving an impression that no-one and nothing would come out well from his examination. His comments about Cowley and Lord Nuffield worried the publisher:

> the most arty of us must hand it to William Morris the Second. He has given employment to thousands, and money to millions; he has provided a cheap means of transport for hundreds of thousands [including an undergraduate Betjeman]. No doubt many persons injured by the engine he has helped to popularize have received the expert attention of the Oxford hospitals which he has so munificently endowed. It was only fitting that the university should honour him with a degree, and the country with a peerage.

> Yet as the lanes of the country have become blue with the fumes of his success, so have the streets of this university life. And the streets are not only full of fumes. Other commercial enterprises have followed in the wake of the successful motor manufacturer. Speculative builders have run up strips of shoddy houses in almost

Oxon, 1938, pp.34–5

every country lane around the town. East Oxford, where the works are, beyond Magdalen Bridge, is indistinguishable from Swindon, Neasden or Tooting Bec. The architectural development of Oxford since the war has completely changed the character of the city.[27]

Osbert Lancaster's cartoons are used as punctuation for the text in an old-fashioned way, full of a sense of the in-joke; but of all the parts of the book, the weakest, the biggest lost opportunity, is Moholy Nagy's photography. Betjeman was impressed with his Leica and his discreet, candid photos of unsuspecting Dons and students and his images "showing the crumbling beauty of stone, the crispness of carved eighteenth century urns"[28]; but in fact, compared with Moholy Nagy's better-known work, the photographer was just going through the motions, using 'modern' camera angles and Cartier-Bresson-type photos of unsuspecting university types. Only one image, of the gates of Trinity College, is the real Moholy Nagy – a negative image of fearsome spikes seen from below at an angle of 45 degrees.

Compared to this, Piper's *Oxon* is a model of integrated modernity and in particular his pictures, about two-thirds of those in the book, both served the text, often going beyond it, and were good in themselves. Piper's style as a photographer suited the guides; Moholy Nagy by contrast feels like an unwilling player of a parlour

One of the interesting features of *Oxon* is the placing of images before the corresponding gazetteer entry as a device to draw the reader on through the narrative.

BULLINGDON

Betjeman, An Oxford University Chest, *OUP 1979 reprint, p.30*

game. Piper's 'Country Deaths'[29] and the double spread of North Leigh[30] both display the style that he was to use and develop continually in his association with the guides. 'Country Deaths' makes disturbing abstracts of the simple black-and-white juxtaposition of dead animals and plants against stone textures; the abstraction of subject and the distancing of black and white make everyday ugliness poetic. 'North Leigh' uses a monochrome villagescape under a burnt-in lowering sky to make a modern version of a Claude or Palmer landscape, free from the sunnyness of the postcard. His surrealist sense of dissonance and his anti-tourist tendencies directed his photography towards a rainy, mildly hostile lyricism.

Piper liked Betjeman's *Devon,* as he notes in his *Oxon,* calling it "the model Shell Guide for all time", and Betjeman liked *Oxon* and Piper and Myfanwy. In 1938 Piper and Betjeman began work on a guide to Shropshire and by 1939 they and Myfanwy were reading the proofs.[31] As they were working on the guide an article appeared in the *Architectural Review* which memorialises a turning point in Betjeman's personality, caused apparently by Piper. The piece, called 'The Seeing Eye: or How to like Everything',[32] is a paean by Betjeman to Piper's openness. "Mr Piper has turned the neglected [architectural] styles into something beautiful and peculiar to himself. Instead of despairing of what we have always been told is ugly and meretricious, he has accepted it at face value and brought it to life.

Left: Osbert Lancaster's cartoons for Betjeman's *Oxford University Chest* show how stuck in a dated humour of knowing mockery Betjeman was when he began working on guides particularly when compared to the rather less mocking though no less critical approach of Piper in his *Oxon.*

Below left: Moholy Nagy's talents as a Bauhaus modernist photographer seem to have been left entirely unused and unexpressed by Betjeman in *Oxford University Chest.*

Below right: Piper's 'Country Deaths' shows his ability to mix current contemporary art ideas, in this case a surrealist fascination with dead animals, with the guide book form, something which made the Shell Guides seem very arty and contemporary in the 1930s.

Betjeman, An Oxford University Chest, *OUP 1979 reprint, pp.48–9*

'Country Deaths', Oxon, 1938, p.6

He has made us look a second time, without any sense of satire, moral indignation, or aesthetic horror".[33]

Working with Piper on *Shropshire* was an epiphany for Betjeman. The "us" of 'The Seeing Eye' is really Betjeman himself, for from this time onward began to emerge the avuncular and enthusiastic character that became his laureate hallmark. But for Piper too, association with Betjeman showed him, in the words of Anthony West, "revelling in this licensed resort to the sustenance that he had been deliberately denying himself in his abstract period, and [made] it clear that it was vital to him to be able to feed his imagination through his eye".[34] West goes on to suggest it was Betjeman who instigated the collaboration with Piper to create the Shropshire guide, and this must have been because of the high standard of Piper's *Oxon*.

Gloucestershire and Shropshire

For Piper and Betjeman, Shropshire was an unknown territory – "It was like going to Brazil or somewhere"[35] – but before it could be finished the war started and the book was cancelled by their new publisher, Faber.[36] T.S. Eliot, director of Faber and Faber, had once taught a very young Betjeman and latterly admired Betjeman's writing. They met again in 1936 and Eliot wanted Betjeman to be a Faber author for his poetry.[37] Betjeman went to Murray's, but in 1938 it was Faber that took on the Shell Guides. Only one guide did appear during this early period of collaboration between Piper and Betjeman, published by Faber, *Gloucestershire* by Anthony West, the son of Rebecca West and H.G. Wells. In the late 1930s he was in his mid twenties and a contributor to the *Architectural Review*, though he was more interested in America than England; he eventually became a novelist and was a staff writer for the *New Yorker* from 1950 to 1972. He was not from Gloucestershire, though from the guide it would seem that he had a very good knowledge of the county.

West was well regarded by Betjeman as a writer and seems to have been an acquaintance with whom, until West left for America, he had some social contact. But all cannot have gone well with *Gloucestershire* for it was extensively revised almost as soon as the Shell Guides were revived in 1949–50. The new *Gloucestershire* was published in 1952. David Verey, who soon after compiled Pevsner's *Gloucestershire* in two volumes (1955), revised the gazetteer, amending some entries, dropping some and adding others. Ten new photographs by Lenn Hallman were also added. One unfortunate casualty of the intervening years was the George Hotel, Mitcheldean, which appeared in both *Gloucestershire* and Piper's 'Fully Licenced' feature in the *A.R.* of March 1940. Described by West as, "the most striking public house in the county",[38] the 1952 entry had to be amended by Verey to, "what was the most striking public house in the county has now had its gables decapitated and a flat roof has

THE SEEING EYE
or How to Like Everything

Right, the railway station at Whittington, Salop.

By John Betjeman

illustrations by John Piper

A TRAIN waits for a long time at Whittington Station, Salop. Many people in their compartments do not use their eyes at all. Though they have the gift of sight, they might as well be blind. One drums with his fingers on an attaché case, another whistles and taps his feet on the floor, a woman stares straight across at the Photochrome view of Bala until it swims out of focus : she dare not shift her eyes in case she should seem to be getting off with one of the men in the carriage. And the fourth member of this unwilling group may be you or not, not necessarily a reader of THE ARCHITECTURAL REVIEW, but someone who takes a look at buildings. I think I am putting the proportion rather high. Suppose there were four a side in this compartment one might say, fairly safely, that one out of the eight present notices his surroundings. Only one out of 300 will be in the least critical of what he sees.

The train still waits at the Station. The barge boards hang over the booking office ; the geraniums flourish against the stucco walls. There are several ways of dealing with the sight. To the small number that look out of the window with any perception, I will give names, in order to help us later on.

Mr. Squinch is a clergyman of the Church of England. He knows architecture as far as Perp and he regards all later than the earliest Perp as debased. The station building means nothing to him. He sees it for a moment, realizes that it is not Norm. Trans, E.E., Dec or Perp nor even a correct revival of one of those styles, so he dismisses it from his mind. Such a building might as well not exist. He thinks of his own church, of the remarkable squint he was able to reveal by clearing away the ugly old eighteenth century three-decker pulpit, of the pale green covers of the English hymnal, the unstained oak of the new choir stalls, the powder blue of the altar hangings and the mats for the kneelers, and here and there a touch of gold on angel and poppyhead to give a luxuriance to the general scene. And since the train has been waiting at the station for half an hour, and since it is four hours since he had breakfast, he is in the mind for visions. He sees England once again as a righte fayre launde with hauberks and crossbows, banners and banner poles, strong castles and stately churches (where the Faith is fully taught and practised) rising above the apple trees, contented peasants tilling the long fields with oxen and knights who go pricking by. The whole thing is very good taste, subdued colours and of sound craftsmanship. Small wonder then, that he does not see the station for what it is and turns the chimney pots in the background into the points of knightly lances, and the blue smoke makes an exterior incense for a cathedral, not of barge board and stucco, but of goodly carven stone.

Mr. Quantity is a more practical man. He is an artist, yes, but primarily a professional man. Indeed he is an architect. He is catholic in his tastes with a small " c." He disapproves of vulgarity and is a member of the C.P.R.E. and has been able to give that body sound, and sometimes indirectly lucrative, advice. His knowledge of architecture is wide but sketchy and he is sounder on the Orders than he is on Gothic. Nevertheless he was able to make a nice little job in unstained oak of Mr. Squinch's choir stalls : a man in his office ran up some quite decent panelling in a late Dee manner. Where are we waiting now ? Whittington. Ah, there's the booking office. A vulgar piece of work, probably by some provincial man. Why didn't he use the local stone ? What *is* the local stone ? All the surrounding houses are red brick. A pity. He was continually advising the use of local stone so as to harmonize with the neighbourhood. A cottage should look as though it grew out of the earth. None of this modernism is necessary. A sense of what is appropriate, restrained and tasteful, be the style demanded Gothic, Queen Anne or even a few years later. Mr. Quantity has had no lunch and he permits himself to replan Whittington as he sits in the train looking out. That station could be trimmed of its fussy detail fairly inexpensively. With a little skill it could be made to look quite passably neo-Renaissance and with a little pale green paint and some Empire timber inside, the interior could be brought up to date. These

Betjeman, November 1939

been built despite every kind of protest".[39] No wonder then that West had left the country.

A sense of awkwardness greets the reader in the acknowledgements of the 1939 *Gloucestershire*. It is written by "The General Editor", Betjeman, and thanks everyone but West. The guide concludes on the same note, with a rebuff to the preceding chapter on 'Dying Industries' by Thomas Hennell – a lament for the demise of rural crafts and a puff for the Arts and Crafts of the Gimsons and Cardew. West calls his chapter 'Living Industry, Another Point of View' and here he dismisses the tweeness of Arts and Crafts and in its place gives an account of Gloucestershire's industrial archaeology

'The Seeing Eye', an article in the *Architectural Review* written by Betjeman and illustrated by Piper, marks the beginning of the partnership between the two men. The article reflects Betjeman's conversion from urbane ironic commentator to positivist lover of middle England through exposure to Piper's undoctrinaire appreciation of ordinary architecture.

and concludes with the development of the aero industries at Gloucester and Bristol. His point is to attack the idea of Gloucestershire as only a rural idyll and to replace it with a more real account of its economy. Both essays were dropped in the 1952 edition and replaced by new writing on 'Cotswold Tradition, Wool and Stone' by Margaret Blundell – a safer, more positive and consensual account typical of the post-war revisions, but also better than a debate in the back pages of a guidebook.

The problem with *Gloucestershire* lay with West. Although he was a very good, honest writer as can be seen in the introductory passages on the county called 'Land' and 'Water',[40] his gazetteer entries were on the whole negative in tone and faintly embarrassed by beauty. He did not have a gift as a gazetteer entry writer nor did he seem to realise that not everything had to be in the gazetteer. One wonders why he bothered with the entry for Alvington, "another place gutted by a main road",[41] other than for personal reasons of regret; or Alderton, "a plain spot with a badly restored church and a mysterious attraction for the speculative builder. At Dixton, two miles off, a manor house proves that builders were not always good architects, even in 1555".[42] Perhaps this entry relates to some argument about old and new architecture between West and Betjeman; but to put such entries on the first page of the gazetteer was not an inducement to the reader, as Betjeman was probably aware. On the following page was another own goal. The entry for Ashleworth reads well: "an unspoilt beauty spot, the church beside a big tythe barn of about 1490. In the direction of Haslefield the old rectory is an early sixteenth century timber-framed house. Ashleworth Quay is a dreamy riverside place with a nice pub." The photograph of Ashleworth tells a different story. Titled 'The rubbish tree', it shows a hedgerow tree in the village adorned with rubbish. The photo was by West. In fact every page of the gazetteer has some disincentive to the visitor quite at odds with the purpose of a guidebook – but not the pundit that West could not resist being, as in the entry for Bishop's Cleve: "suffers from the law of beauty spots, that people run up the ugliest houses to enjoy them from, so this is now rather a nasty place".[43]

All this must have been doubly galling for Betjeman, for in the midst of all West's ambivalent negativity is Betjeman's own entry and perambulation of Cheltenham, not to mention another favourite of his, Sezincote, for which he chose the steel-engraved image and wrote the entry. Betjeman had first written about Cheltenham in a poem for the *Cherwell* in 1927. His piece in *Gloucestershire* was, at that time, a definitive statement of his admiration for the place. The section closely resembles the layout, typography and form of his 'Architectural Tour' in *An Oxford University Chest*[44] but is better written in the style we now associate with Betjeman.

Gloucestershire, 1939, p.43

'The rubbish tree', Ashleworth, Gloucestershire, 1939, p.16

By 1952, this pub had a flat roof but here we see it as it was in 1939, the very essence of the slightly down-at-heel, Dylanesque building that all involved in the early Shell Guides loved and feared would be lost to the modern world. Rightly, as it turned out.

West's *Gloucestershire* had a tendency to forget it was a guide, and thus intended to encourage tourism, in favour of 'telling it how it is'. Here, the illustration to the "unspoilt beauty spot" of Ashleworth is this image of spoliation.

Detached houses in the Park, c. 1830.

Prestbury Road, c. 1830.

Early Victorian 'Gothic.' A house in the Park, c. 1840.

SOME OF THE MANY GOOD GEORGIAN STREETS AND BUILDINGS OF CHELTENHAM

* denotes a photograph in these pages.

NORTH OF THE HIGH STREET:

*Clarence Square: *various dates from* 1820–40.
Columbia Place: *early Victorian copy of Sir John Soane's style.*
Evesham Road: *various villas, c.* 1830.
Liberal Club: *chaste classic composition, c.* 1830.
Masonic Hall: *skilful treatment of blank wall spaces,* 1817.
Pittville Circus: *early Victorian houses in various styles.*
*Pittville Lawn: *noble terrace, c.* 1830.
Pittville Park: *terraces, c.* 1830.
*Pittville Pump Room and Gardens: *well laid out gardens, ponds, shrubs and trees leading up to Pumproom* (J. B. FORBES *architect,* 1825), *with splendid interior.*
Portland Street: *good Georgian terraces, minor architecture, with a late Georgian-Perpendicular church and a charming little house called 'Gothic' opposite.*
*Prestbury Road: *on the left-hand side going away from the town a row of perfect* 1830 *stucco semi-detached houses, a model for modern architects and local authorities.*
Wellington Square: *various dates from c.* 1830.

SOUTH OF THE HIGH STREET:

All the places mentioned here were built somewhere between 1820 and *c.* 1850, unless a particular date is mentioned.

Berkeley Place: *on the road to* Oxford, *stone in the* BATH *manner.*
Cheltenham College (Boys): *the older part of the buildings* (1841–3) *in an original Early Gothic Revival manner, by* J. WILSON *of* Bath.
*Christ Church: *a very original effort in Gothic Revival by* F. JEARRAD. W. *Front most imposing. Interior spoiled.*
Echo & Chronicle Office: *the interior of this simple classic building has been modernised.*
Fairlight Place: *typical of many small less distinguished* Cheltenham *streets: Georgian traditions surviving into Victorian times.*
General Buildings, *near* Imperial Square: *a charming Georgian Gothic house, well-preserved by an* Insurance Company, *which uses it as offices. An example of how well stucco buildings look when they are kept in repair.*

Left: In 1935 and then again in 1937 Betjeman had used the idea of a printed perambulation around a town as a way of talking about groups of architecture much as Pevsner was to do in his Buildings of England. With his tour of Cheltenham Betjeman also provided the images. They are not very good, being shot from an angle and slightly too far away. His intention was sound though as these perambulations were his most determined attempt to make the guides what he suggested they would be at the outset – guides promoting a good Georgian architecture which he took to be the best of British urbanism. He calls the terraces on Prestbury road "a model for modern architects and local authorities".

Three photos by Betjeman: some of the many good Georgian streets and buildings in Cheltenham, Gloucestershire, 1939, p.26

On the promenade, the charming little Imperial Spa building (1818) has been demolished in favour of an unharmonious cinema; the Pittville Estate, Cheltenham's grandest Georgian housing scheme, has been broken into by ill proportioned villas. The statues have been ripped off the parapet of the Pittville Spa and cut in half, windows leer rakishly through pediments, porticoes have been stripped of their pillars, decent buildings have been jazzed up with strange painting schemes, the loveliest crescent in the town has not been improved by the dumping of a bus depot into the gardens in front of it, and one of the most distinguished squares is now dominated by a block of modern flats in Wembley Exhibition style: but Cheltenham is now aware of its beauty.[45]

Betjeman's entry, running over eight pages, full of energy and positive ire was (he must have felt) lost in a sea of equivocation; he had even taken his own photographs and carefully selected Victorian advertisements and tradesman's cards to illustrate the piece. But Luckily for West and Betjeman, *Gloucestershire* was the first Shell Guide published by Faber and Faber whose chief designer was David Bland; and Betjeman also was at the height of his printing-and-typography enthusiasm.[46] The result was the best-quality production of any Shell Guide ever published and a much more professional design standard throughout. The book was priced at a shilling more than earlier guides, at three and six, but it was a hardback with dustcover and the novel feature of a spiral binding inside. The paper used for the pages was a dense, smooth cream stock with a slightly lighter stock for the dustcover. The pages took photographs very well and these in turn were printed in rich blacks and whites – far more tonal than the earlier guides, or many of the later; the print was very dark and clear too. The cover and title page were laid out in a very restrained and disciplined manner compared to Betjeman's work – though it is in his style, suggesting a steadying hand from Faber. The typography has similarities to John Rayner's *Hampshire* but, again, is tighter with more space; the text was in Monotype Plantin, a pre-war arts and crafts, vernacular-revival face of 1913 that was influential on Times New Roman because of its legibility: together, these allowed the gazetteer to be made small and dense. The covers are the same image of the chancel of Gloucester Cathedral reproduced in violet from a Victorian print, over which is printed the italic titles; and this is separated from the title page by an extravagantly empty page that in a very small, reversed-out, sans-serif display face quietly announces *Gloucestershire* a Shell Guide, followed on the reverse by a very tasteful set of publishing details. The title page is mainly taken up with a nicely over-square photograph of a Cotswold field edge, worthy of Paul Nash but by Frances Hope. Even the reproduced Bartholomew's maps are better than usual. It is hard to convey in words the quality of the Faber *Gloucestershire* except to say that it is rather like the difference

between an interesting person with some eccentricities of dress and the same person looking good. *Gloucestershire* was the first guide to use the hardback design that featured in all subsequent guides, prior to the softbacks of the 1980s. It is clothbound in cream with no title save for the spine, where the word "Gloucestershire" is reversed out against scarlet in a bold, heavy serif, upper-case face and the words "SHELL GUIDE" printed in a scarlet body text italic.

Despite, or perhaps because of, the shortcomings of West's *Gloucestershire*, what is clear is that from rather confused beginnings of style and content the Shell Guides had developed into a very effective format for a guidebook. The format had several features that together are more than the sum of their parts. The gazetteer was the most effective part of this combination since, even badly written, it offered brief snippets of information that quickly told the reader about where they were, or wanted to visit; and being surrounded by other snippets naturally encouraged the reader at least to tour the county. Of almost equal importance were the plenitude and the positioning of images in the guides. Though the gazetteer gave condensed information a picture couldn't deliver, the images in the guides provided context and atmosphere and an alternate vehicle for more literal extra information. The larger images in the introductory section and spaced throughout the gazetteer had to be good images in themselves but also had to convey the mood of the county and suggest ways to look at it; they had to grab the viewer. The minor images scattered in the text of the gazetteer had a different task: either to give an image to a place in the gazetteer that added to the text entry; or to do the same for an entry elsewhere, to make the reader flick through from the image to the entry. Another task for the inter-textual images was to show a detail that a gazetteer entry description in itself might not be able to convey; these often took the form of anthropomorphic images of memorial sculpture or drawings and old prints to show a more poetic way of seeing the real, as in the case of the entry for Moreton Corbet,[47] which appears on page 41 of *Shropshire*. It is illustrated by a Victorian print of a ruined mansion on the next page and is followed by a photograph of the ruin on the page after that. This page ends with a puzzling detail of a sculpture in an arch that refers to an entry on the page beyond for Neen Sollars.[48] The design of the gazetteer texts and images had to both make the reader read an entry while at the same time encouraging the most promiscuous kind of flicking through.

Around the central gazetteer are introductory and contextual chapters and these were the least successful feature of the early guides; so as the gazetteer flourished they mutated from accounts of sporting activities, ferry times and flora to others of industry or history of sculpture; and finally withered into an introduction to the layout of each county, with the occasional essay like *Oxon*'s 'Deserted Places'. Another element of the format was the reproduction of

Gloucestershire, 1939, cover

Seven Mile Plantation, Badminton, Gloucestershire, 1939, title page

graphic imagery, introduced by Betjeman to foster his interest in evangelising the love of neglected Georgiana and Victoriana. His old prints and trade cards were effective both as part of the entertainment and as propaganda. The also lent to the guides something of the respectability of an antiquarian bookshop, giving them an aura of seriousness that the images themselves were not intended to imbue. With the inclusion of artists as authors, the guides also began to include sketches and reproductions of paintings. It was the sketches that were more successful for they added to the bogus antiquarian respectability of the guides something of the sense of bohemian creativity of the artist's sketchbook. The format of the Shell Guides by 1938 both flattered the aspirations of their supposed readers towards learning and artiness while pandering to and encouraging their page-turning shallowness. By the beginning of

the war in 1939 Faber had buffed up the emergent Shell Guide formula to give the guides a sense of durability and with that, respectability; the guides became books not magazines.

There is no evidence of Piper's involvement with West's guide; but since *Oxon*, he and Betjeman had been working on the guide to *Shropshire*, a process whose pleasures are memorialised in Betjeman's 'The Seeing Eye: or How to Like Everything' in the *Architectural Review* of November 1939. In fact, the guide had progressed to the stage where the Pipers and Betjeman were correcting proofs. By then, with the start of the war in September, Faber had decided to call a halt to the production of further guides because, "our own feeling is that no one who cannot use a car at present is likely to think of buying guides".[49]

Perhaps the rarest Shell Guide is the 1939 *Gloucestershire* since production ceased in the year of publication. It was also the first Shell Guide to be designed under the direction of David Bland of Faber and shows how much improvement to the design of the guides Bland achieved. *Gloucestershire* was printed on thick cream paper and designed with a clarity and attention to detail that had eluded the earlier editors and publishers of the guides.

67

NOTES

1 Richards, November 1938
2 Richards and Ravilious, 1938
3 Betjeman, 1938
4 *Oxon*, 1938
5 Spalding, 2009, p.107
6 From Anthony West's monograph on Piper (West, 1979), it is clear that Piper was fascinated by scarecrows and identified with them in some way, since he took photographs of them throughout his life.
7 *Oxon*, 1938, p.23
8 *Oxon*, 1938, p.14
9 *Oxon*, 1938, p.19
10 *Oxon*, 1938, p.19
11 *Oxon*, 1938, p.18
12 *Oxon*, 1938, p.23
13 *Oxon*, 1938, p.26
14 *Oxon*, 1938, p.27
15 *Oxon*, 1938, p.20
16 *Oxon*, 1938, p.20
17 *Oxon*, 1938, p.37
18 *Oxon*, 1938, p.6
19 *Oxfordshire*, 1953
20 *Oxon*, 1938, p.20
21 *Oxon*, 1938, p.20
22 *Oxon*, 1938, p.20
23 *Oxon*, 1938, p.21
24 *Oxon*, 1938, p.26
25 *Oxon*, 1938, p.34
26 Quoted in Peterson, 2006, p.29
27 Quoted in Peterson, 2006, p.9
28 Quoted in Peterson, 2006, p.31
29 *Oxon*, 1938, p.7
30 *Oxon*, 1938, pp.8–9
31 Peterson, 2006, p.64
32 *Architectural Review* 86, November 1939, pp.201–4
33 Extract from 'The seeing Eye…' quoted in Peterson, 2006, p.219 – Peterson has picked the operative passage of Betjeman's often-awkward text, as he frequently does in this great book.
34 West, 1979, p.93
35 Quoted in Spalding, 2009, p.112 – from *Piper's Places: John Piper in England and Wales* (Ingrams and Piper, 1983, p.47)
36 Faber remained the publisher of the Shell Guides until their demise in 1984.
37 See Lycett Green, 1994, p.142
38 *Gloucestershire*, 1939, p.42
39 *Gloucestershire*, 1952
40 These were retained in the 1952 edition.
41 *Gloucestershire*, 1939, p.15
42 *Gloucestershire*, 1939, p.15
43 *Gloucestershire*, 1939, p.17
44 That in turn was based on researches which produced the article 'Ecclesiastical Typography' for *Typography* No.6, 1938.
45 *Gloucestershire*, 1939, p.21
46 He joined the Double Crown club in 1938.
47 *Shropshire*, 1951, pp.41–3
48 *Shropshire*, 1951, p.44
49 Richard de la Mare to John Betjeman, 26 September 1939 from Faber material held in University of Victoria, Canada, quoted in Peterson, 2006, p.306 – the War began on 1 September 1939.

When Faber and Faber took over the publishing of the Shell Guides in 1939 they redesigned the layout, opting for a standardised hardback with the county title on the spine. *Gloucestershire* was Faber's first guide and its redesign by David Bland tidied and tightened what had been the custom in the early guides by using crisper type, better laid out, and better (blacker and whiter) printed photographs which instantly seemed more modern and authoritative. In doing so, Bland made the rest of the guides look like magazines. Faber quickly rebound all existing unsold copies of the guides in the new style, though retaining their spiral bindings within the new hardcover, before shutting down the series at the outbreak of war. The newly bound guides and *Gloucestershire* particularly set the style and standard of publishing for the guides of 1951 and after.

THE WAR, MURRAY'S ARCHITECTURAL GUIDES AND SHROPSHIRE

BOTH BETJEMAN AND PIPER had what people used to describe as 'a good war'; in fact they became famous. Betjeman volunteered but was unfit for service. However, he found work in the Ministry of Information and subsequently was appointed as a press officer to the British Ambassador in Dublin for the first part of the war, returning to England in autumn 1943. The following year he returned to the Ministry of Information only to be posted to P Branch of the Admiralty, and wrote book reviews for the *Daily Herald*. By the end of the war he was working for the British Council. Piper on the other hand was constantly threatened with call-up but found continual work as a war artist under the patronage of Kenneth Clark until he was finally asked to work on a project for the Ministry of Aircraft Production, in the second half of 1941. From then on he was classed as being in a Reserved Occupation; essentially he was a war artist. Within these roles both Piper and Betjeman were able to develop both their reputations and their personal style. Betjeman continued to write as a poet, an historian, a journalist and as a broadcaster while Piper's art developed through war commissions like painting the devastated Coventry Cathedral in November 1940, painting Windsor Castle and park for the Queen in 1941 and exhibitions like the group show with Moore and Sutherland at Temple Newsam House outside Leeds, June 1941.[1] But Piper also managed to continue working for the *Architectural Review* and on various book projects, including *British Romantic Artists* in 1942 for the Britain in Pictures series and *English, Scottish and Welsh Landscape Verse*, an anthology by Betjeman and Geoffrey Taylor published in 1944. He was the subject of a book in the Penguin Modern Painters series produced under the editorship of Kenneth Clark and written by Betjeman, published in 1944.

Piper's experience as a war artist had a profound effect on his work. In late 1939 he was escaping from abstraction but his landscapes still had the abstractionist's love of forms in composition, as can be seen in his 1939 *Autumn at Stourhead*. His style still veered between the influence of fellow British artists like Nicholson and Wood and continental styles: Piper's vision of Stourhead is seen through the lens of the Italian Lakes; the colouring of this work is essentially brightly lit and its atmosphere has the stillness of a dream. But dating from his visit to a blitzed Coventry in 1940 his whole palette darkens and his blocky abstract forms become Mannerist chiaroscuro masses of darkly vibrant colour.

But though this darkness was no doubt appropriate to the war,

In 1939 Piper's landscapes had clear influences from the surrealists, notably the stageyness of de Chirico; but after his visit to the just-blitzed Coventry, and under the influence of Samuel Palmer, Piper's work became much darker, more architectural with a much greater use of line and scrafito to give human character to what had been sunny, blocky, forms.

Autumn at Stourhead, 1939, 25x30 inches, plate 2 in West, 1979, © Manchester City Galleries

Seaton Delaval, 1941, 28x36 inches, plate 3 in West, 1979, © Tate

Piper had also moved toward an earlier dark view of the world. Later in his book *British Romantic Artists*, he lucidly explains himself:

> Romantic art deals with the particular. The particularisation of Bewick about a bird's wing, of Turner about a waterfall or a hill town, or of Rossetti about Elizabeth Siddal, is a result of a vision that can see in these things something significant beyond the ordinary significance; something that for a moment seems to contain the whole world; and when the moment is past, carries over some comment on life or experience besides the comment on appearances.

> Abiding also in the Romantic painting of this country is the sense of drama in atmosphere, in the weather and the seasons. As a race we have always been conscious of the soft atmosphere and the changeable climate of our sea-washed country, where the air is never quite free from mist, where the light of the sun is more often pale and pearly than it is fiery. This atmosphere has sunk into our souls. It has affected our art as it affects our life.[2]

In rediscovering English Romanticism in time of war, Piper seems to have found a way of taking the sense of much of European surrealism and expressing it through an interpretation of an earlier English vision of the world, that of Blake and more particularly, for Piper, Samuel Palmer. In doing so, he made modernism his own — meaningful to him and his particularly English view of the world as he saw it. These opening paragraphs of *English Romantic Artists* give the coda to all his later work whether painted, designed or photographed, for Piper like Nash saw spirit vibrating through the ordinary things of man and nature.

Nor was he the only one, for the war years were a period of absolutely taxonomic examination of the minutiae of Britain. Whether it was the meticulously recorded and analysed banalities of the Mass Observation work for the Ministry of Information, or the endless popular literature that familiarised the population with every aspect of British cultural life from *Popular Art* through *Medieval Carvings in Exeter Cathedral*, *The Anatomy of the Village*, *Early Britain*, *Henry Moore* or *A Picture Book of the Whole Coast of Britain and Wales*, Britain was obsessed with finding its essence in the particular. Everything was considered to have some kind of genius loci. This faith in the atomic construction of the British soul from a periodic table of ordinary things lying around our land and built environment also extended to the proliferation of whole new areas of academic expertise. History developed local history; antiquarianism and classical archaeology spawned British archaeology; natural history spawned the particularly British science of the Collins New Naturalist series. And in the end, policies for the future were divined from this surreal sense of what the Nation was. From Thomas Sharp's *The Anatomy of the Village* came the city plans for Exeter,

Durham and Oxford, and ultimately the County of London Plan. Everyone, but more particularly the new media class that encompassed the BBC, the Ministry of Information and the Council for the Encouragement of Music and the Arts (*CEMA*), amongst others, was influenced by and implicated in this culture, whether they liked it or not. For Orwell it was 1984 but for Dylan Thomas it was Llareggub. This taxonomy of the significantly ordinary became the way to express pleasure in the dull and unchangingly familiar. Ordinary things, seen through the Romantic eye, could suddenly provide a richly surreal landscape.

Piper and Betjeman were part of this cultural ecology, consuming energy to give it back in another form, taking ideas from all aspects of the culture and producing from them a route to interpretation for the 'general reader'. Whereas in 1939 they had been producing guides for the motorised and youthful intelligentsia, after passing through the war they had absorbed this new culture and were more interested in being optimistic than smart; more interested in celebrating the ordinary country than seeking their own unique untouched places; and more interested in a general reader than 'people like us' — generally, but not entirely.

The cancellation of *Shropshire* by Faber at the start of the war was a blow to Piper and Betjeman. They seem to have thought that the project would not be revived by Faber or Shell, not least because a few months after the start of the war their patron, Jack Beddington, left Shell to become director of the films division of the Ministry of Information, taking over from Kenneth Clark. Neither dropped the idea of making guidebooks and in 1943 an opportunity presented itself.

Jock Murray, Betjeman's publisher, became interested in using photographs being made for the National Buildings Register project to illustrate a revived series of his company's famous guides, Murray's Handbooks for Travellers, which covered most parts of Britain until their publication ceased before the First World War. At some point during 1943 he discussed this with both Betjeman and Piper and also with John Summerson. They were all very enthusiastic, Summerson seeing the guides as architectural guides and Betjeman and Piper as more pictorial guides — in fact Betjeman called them pictorial guides in his correspondence with Murray.[3] In 1944 Betjeman proposed that he be general editor and Summerson be "head of architectural pictures";[4] but in the end Betjeman and Piper became joint editors. Summerson proposed Kent for the first guide, but Betjeman and Piper proposed Shropshire, a guide that almost existed but would need new images, and Bucks, which they both knew well. In the end, Murray took up the idea of a guide to Bucks and Shropshire but meanwhile, at Summerson's suggestion, he contracted Marcus Whiffen to start doing the research for Bucks. Piper and Betjeman's work on Shropshire was owned by Faber and Shell so, though Betjeman thought they could do the guide and proposed a visit with Piper to re-photograph the county, the idea seems to have been dropped; but Murray was willing to let them work with Whiffen on Buckinghamshire. Betjeman's letter makes it clear that he and Piper had no intention of letting this happen:

> I am not hopeful, I fear, that Whiffen will produce good photographs of Bucks. I fear he is primarily a writer – and, as such, very good. It is agreed that these Guides shall be, primarily, visual records of the county and I am sure that if you stick to the NBR or even a preponderance of NBR photographs you will produce something halfway between Batsford and *Country Life*. I am quite sure that J.P. is right in saying that they must depend primarily on the photographer's eye for their effect and they must show the county as it is, rather than as the SPAB or the Fine Arts Commission or anything else would like it. But they must show what is beautiful in it, regardless of date,

association or antiquity. It so happens that old buildings are the most beautiful, but you can with a camera make even an old building look dull and ugly as NBR and Whiffen show. However, I feel we must give Whiffen his chance. But I think you must be prepared to risk a loss there and use him only for captions. Don't publish the book just for the sake of beating Batsford's to the post. It won't be worth it. And it won't beat them. It will be Batsford's...[5]

Murray seems to have agreed to all of them working on the project. Marcus Whiffen resigned from it in July 1947, stating in a letter to Murray, "It is not merely that the selection of subjects has been altered, but the whole idea of the book has changed."[6] *Murray's Buckinghamshire Guide*, edited by John Betjeman and John Piper was published in July 1948. In the interim between the original proposal for guides to Buckinghamshire and Shropshire, Murray also agreed

Betjeman and Piper's Murray's Architectural Guide project was not a sponsored tourist guide like the Shell Guides and so could be openly critical of architecture and society. Of this new suburban street in Amersham they say, "A distinct Buckinghamshire style, which this book has been at pains to exemplify, has here ceased to exist". Their deep cultural hostility to the suburb of the common man and more liberal approach to more individualistic, 'good class', architecture can be seen in their positive account of 'Metroland' which includes other similarly non-local styles of suburban house in the generic vernacular revival and modernist styles.

Images 157 and 158, Murray's Buckinghamshire Guide, *1948, p.108*

METROLAND (157/165). The nearness to London of the airy Chiltern Hills, and frequent trains to and fro, have turned parts of south-eastern Buckinghamshire into a dormitory. The first dormitory houses to appear were near the Metropolitan railway stations of Chalfont, Amersham, Missenden and Wendover, and those beside Great Western and Great Central stations of Gerrards Cross and Beaconsfield were built next. They were 'good class' and architect designed, since the railway fares meant that most residents were wealthier business executives and professional people. The Garden Village as opposed to the Garden City was the aim of the builders. Houses deliberately 'quaint', with a detail here and there suggesting tiled, half-timbered, Quaker, and Georgian Bucks, stood in ample gardens of flowering trees bordering commons where well-worn footpaths traversed the bracken. They were thought of by their inhabitants as very much in the country. Even in the mid-wars period, in the more exclusive parts of Amersham and Beaconsfield, large country houses were built, sometimes escaping into a mythical past, in a style more antique than the oldest timber manors in the county; sometimes escaping into a mythical future of fresh air, no black-outs and everlasting sunshine. Both were good of their kinds. But the individuality of Buckinghamshire building styles was disappearing.

157. At Gerrard's Cross

158. 'Normandy', Amersham (c. 1930).

Images 165, Murray's Buckinghamshire Guide, *1948, p.112*

Image 163, Murray's Buckinghamshire Guide, *1948, p.111*

to let Betjeman and Piper do a guide to Berkshire and to revive a 1935 Shell Guide project, a guide to Lancashire by Betjeman's friend Peter Fleetwood-Hesketh (which was finally published in 1955 after Betjeman and Piper had begun working on Shell Guides again). In 1949 after the success of *Buckinghamshire*, a new guide to Somerset was contemplated; but after *Berkshire* Betjeman and Piper decided not to continue with the project as it took, they said, too much time and was not sufficiently remunerative.

Murray's Buckinghamshire Guide came out in 1948 and cost 15 shillings. Compared to the Shell Guides it was very restrained, being printed plainly in Times Roman on a cream paper for the text and a glazed white paper for the photographs. Maps were reproductions of the O.S. half-inch map overlaid with a numbered grid. As well as an introduction and a 'Gazetteer to All Parishes', the main feature of the Murray Guides was a 112-page photo section. This was a captioned photo essay on the history of architecture in the county, from a brief description of the landscape through to recent buildings. The declared intention of the guide was: "only to illustrate, or mention at any length in the gazetteer, those objects which struck us as beautiful";[7] to "illustrate pictorially as much of the variety of Bucks as would lend itself to illustration and describe the rest in the gazetteer";[8] and "only mention what is characteristic of Bucks".[9] The subtext of the guide is that the present day (1948) suffered from the disappearance of local traditions and materials, as represented by Amersham in the last of the 165 photographs. The caption begins, "The last picture shows the All-English style: of the small car, classlessness and the common man" and ends, "A distinct Buckinghamshire style, which this book has been at pains to exemplify, has here ceased to exist."[10] The gazetteer is laid out in two columns of Times Roman rather than the Shell Guides' three of Plantin, but essentially the gazetteer is the same, only with longer, more architecturally focussed entries. However, in the Murray's Guide the gazetteer seems like an index because it is not the main vehicle for ideas: the pictures are. In Murray's *Buckinghamshire* the relationship that exists between the images and the accompanying text is the reverse of that of the Shell Guides – the images dominate the narrative and the page with the captions providing, despite their length and erudition, a supporting role.

The Murray's Guides are in this respect experimental, recognising a new truth in the early Media Age of film and photo magazines like *Picture Post*: that images are more important than even the best text. In *Buckinghamshire*, Piper provided around 60 of the photographs, all of which are beautifully and darkly toned; and whenever these are of sculptural subjects, every effort is made to bring them to life as can be best seen in the green man's face in the poppy-head pew-end at Ivinghoe.[11]

Toward the end of the guide there is a very positive section on Metroland, showing elegant pre-war suburban houses and then,

Image 24, Murray's Buckinghamshire Guide, *1948, p.16*

surprisingly, an International modernist house at Chalfont St Giles by Medelsohn and Chermayeff. As with the Shell *Gloucestershire*, the images are strongly tonal blacks and whites, not the muted tones of many other austerity-regulated photo illustrations. As well as a number of Katherine Esdaile inspired sculptural examples, *Buckinghamshire* also illustrates Marlow Bridge and work by Soane, a 'Pisan' revival church and West Wycombe Mausoleum, representing Betjeman's expanding architectural interests; while Piper's are represented by stained glass, old Manors, and distressed seventeenth-century barn doors.

This is one of Piper's best photographs, illustrating precisely his ability to bring sculpture to life and in the process revealing something of the deep surrealism of English art.

In the Murray's Guides, Betjeman could celebrate Victorian architecture with an audience he knew would be able to appreciate his enthusiasm for its less well-known practitioners and styles. Here he reveals the Pisan style and the architect of the Danube bridge at Budapest.

Image 137, Murray's Buckinghamshire Guide, 1948, p.94

Image 138, Murray's Buckinghamshire Guide, 1948, p.95

Piper used the Murray's Guides to elaborate on his interest in old houses and barns. Beachampton Hall Barn was particularly attractive to him as it combines neglect with architectural features and the implicit suggestion that it could be made into a house again.

Beachampton Hall Barn, images 54 and 55, Murray's Buckinghamshire Guide, 1948, pp.38 and 39

West Wycombe Mausoleum, images 97 and 103, Murray's Buckinghamshire Guide, *1948, pp.65 and 69*

Some of the images in *Buckinghamshire* are striking in their modernity – notably Avery Colebrook's[12] shots of West Wycombe Mausoleum which have remarkable depth of field and resolution and explore the full range of tones and compositional possibilities of shadows. In their next Murray, *Berkshire*, Betjeman and Piper acknowledge Colebrook for his "exciting" photographs of Windsor and introduce a new technique, colour photography, into their nineteenth-century stained glass section with an image taken by the famous colour photographer Percy Hennell.

Looking at Colebrook's and Hennell's images, it seems clear that Piper learnt a lot from them as their techniques and compositions appear in his later photographic work, while Piper's image 164 of the Madonna window at the White House Wantage – by the architect Baillie-Scott, another Betjeman favourite – is in Piper's most neo-Romantic style.

Though Betjeman and Piper abandoned the Murray's Guides after *Berkshire*, they used the opportunity to look at their own Home Counties and to push their idea of a guidebook to a more modern and experimental place. Their guides had expanded to include a wider range of architectural styles, from suspension bridges and Pre-Raphaelite interiors to barns. They had also pushed their use of imagery to a new, more directly narrative level and recognised new photographic methods to help in this process. Altogether the

Our Lord Blessing Children, Ford Madox Ford at Brightwalton, image 147, Murray's Berkshire Architectural Guide, *1949, p.97*
See colour image, page 134

These images by Avery Colebrook show one of Betjeman's favourite buildings, the Mausoleum at West Wycombe, which contains the hearts of members of the Hellfire Club. The photographs are unusual choices by Betjeman and Piper because they try to show the context of the site at some cost to the description of the building; but for their tonality and depth of field alone Piper would have loved them.

Piper was very suspicious of colour but where he did use colour images in later Shell Guides they were often paraphrases of this image by Percy Hennell, who produced a number of colour-photograph-illustrated books in the war.

Murray's Guides were a leap forward from the pre-war Shell Guides and their influence on later guides was evident right up to 1984 when the Shell series ceased. One aspect that was a hangover from the earlier guides was Betjeman's unshakeable conservatism; the last image in the Berkshire guide is the Harwell Atomic Research Establishment. Seen as a thin stripe of huts on the horizon of a field, the caption reads:

> Post war Berkshire's crowning state monument is Harwell Atomic Research Establishment. It was built on the downs by order of the Ministry of Supply which overrode other ministries and local objections. … Its prefabs and factories spread over the Downs and higher into the skyline. Its service to Berkshire is that the scientists in it are engaged in slitting the material of which the world and its inhabitants are made.[13]

Pevsner

The Murray's Architectural Guides are better architectural guides than the Shell Guides: that was their focus and they had higher production values, if not design. Undoubtedly, with the extended, captioned photo essay that is the core of each book, they provided an authoritative, accessible and beautifully captured history of architecture that was better than any other widely available architectural guide, including Pevsner's: even Pevsner himself admitted in his own guide to Buckinghamshire of 1960[14] that, "The most enjoyable book on the buildings of Buckinghamshire is John Betjeman and John Piper's *Murray's Buckinghamshire Architectural Guide*".[15] To be sure, Pevsner would have been aware of Murray's Guides. He knew Betjeman and Piper from his time at the *Architectural Review* and, by 1948, he was researching Middlesex for his own series of guides, the Buildings of England, a version of the German series of Architektführer, Georg Dehio's *Handbuch der deutschen Kunstgeschichte*, that he had been trying to get going in Britain since 1935. It was not until 1945 that he had come to an agreement with Allen Lane at Penguin to back the series, after the success of his 1942 *Outline of European Architecture*. Lane already published a series of Penguin guides to the counties, edited by Blue Guides editor L. Russell Muirhead, a direct inheritor of the Baedeker mantle.

The Penguin guides were short and aimed at walkers, cyclists and motorists and were organised like a Baedeker with tours and a good map of the area. In 1939, they cost sixpence. Set against this backdrop, Pevsner could not hope to produce a Murray-type guide: he was compiling a cheap paperback as a companion to an existing series of guides; the first editions of 1951, *Cornwall*, *Middlesex* and *Nottinghamshire*, sold for three shillings and sixpence compared to Murray's, by then, eighteen shillings. Because of cost, the early Pevsner's guides had very few photographs (all from cheap sources),

Piper and Betjeman were ahead of their time in their architectural tastes as seen here in an early rediscovery of the romance and charm of "craft-movement villas usually found in garden cities and garden suburbs".

The White House, WANTAGE (**163, 164**), was built for the chaplain of the community of St Mary the Virgin by M. H. Baillie Scott. It is a prototype of well-designed, craft-movement villas usually found in garden cities and garden suburbs. Its style is a popular architectural expression of the Morris movement. The architect has designed door-handles, grates, fender, fabrics, and even the stained-glass Madonna in the priests' private chapel, (**164**).

164

The White House Wantage, Images 163 and 164, Murray's Berkshire Architectural Guide, 1949, p.107

Harwell, image 171, Murray's Berkshire Architectural Guide, 1949, p.112

Betjeman was both terrified by and horrified with Harwell Atomic Research Establishment. It exemplified the ugliness and menace of the future.

a small map and very pithy, simply descriptive entries. At that time the entries didn't even have a reference to help you find them on the map. They were not the cultural lions they were to become, let alone the Holy Records they now are. That said, in 1955 Penguin published new county guides "compiled" by F.R. Banks which were much more detailed than their Russell Muirhead predecessors because of the new standard set by their new companion, Pevsner's Buildings of England.

The prolonged period of cultural introspection engendered by the practicalities of total war – and egged on by the gentle propaganda created by numerous government-funded cultural recording projects, combined with the simple desire to move freely as catalysed by the ending of hostilities in Europe – created a ready market for travel guides. Even if actual travel was restricted still by rationing and a general lack of money there was, publishers felt, a market for the travel guide, suggesting immanent departure, as much as the travel book suggesting more distant possibilities. Ideally the two forms could be combined.

In 1946, a new series of guides that aimed at just this market was published by the imprint of an enterprising émigré from Budapest, Paul Elek. Elek's Vision of England series ran until 1957 and was by and large organised by county, though there were guides to

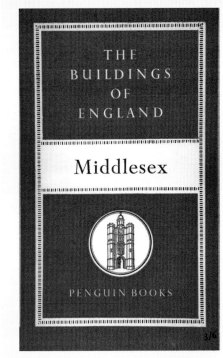

Cover of Pevsner's Middlesex, *1951*

Cover of F.R. Bank's Kent, *1955*

Nellie Kirkham, Derbyshire, *London: Paul Elek, 1947, plates 7–11: Black Rocks nr. Cromford by W.A. Poucher; Chelmorton Low by John Armitage; The Curlew, by John Armitage; Moors above Bamford Edge by Richard S. Howes; Farmhouse below Cratcliffe by W.A. Poucher*

7 The wind-blown summit of Black Rocks near Cromford. *W. A. Poucher, Ph.C., F.R.P.S.*

8 Chelmorton Low, a typical stretch of land in the heart of the limestone country. *John Armitage.*

9 The curlew, the bird of the moorland —these birds are steadily increasing in numbers in Derbyshire. *John Armitage.*

10 On the gritstone moors above Bamford Edge—this is typical of great areas of the northern moors of the country. *Richard S. Howes.*

11 Derbyshire farmhouse sheltering beneath the rocky heights of Cratcliffe. *W. A. Poucher, Ph.C., F.R.P.S.*

Pevsner's Buildings of England began life in a modest way and were not really in any way equivalent to the Shell Guides. In the beginning, they may have been seen by the publisher as a partner to the Penguin county guides that started in the 1930s and were modernised in the mid 1950s.

The Elek guides were in some ways better photo guides than the Shell Guides because they were neither in thrall to architecture nor acting as a motorist's guide. These factors meant they were free to represent all aspects of 'the country' and in this example this means open country: remote tracks, birds and isolated farms set in rugged landscapes where the land is the star rather than the farm.

areas, such as *The Black Country* (1946). The series was edited by Clough and Annabel Williams-Ellis, though they were as much *bona fides* as editors since layout was by Peter Ray, photography edited by Malvine Leonard and covers designed by Kenneth Rowntree (who also did work for Shell) which left about 40 pages of text and some illustrations to be commissioned and edited. The Elek guides were influenced by pre-war Shell Guides but not so much that they were an imitation. They were exactly the same size and with about the same balance of text to image: *Derbyshire* had about 35 pages of text and 64 images, and in addition 8 line drawings and coloured illustrations. Like Hobhouse's Shell Guide in the thirties, there is a section on the great houses and the book only really covers the area now occupied by the national park. Some things were rather better done by the Elek guides than Betjeman's Shell Guides. The map, for instance, is a good colour reproduction of an Ordnance Survey one-inch map rendered at three-miles to the inch. Like those of later Shell Guides, the cover is a mixture of good type and layout, illustration and photography suggesting a mixture of artiness and history; the most successful aspect of the Elek guides was the use of photographs in a self-contained group.

These were reproduced at a larger size than in the pre-war Shell Guides, most occupying half a page. The images were by a number of well-known photographers including, in the case of *Derbyshire*, John Armitage and the 'mountain' photographer W.A. Poucher as well as archive material from *Country Life*, the Courtauld Institute and the National Buildings Record. The selection of the images is almost as good as the later thirties Shell Guides and only limited by the lack of a link between the photographer and the particular book the image is in; they are certainly not tourist images. The best of the photographs show things not shown in the Shell Guide for Derbyshire but that were in *Bucks* and *Oxon* and *Gloucestershire*: good villagescapes, church interiors, particularly Esdailesque sculptures, churchyard sculpture and – unlike almost any Shell Guide – views from the tops of hills ascended by walkers.

Despite all these merits, the Elek Vision of England guides are guides to be consumed before leaving home because they rely on a narrative form. Consequently, whilst information is richly provided, it is difficult to extract with many index entries on individual places running to four widely spaced references in the text. This is not to say that the guides are badly written or lack eccentricity or poetry; when you find it, the entry for Eldon Hole is as good as any in a Shell Guide:

> In these days it is not looked on as a difficult trip, and the only danger is from falling stones dislodged by the swinging ladder. The first ninety feet at the northern end are negotiated with the aid of a hand-rope, which brings you to an extensive ledge where the rope ladders for the rest of the descent are fixed. At the bottom you share the stony

floor with dead cows and anything else that happens to have tumbled in; a short passage takes you to a really magnificent cavern whose vast dome soars more than one hundred feet above your head.[16]

Shropshire at last?

In fact, in 1946 Elek tried to buy the manuscript for Betjeman and Piper's *Shropshire* from Shell for the new Vision of England series but it was lost and therefore unavailable. The effect of this request and the subsequent success of Elek's guides – rapidly expanding to cover many counties between 1946 and 1950 and indicating that, at 12/6d, this kind of book would sell – prompted Shell and Faber to revive the Shell Guides. This though didn't happen until 1950 after Betjeman and Piper had abandoned writing Murray's Architectural Guides (though they edited the last of the series, Fleetwood-Hesketh's *Lancashire*). This didn't seem to affect Murray's relationship with Betjeman and in fact it thrived as Betjeman's poetry became very successful.

As the admirable Peterson notes in *John Betjeman: A Bibliography*, "*Shropshire* has an exceptionally long and complex production history"[17] but this need not detain us more beyond noting that whilst the original proofs were found and revised, most of the images were lost. This was probably a bit of a godsend for it allowed *Shropshire* to be given the reconsideration of its authors with a decade more experience than there had been in 1939. In a letter to Piper in 1955 about his Shell film series *Discovering Britain*, Betjeman said, "I don't think I've enjoyed anything so much since our Shell and Murray Guide days".[18] There is no doubt that their relationship was very close at that time, with Piper discovering his architectural and Romantic voice and Betjeman re-forging his persona with an openness and generosity and public optimism from his friendship with Piper. There were third and fourth characters that must be considered in relation to *Shropshire*. Myfanwy Piper made critical contributions to the manuscript in 1939 and probably again in 1950; but the unsung member of the post-war Shell Guide team is David Bland of Faber and Faber.

The key difference between the pre Faber Shell Guides and those they published is professional attention to detail and this for many years was down to David Bland. When the guides came to Faber he probably took the rational decision to put a hard cover around the fragile covers of the spiral bindings of the guides they inherited from earlier publishers. The hard cover he used was very similar (down to the form of the titles on the spine) to that used by Bartholomew on their luxury hard-cover linen-backed versions of their half-inch maps (also used in the guides). When *Gloucestershire* was to be published, Bland used a very good paper stock that was durable and would take a photograph and made sure that the whole was spaciously and seamlessly laid out in contrast to the, at times, obvious cut and paste of earlier guides; and typically for a man with a letterpress background, he took great care to have good typography and not too many different fonts, unlike Betjeman.

Bland had an unusual career. At Bristol Grammar School in the twenties he became friends with Vivian Ridler and they started doing printing as a hobby. Soon they moved on to printing the parish magazine and then started their own company, the Perpetua Press. In their early twenties, in 1935, their *Fifteen Old Nursery Rhymes* was judged to be one of the fifty best books published that year. Vivian Ridler went on to join the Oxford University Press, eventually becoming its printer. Bland joined Faber in the late 1930s and likewise enjoyed a long career there as a production manager.

Bland's work on *Gloucestershire* was, in modern terms, graphic design; and like a graphic designer he simply orchestrated the materials regardless of content. Content was the job of Betjeman and Piper but this disinterest in it allowed Bland to be very exact in his judgements. In 1954 he was one of the three judges of the National Book League exhibition the Best 100 British Book Designs of 1953, an accolade he'd received for his designs for *Shropshire* in the exhibition of 1952. In the text of the catalogue some entries carried comments by the judges and from these one can see the kind of attention to detail Bland might have applied to his own work. Of Andre Deutsch's version of Trollope's *The Two Heroines of Plumpington* they note, "The rules in the headlines are perhaps a little emphatic" and of Routledge and Kegan Paul's *British Caving*, edited by C.H.D. Cullington, they state, "No evident need for the rule under the headlines. The letter-spacing of lines in capitals and in small capitals appears to be uneven throughout the book. The head margins are too deep. Off-centre style not consistent throughout. Good presswork."[19] A further insight into the mind of David Bland can be taken from his gazetteer for the Isles of Scilly in Betjeman's *Cornwall: A Shell Guide*, of 1964. Here his writing is clear but not much more, and scarcely does justice to the photographs accompanying the text, all his design:

> Hugh Town is on an isthmus with beaches fore and aft. It is full of decent low-built, early nineteenth century houses of granite; and even those built by the Duchy of Cornwall during this century are unexceptional…[20]

Bland was concise, careful and correct and in this he was a counterpoint to Piper and Betjeman's subversive double act, which cast Piper as straight man to Betjeman (whereas in fact they both created their material). With Betjeman and Piper's excellent copy and Bland's dry design style, *Shropshire* turned the Shell Guides from something akin to a special magazine supplement into a book that was richer than any other guide of the time — more evocative than Pevsner's descriptions; more descriptive than the Williams-Ellises' Vision of England prose; a more poetic conjunction of text,

illustration and photography than their own Murray's Architectural Guides. In short, different from and better than any other guide to Britain at the time. Published in October 1951, by December the 5th it had sold 800 copies.[21]

Actually *Shropshire* was less luxuriously printed than *Gloucestershire* using glazed 'white art' paper, except for the endpapers. It was also shorter than Elek and the Williams-Ellises' Vision of England guides, whilst being sold for the same price. And every copy carried an errata insert of the utmost elegance explaining that the number codes given in the gazetteer relating to the map were three digits out thus, "for 10 read 13".[22] These were not its only faults and Peterson notes that, "not all readers welcomed the book's unusual appearance"[23] and quotes a letter by Bland to Arnold Brigden that rather lamely states, "you must realise that these books are intended as pieces of advertising, not just as ordinary guidebooks"[24].

Shropshire is most like Piper's earlier *Oxon*, combining line drawings, ink and wash illustrations, lino cuts, reproductions of old steel engravings, aquatints, wood engravings and rather surreal photographs of sculptures. In addition there are new kinds of image: diagrams of sections through the topography of the county, close ups of cast-iron railings and bridge signs, canal locks as well as others of old railways and stations and stopped-up Romanesque doors to churches.

The text design varies from a tight three-column 9pt Plantin layout for the gazetteer to a two-column 11pt layout for the section on Shrewsbury. Titles vary from copperplate for in-text titles to heavy display faces for major titles. What might be construed as most upsetting is the subtle irreverence of, for instance, the title page of the long entry on Shrewsbury. The city announced in a florid copperplate cartouche with an elegant but empty couple of lines from Housman, the pair verging on parody. Below, the two-column layout is introduced and immediately broken by the insertion of a just-too-wide photo of the "Central boot repairing depot", a decrepit eighteenth-century shop — the image being captioned simply "Shrewsbury".

The whole page reads a bit like the work of a younger Betjeman put through a filter of a more subtle and older satirist. In view of the kinds of judgements made by the judges of the British Book Design Exhibition in 1954, it is not surprising that not all were happy with this earlier book — although actually the judges of the National Book League loved it.

Perhaps one reason for this was the combination of economy of means and plenitude of culture that the book delivers, for although it is shorter than the books in the Elek Vision of England series it has far more content and this is really because of Bland. His use of paper allowed the gazetteer to be printed in a small point size; it also 'took' photographs well and, by extension, Piper's dark,

Aquatint of Coalbrookdale by De Loutherburg, p.25

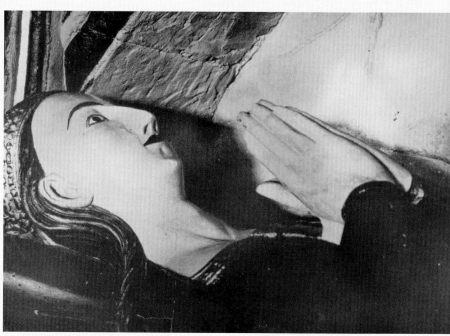

Cornewale effigy at Burford, "the authors", p.20

Cover

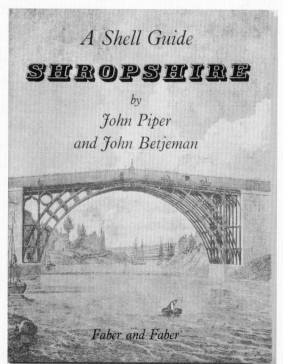

Front endpapers of Ironbridge

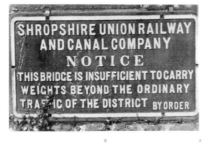

Above: Iron Tombstones at MADELEY.
Below: Notice on a Shropshire Union Canal Bridge.

SHROPSHIRE UNION RAILWAY
AND CANAL COMPANY
NOTICE
THIS BRIDGE IS INSUFFICIENT TO CARRY
WEIGHTS BEYOND THE ORDINARY
TRAFFIC OF THE DISTRICT BY ORDER

Opposite : One kind of Shropshire scenery. CARDING MILL VALLEY, CHURCH STRETTON

Shropshire Cast Iron, by "the authors", p.9

Lock at Wappenshal, "the authors", p.29

Shropshire Outlines, p.7

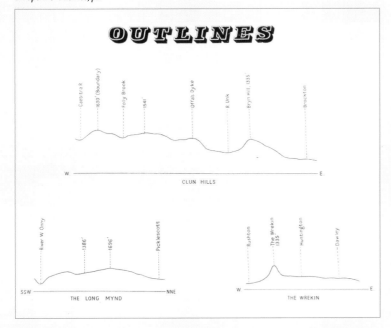

Bucknel Station, "the authors", p.18

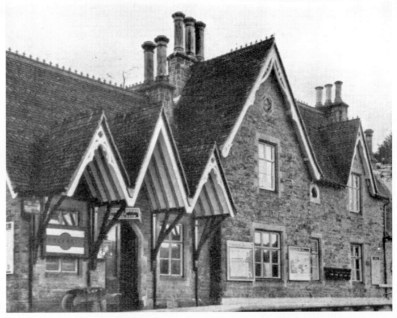

Shropshire and Montgomeryshire Railway Llanymynech, "the authors", p.36

Romanesque door aperture at Tugford, "the authors", p.59

Previous pages and left: All these images from *Shropshire* (1951) were either selected or photographed by "the authors". Probably the photographs were taken in 1939 when Piper and Betjeman travelled the county in the full flush of their guidebook enthusiasm. The diversity of the imagery, and their historical and cultural references, gives a clear sense when seen together of the breadth and depth of the intellectual ambitions of the post-war Shell Guides.

Wroxeter, wood engraving from Salopia Antiqua

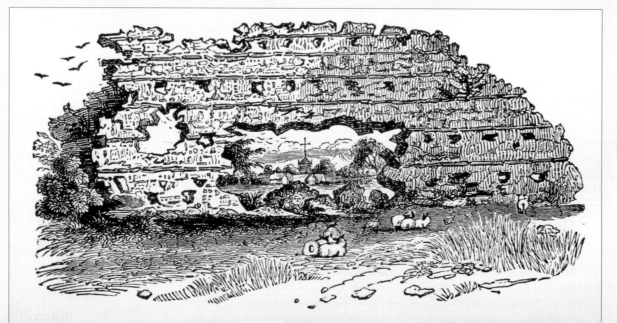

contrasty graphic imagery. Taken together these design decisions facilitated the novel design idea that every available surface of the book should be covered with material that gave local timbre to the voice of the text. The credit for this idea must go to Betjeman first, but Piper brought to it the idea of the artist's sketchbook and Bland showed them how to pack it all into a small suitcase.

Though Bland, Piper and Betjeman's extensive use of every illustration type on every available surface in every size was a rare example of a book subjected to total design, the real reason for the book's success is the way that copious illustration is pitted against an extremely pared-down idea of a guidebook, an essence of the thirties Shell Guides. The book begins with a double-page spread describing the county, with diagrams and in three columns of text. This is followed by an equally minimal summing up of the county in four photographs on the next three pages, from the general view of the Long Mynd at Carding Mill Valley to details of grave railings at Madeley. Then follows the gazetteer, indexes and maps. *Shropshire* is really a gazetteer with photos and this is far more radical, though tidier, than the hedging around of the gazetteer in the thirties guides with sections on golf, flowers and lost industries. The addition of Bland to Piper and Betjeman led to a design for *Shropshire* that became the template for the subsequent Shell Guides. These relied on the chief skill of their editors: the conversion of what in ordinary guides was a long, illustrated narrative into a series of poetic telegrams of text and image arranged in a rhythm where the constant refrain of short text was laid over by another pleasantly distracting beat of constantly changing images and image media.

In the end, the key to the future success of the Shell Guides was that a format had been found that packed in information, both textual and pictorial; and this was simply the gazetteer of short entries supported and visually driven by images, which led the reader into the text. There is more to this format than meets the eye.

The problem of representing a large physical subject, its history and culture is the problem of the guidebook; the giving of coherence to the random accretions of time and culture to a random piece of land with its own physical incoherencies of hills, rivers, mountains, forests and meadows. The traditional solution to the problem has been to describe a journey, thus providing an excuse for a constrained narrative through a land. This option was not really available to the Shell Guides since they were expressly made to encourage motor exploration – and in any case, an itinerary smacks of tourism whereas lack of structure stands for travel. The apparent advantage of a gazetteer is its randomness, being organised around the comprehensible but very detached-from-reality form of the A–Z. But once one accepts that a place can be organised not by reality but by a system that makes retrieving information simple, the gazetteer has many advantages. In the narrative of a journey places are described as they are arrived at, but this excludes many places

Shrewsbury

High the vanes of Shrewsbury gleam
Islanded by Severn stream.
A. E. Housman.

The full Severn makes a more than hairpin bend, very nearly completing the circle, and on the mound of the peninsula the hill-town of Shrewsbury rises. The one pregnable side of the town, where there is no natural fortification of water, is occupied by a pink sandstone Norman castle (containing a round Georgian room designed by Telford) and a large and handsome Tudor-style railway station. There is, of course, the usual sprinkling of suburbs in all directions, the most unpleasant development being that in a northerly direction. Two bridges, both of classic beauty, cross the Severn into the city. The English bridge from the east was designed by John Gwynne in 1774 (he also built Magdalen Bridge, Oxford, and the bridge at Atcham), and the Welsh bridge rebuilt in 1795 by Mylne, the designer of old Westminster Bridge. The bridges symbolize the eternal conflict between England and Wales, whose history involves much of the history of Shrewsbury and the whole county; in Shropshire you will find someone called Edwards calling himself English and someone called Smith calling himself Welsh. The Welsh wars, the Wars of the Roses and the Civil Wars swayed to and fro over Shrewsbury, and the unravelling of their complications is more a matter for history books than a guide book. David, brother of Llewelyn and the last of the Celtic Princes of Wales, was dragged at a horse's heels through the Shrewsbury streets and hung, drawn and quartered here in 1283. Harry Hotspur was slain at Battlefield outside the town in 1403. Henry Tudor stayed in Wyle Cop, a Shrewsbury street, on the way to Bosworth. In August, 1551, the sweating sickness, which spread all over England, broke

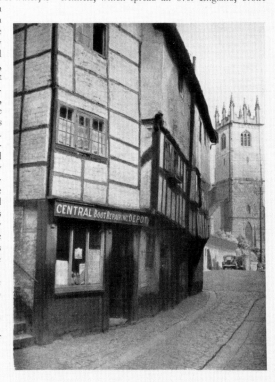

SHREWSBURY.

51   F*

Title page to 'Shrewsbury', Shropshire, 1951, p.51

Betjeman and Piper liked to make provocative, subtly subversive layouts of images playing against text and the expectation of the reader. Here, is Shrewsbury unspoiled and quaint or just decrepit?

not visited. A subsequent form of travel narrative is the narrative of the native where a whole area is described and this is usually done through headings that organise the information in packages like centuries or wars or great families or agriculture or industry. All these have the disadvantage of presenting information about places in a way that disaggregates them; the information about a village appears under many different subject headings and thus either a whole book has to be read or information sifted out using an index. A gazetteer concentrates all the information about a location into one place with its name on.

One function of the narrative structure of travel guides is simply to guide the reader to the most interesting places and a gazetteer has the disadvantage of eradicating this structure. The solution to the problem in the Shell Guides evolved slowly, but by *Shropshire* it was well developed: strong images placed out of gazetteer order in the text that, through their immediate appeal, drag the reader to the gazetteer entry elsewhere. This combination in the Shell Guides of image and gazetteer entry gave the reader an intuitive way into an incoherent county; but as a format it has some risks, the biggest being dull pictures and, worse, dull and irrelevant entries. This risk puts the onus on good editing and good editors and in fact the image and gazetteer format also has some unexpected advantages in this respect for the editor. Because all the images refer only to particular gazetteer entries, some weak pictures can be accommodated since they have a tendency to disappear in a book where pictures are not looked at in any order. Likewise, dull gazetteer entries also disappear partly because they can be overlooked and partly because a good image ameliorates the dullness of text in the same way that all the elements of an opera can make some poor lyrics irrelevant. The format of the Shell Guides arrived at in *Shropshire* was perfect for a guidebook for it gave the information while making the reader feel empowered and free.

The only real risk came in the form of the gazetteer entry. It didn't matter if it was occasionally dull, but it did have to be as short as possible to allow for a short book and to hold the attention of the reader. It might be thought that negativity in gazetteer entries would be a problem but while this is true if there is a preponderance of negativity (as with some of the Shell Guides), it was important that some existed to demonstrate the critical independence of the author(s). This is why in Betjeman's entry on Shrewsbury it is good that he says, "One's first impression of Shrewsbury from a distance is elation. One's next impression is of disappointment at the untidiness of the architecture of the main streets".[25] Or why in his entry on Ruyton of the Eleven Towns it is fine to say, "It looks rather passé, but has a factory. Some faded brick houses and Inns. Church scraped, bad modern glass. The fragment in the churchyard was a castle. Ruyton Towers on the Knockin road is a large house in red sandstone with plate-glass windows in a late

Victorian–Norman manner with a conifer in the background".[26] There is also the consolation that these remarks are prefaced by, "Large main-road village with character" and that the entry is surreally funny from the place name to the conifer by way of the Knockin road. Actually the secret of the gazetteer entry is that it has to be short, imagistic, interesting and, especially if not that, funny. Betjeman was a great gazetteer-entry writer because even at his most desperate for material he was a poet of the telegram kind (in the manner of Robert Benchley's telegram home about Venice: "Streets full of water. Advise."). His entry for Rodington has just this quality, but it also contains another game which he often plays on the reader: he says something is dull whilst making it seem quite different: "Silver birches; flat country; red-brick cottages; Rembrandt views of canal bridges, locks and wharves. Church: Victorian, but of no interest".[27] Laid out in the book, this entry ends with the words "but of no interest" on its own line and thus seemingly and at first glance referring to the whole.

In fact, after the design principles established in *Shropshire*, the difference between a good Shell Guide and an indifferent one was, in the end, narrowed down to the quality of the gazetteer entry. The best are short poems that make ordinary places a pleasure to read about and thus desirable to visit. One reason the gazetteer entries were so crucial was that the team of Betjeman, Piper and Bland was always able to deliver books which were a visual treat; and as the series developed after *Shropshire*, this was mostly down to Piper's great skills in taking, choosing and editing images.

NOTES

1 26 paintings
2 Piper, 1942, p.7
3 Letter from J.B. to Murray, 15 September 1945 – Lycett Green, 1994, pp.359–60
4 Letter from J.B. to Murray, 21 June 1944 – Lycett Green, 1994, pp.344–5
5 Letter from J.B. to Murray, 21 June 1944 – Lycett Green, 1994, pp.344–5
6 Lycett Green, 1994, pp.394 – footnote by the author to a letter from Betjeman to Murray of 8 June 1946 which criticises Whiffen's judgement, declining to meet him on the 14th of the month and criticising Whiffen's photographer Herbert Felton.
7 Betjeman and Piper, 1948, p.vii
8 Betjeman and Piper, 1948, p.viii
9 Betjeman and Piper, 1948, p.ix
10 Betjeman and Piper, 1948, p.112
11 Betjeman and Piper, 1948, p.16, image 24
12 Avery Colebrook took almost as many pictures as Piper in *Murray's Buckinghamshire Guide*.
13 Betjeman and Piper, 1949, p.112, image 171
14 Researched by Mark Girouard
15 Pevsner, 1960, p.43
16 Kirkham, 1947, p.20
17 Peterson, 2006, p.64
18 Lycett Green, 1995, p.54
19 National Book League, 1954, pp.15 and 28
20 Betjeman, 1964, p.134
21 Peterson, 2006, p.66
22 *Shropshire*, 1951, p.65
23 Peterson, 2006, p.65
24 Letter from D. Bland to A. Brigden, 25 July 1956, quoted in Peterson, 2006, p.65
25 *Shropshire*, 1951, p.52
26 *Shropshire*, 1951, p.49
27 *Shropshire*, 1951, p.49

HEREFORDSHIRE, WORCESTERSHIRE, NORTHAMPTONSHIRE

THOUGH *SHROPSHIRE* WAS an apparently new Shell Guide, it was in most respects a redesign of the almost-published 1939 proofs for *Shropshire*. Nor was it to appear without successors soon to follow. As was usual with the guides, forthcoming titles were advertised opposite the title page of *Shropshire*. These were to be revisions in the new Faber format of guides that Betjeman liked: *Devon, Oxon, The West Coast of Scotland* (which also became a good seller in the fifties[1]) and Anthony West's *Gloucestershire*. Though West's guide was the first Faber guide and featured a complete gazetteer, unlike its predecessors it was very negatively written. By the early fifties West had emigrated to America to work at the *New Yorker* and didn't want to redo the guide so the job was passed to a new author, the architectural historian David Verey, who much later compiled the two-volume Pevsner for Gloucestershire (1970). The alterations to *Gloucestershire* were not only in the gazetteer but also included the removal of the sections about industry. These had been provocatively political in their analysis with West attacking the conceptualisation of the county as a "for ever rural" place, pointing out that it had several hi-tech industries including aviation. In fact, with the exception of *Devon*, all the revisions had some element of moderating the content of the earlier guides. Stephen Bone's *West Coast of Scotland* was cleared of its most intrusive anti-Englishness, though it is still there if you look; Piper's *Oxfordshire* was re-written in less snobbish terms and included a contrite apology by the author.

This left *Devon*. The original guide was early in the series, short and incomplete in its gazetteer, and a bit inaccurate since Betjeman had not visited all the places he wrote about; so the new guide had to be longer, more authentic and comprehensive in its coverage. *Devon* was slated to be redone by Betjeman, but in the end it was revised by Brian Watson with the aid of "Dr Pevsner's Architectural Guide to Devon".[2] Watson began his revision in 1950 but by 1953 it was finished. According to Peterson,[3] W.S. Mitchell of Shell and Betjeman were not happy with the revision and Betjeman revised some of the entries and was much involved with the design prior to publication; but then, it's hard to imagine that Betjeman would be happy with any revision of his work. Much of the feel of the original guide was retained but the new guide was about half again longer – though still not a complete gazetteer of the county, which is very big and required two Pevsners. This lengthening quickly became a feature of the new and revised guides as they had to compete with the comprehensiveness of Pevsner's guides.

These early revisions set the tone for the post-war series so that not only were the thirties guides redone, with the exception of *Somerset* and *Hampshire*,[4] but later guides like *Suffolk* were also revised. Some, like *Devon*, were revised several times by different authors in different decades. The revisions in themselves were interesting because early on in the fifties a decision was made to keep the most flavoursome elements of the previous editions.

Consequently, all the revised editions – with the exceptions of *Cornwall* and the late edition (1975) of *Devon* by Ann Jellicoe and Roger Mayne – are more complex views of the counties they represent than may appear at first glance, because they are a palimpsest of different views made at different times.

Faber's cautious revival of the series by revision allowed them to commission new guides that would feed into the series after the easier-to-achieve revisions had been published; and by the mid fifties new guides and the results of the continuing revision process began to appear together. The first genuinely new title of the post-war Shell Guides was *Herefordshire* by David Verey in 1955, followed by another revision, *Wiltshire*, again by Verey in 1956, *Norfolk* in 1957,

In *Herefordshire*, Betjeman and Piper reinstated the Edward Bawden cartoons based on the formula of a place name taken from the guide that could be used to relate to petrol. For example, in *Gloucestershire* Stow-on-the-Wold becomes Shell on the Road. In *Herefordshire* the joke is more obscure with the pay off being the penultimate line "and Humber 3 miles from Leominster, Herefordshire" not Yorkshire or Lincolnshire as might be expected.

and *Mid-Wales* in 1960, also by Verey – who was again standing in for someone, in this case John Piper. It's hardly surprising then that Betjeman called him the Verey Light since – with the exception of Brian Watson's *Devon*, and *Norfolk* by Betjeman's old girlfriend, Wilhelmine Harrod, and C.L.S. Linnell – Mr Verey carried the Shell Guide load through the fifties.

Verey's *Herefordshire* was the first guide to include every parish in the county as opposed to most, and it also reinstated the convention of an Edward Bawden cartoon advertising Shell in the endpapers of the book. More significantly, *Herefordshire* initiated a move toward guides to counties that fell outside the normal tourist ambit.[5] Together with the move toward a more restrained but definite visual modernity in the covers – *Herefordshire*'s was initially an abstract image of apples on coarse yellow paper and then a rather complex mix of graphic layout and photography – the coverage of all parishes and the use of an expert author were a measure of the increased seriousness of the guides. This Piper later ascribed to his influence – at the cost of Betjeman's enthusiasm – in a letter to David Bland in 1966: "I feel to some extent responsible for the present, possibly over-serious style".[6] The drift toward seriousness was probably in part a response to Pevsner's Buildings of England and in larger part due to Piper's nature, as evidenced in his early sketchbooks of tours in England and his interest in topographic books. *Herefordshire* and all Verey's Shell Guides have the quality of, where necessary, being better than the Pevsner's dry airless format – even though he later jumped ship and wrote one – as this entry for Shobdon shows:

> This place is a monument to the 'folly' of a certain mid-eighteenth century Lord Bateman, who had the fashionable idea of making the Romanesque church into a romantic view. He therefore pulled it down and re-erected the chancel arch and two doorways, which all dated from 1140, on top of a hill. This has caused anguish to generations of antiquarians who have had to witness the gradual disintegration of the carvings, now for 200 years exposed to the elements. The church he built in its stead is very pretty, with enormous pews painted white making a strange Rococo–Gothic setting for the Romanesque–Celtic font. There is, among several monuments to the Batemans, a good Nollekins. The Bateman's house has now been demolished.[7]

Although few new guides were published in the fifties, it was for a variety of good reasons. Economically the country languished in Austerity until at least 1955, despite the easing of rationing. It wasn't until 1956 that the post-war boom really began to affect consumers and private-car ownership began to increase rapidly. Equally Betjeman and Piper had other fish to fry with Betjeman's burgeoning success as poet, media personality and, increasingly, leading voice of

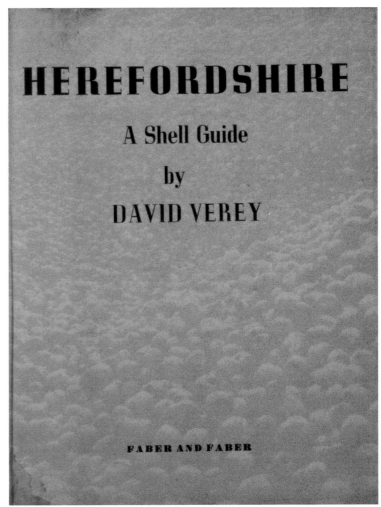

Herefordshire, 1955, cover

architectural conservation and Piper's inexorable progress toward becoming a kind of artist laureate. Producing an ever-greater range of work, from stained glass for Coventry (1957–61) to covers for work by Britten, he was the New Elizabethan artist for the New Elizabethan technocrats. The beginnings of an economic boom in the mid-fifties led to an increase in consumption of petrol and guides, and this led to more commissions. But as with all books there was a long lead-time so it was not really until 1960 that properly new guides began to appear in any number. By then the revisions of the early fifties were also invalid and titles that were to be revised needed to be done in depth to cope with the rapid modernisation of Britain's road infrastructure. Betjeman knew this only too well from his involvement with the Royal Fine Arts Commission, a body that spent much of its time discussing street lighting and bridge replacement schemes in small towns and villages up and down the country.

Herefordshire's original cover was one of the most modern and striking of all the Shell Guide covers; but it was quickly dropped in favour of a less artistic but more appropriately guidebook-ish style showing two photographs relevant to each county.

87

Between 1960 and 1968 ten new and revised guides were published beginning with *Mid-Wales* and followed by *Suffolk, Rutland, South West Wales, Cornwall, Worcestershire, Lincolnshire, Northampton and the Soke of Peterborough, Essex* and *Wiltshire*, again. The motoring context for these new guides was the introduction in 1959 of the Mini and the Ford Anglia followed in the early sixties by the Cortina and the Austin 1100/1300, or big Mini. In addition, the post-war gloom of boarding houses and hotels was being superseded by holiday cottages rented through *The Lady* and overnight stops at Trust House Posthouses – as near to Motels as England got.

David Verey's *Mid-Wales* (1960) marked a significant shift in the Shell Guides. There had been only three new titles since *Shropshire*, and the third of these, *Mid-Wales*, was originally supposed to be written by Piper[8], a natural title for him to pen since he had developed a strong affection toward Wales. It would have been his fourth guide if one includes his revision of *Oxon, Oxfordshire*. In the end, though he didn't write the guide, he did edit it. Pictorially, it is a tour de force, a new essay in Piper's emerging picture-editing style, and on the strength of this in 1959 he was made assistant editor of the guides.

The balance of power in the guides was shifting away from Betjeman and it is clear that his interest in the guides after *Shropshire* was diminished from his disinclination either to undertake re-writes like *Devon* and later, in 1955, *Cornwall* or to author new titles like *Surrey*, which though planned with Piper in the mid fifties never came to fruition. It is telling that in a letter to Piper in 1955 about his pleasure at his new film series *Discovering Britain* he refers to the Shell Guides as if they were work in the past: "I don't think I've enjoyed anything so much since our Shell and Murray Guide days."[9] That said, in 1960 after five years in preparation H.J. Willmott's manuscript for *Cornwall* was judged unusable and Betjeman stepped in and wrote possibly the best Shell Guide of the whole series. But this was Betjeman's last great effort with the guides and one that he found dispiriting as a process despite others' pleasure in the final work. Piper thought it "by far the best of the lot".[10] This is not to say Betjeman gave up on the series and after *Cornwall* he was closely involved in two new guides, *Worcestershire* and *Northamptonshire and the Soke of Peterborough*.

Shortly after *Cornwall*, James Lees-Milne had submitted his manuscript for *Worcestershire* to Shell and they had taken exception to his remarks about Worcester: "it had been sacked five times in its history, by Romans, Danes, Saxons, Welsh and Roundheads but never so disastrously as by the present mayor and corporation".[11] Betjeman was outraged by this intrusion into authorial freedom by his sponsor, especially after arguments about production details in *Cornwall*, and threatened to resign. Shell and Betjeman compromised and a new wording to the entry was agreed which said the same thing less forcibly but this episode was another straw. Lees-Milne

Radnorshire under snow, from the road between Presteigne and Knighton, Mid Wales, *1960, p.12*

was a bit of an anachronistic author for the guides by that time. He had negotiated many transfers from impoverished owners of, in his judgement, appropriately tasteful and decayed stately homes into the stewardship of the National Trust, in the process moving the Trust from being a landscape preserver to being a guardian of the national patrimony. He was also a dyspeptic snob and known for it, so it might have been expected that most of *Worcestershire* would be in that vein; but in fact he had a great talent for the gazetteer entry, so much so that Betjeman wrote to him saying, "We (Mr Piper and I) think your guide frightfully good and the best in the series to date".[12] His entry for Tenbury Wells made Betjeman go and stay there. Of the Wells he says, "The waters are particularly beneficial for glandular swellings, congestions, scrofula and scurvy. The baths no longer function, but there are some engaging remains (c1911) in a rusty tin pagoda tower and adjacent structures of tin with multi-coloured brick entrance, a sort of expensive prototype of the Nissen hut"; and of the town he concludes, "The number of inns makes Tenbury a happy, lethargic town".[13]

The entry, surrounded by images of disused locks at Stourport, "Venice of the Midlands", and a cast-iron bridge over the Severn, is an indicator of how much the guides had moved forward from the early metropolitan archness of Byron's *Wiltshire* and Hobhouse's *Derbyshire* to become a hymn to the unordinary everyday in everyday rural England. The feeling of sun, slowness and gentle decay summoned by Lees-Milne stands for most of the guides in this period and this no doubt is why Betjeman was so angered by Shell's editorial interference at the comments about Worcester. These were no more than an expression of the upset felt by many at the destructive powers of the modernisations of local authorities acting on the instructions of central government and a criticism that would guarantee the credibility of the rest of the gazetteer.

Betjeman had been pushing this combination of love and despair for the countryside in the guides for some time, partly from his involvement in the creation of the Victorian Society and the unsuccessful defence of Euston Arch and Bunning's Coal Exchange,

An early example of Piper's ability to take a counter holiday image and use it to demonstrate the timeless beauty of a county and, inter alia, to challenge conventional notions of rural beauty.

both in London, and partly from his depressing meetings at the Royal Fine Arts Commission, which presided over the tiny cuts of the modernising of towns and villages. A measure of this can be taken from his comments to Willmott, *Cornwall's* inept reviser: "What has not been done is an adequate description of what the place looks like now. Is it ruined with poles and wires? Has an old bridge been destroyed and a concrete one put in its place? Have hideous shop-fronts defaced some Georgian town mansion? Are there bungalows outside the fishing port you describe?"[14]

The final straw came with Juliet Smith's *Northamptonshire and the Soke of Peterborough*, published in 1968. In 1963, aged 22, Juliet Smith was offered the authorship of a Shell Guide to Northamptonshire and an area of 30 parishes formerly part of the county that had just been transferred to Huntingdonshire, the Soke of Peterborough. This guide, and *Rutland*, published in 1963, were, in title, a kick against the modernisation of county boundaries, a typically just-ahead-of-its-time gesture of the guides. (Now, thank goodness, this is a particular stone that is being rolled back.) How did she get the job? She was intelligent – Candida Lycett Green mentions that she "envied her cleverness"[15] – knew the Betjemans and wanted to write a guide. Cynically, one might suppose that this was a typical Betjeman manoeuvre involving a well-connected pretty daughter of a friend's family. However, Betjeman was equally able, and known, to be generous and helpful to young people; and since she had suggested a guide to a very 'unknown' county he was probably as attracted to the quixotic in the idea as he was to the guide for *Rutland*.

Northamptonshire, as Smith says, "deserves to be far more widely known" because "I have visited every village in the county and have also described some of their hamlets which I particularly liked. The main impression which I have received was one of the continuity of English country life. The ancient buildings, changed, beautified or sometimes disfigured by successive generations, have made the past seem very close, and our remoter history lies only inches beneath the turf of Castor or Borough Hill."[16] In these remarks she sums up the appeal of the Shell Guides and the thing that, inter alia, most tourists in England were searching for beyond "the white heat of the technological revolution" of the sixties metropolis. Finding it in the Midlands, that is to say anywhere in rural England, was the gift of the Shell Guides far more than a revision of the old tourist haunts of the west – though they did this too. Smith's entry for Fotheringay,

In the fifties the Shell Guides became a champion for industrial archaeology, then an emerging and liberal approach to British history. In fact, the guides championed all the new ways of appreciating the diversity of the British built environment, making them far more inclusive than similar works by Pevsner, the Ministry of Works or the National Trust. These latter all lagged behind the Shell Guides, which benefitted from their connection to the forward-looking *Architectural Review*.

Cast-iron bridge over the Severn, Worcestershire, 1964, p.75

Stourport, "Venice of the Midlands", Worcestershire, 1964, p.74

Edwin Smith was a popular photographer amongst the East Anglian and East Midlands guide authors for he was the best photographer of their domain; but his style was the tonal and technical opposite of Piper, being both evanescent in tone and rather artificial in his manipulations of the negative. Piper is reputed to have positively disliked him though he was generous enough to often use his work.

Fotheringay, by E. Smith, **Northamptonshire and the Soke of Peterborough,** *1968, p.56*

NOTES

1   According to Chris Mawson's Shell Guides website (www.shellcountyguides.co.uk).
2   *Devon*, 1955, p.5
3   Peterson, 2006, p.21
4   A revision of *Hampshire* was begun by John Arlott but he never finished the manuscript.
5   Consequently, as Mawson notes, sales of *Herefordshire* were small.
6   Lycett Green, 1995, p.256
7   *Herefordshire*, 1955, p.53
8   According to Mawson, he was offered this in 1956 but because he and Betjeman were thinking of doing *Surrey* the work was given to Verey.
9   Letter to Piper of 16 July 1955 quoted in Lycett Green, 1995, p.54
10 Letter from Piper to Betjeman of 26 June 1973 quoted in Peterson, 2006, p.19
11 Footnote in Lycett Green, 1995, p.276
12 Lycett Green, 1995, p.203
13 *Worcestershire*, 1964, p.75
14 Peterson, 2006, p.16
15 Lycett Green, 1995, p.269
16 *Northamptonshire and the Soke of Peterborough*, 1968, pp.9–11
17 *Northamptonshire and the Soke of Peterborough*, 1968, p.57
18 Lycett Green, 1995, p.268
19 Lycett Green, 1995, p.256
20 Lycett Green, 1995, p.256
21 See 'Northamptonshire (& the Soke of Peterborough)' in the 'Bibliography' section of Chris Mawson's Shell Guide website

placed opposite Edwin Smith's almost mystical image of its church, in its own way stands for the unique quality of the guides when compared to Pevsner or any other guide. It begins:

> The famous castle is now only a grassy mound overlooking the Nene, and the sheep graze where Mary Queen of Scots, "passed out of th' entrie into the hall within the said castle of ffotheringhaie before mentioned with an unapauled countenance stepped up to the scaffold in the said hall and there made for her death."[17]

Betjeman had given Smith very good and balanced advice about guidebook writing, commending Piper's recommendation of Scarfe's *Suffolk*, "as a model of condensed writing" after an extended essay of his own views. This included: "and for adjectives, avoid dead ones like 'fine', 'ancient', 'magnificent' and instead use words describing shape and colour, tall, fat, thin, square, pink, brown, red, mottled with moss etc. And don't be frightened of saying a place is hideous if you think it."[18]

This last advice caused a familiar row between Betjeman and Shell over what Lycett Green describes as "a defamatory reference to the Norwich Union Society Building in Northampton which Juliet Smith had made in her *Northamptonshire*".[19] This led Shell to ask for its removal as it had similar remarks in the guides dating back to Hobhouse's comments about Matlock in the thirties. On this occasion Betjeman chose to resign, giving the editorship over to Piper. In a letter to Piper he said, "As one gets older one can't work so fast, one's ideas run out".[20] Though a truism of a sort, it was far from true of Betjeman and was simply a good thing to say to allow him to move on. More telling of the incident is that after 1967 he expressly instructed Shell to disassociate his name from the series.[21]

After Betjeman's resignation, Piper edited 17 new and revised guides before the cancellation of the series – and Betjeman's death – in 1984; but it was in the period from 1960 to 1967 with Betjeman still on board that the Shell Guides went through an authorial development that remained constant through to the last guide, *Nottinghamshire*.

RUTLAND, SUFFOLK, ESSEX, LINCOLNSHIRE, STAFFORDSHIRE AND NOTTINGHAMSHIRE

THE SHELL GUIDES OF the sixties were the product of what Betjeman and Piper had learnt in revising the guides of the early fifties and differed considerably from new Shell Guides published later in that decade like *Norfolk* (1958), by Wilhelmine Harrod and C.L.S. Linnell, which ran to 88 pages[1] and followed the format of *Shropshire*. These newer sixties guides were longer – Norman Scarfe's *Suffolk* published in 1960 ran to 120 pages. The increased length of the guides was a symptom of a new policy of the editors to allow the authors to write as much as they felt to be necessary and was accompanied by a similar increase in the number of images: *Norfolk* began with about 90 images, which rose to nearly 200; *Suffolk* concluded with around 190. But this policy also caused friction between Betjeman and Piper and their publisher Faber and Faber.

Piper seems to have been caught in the middle. In February 1966 he wrote to David Bland, "I believe the public would prefer the county guides to be more larky, with more old engravings and line drawings, and maybe quotations and humorous drawings – more like they were when they first started. I feel to some extent responsible for the present possibly over-serious, style".[2] This is a strange letter because the fact was that the longer guides were a success: as Chris Mawson notes on his website, *Suffolk* was both a critical and sales success. Reading between the lines one might suggest there was tension between Piper and Betjeman over the less frivolous style for the guides, a style Betjeman could lay claim to, as well as some tension with Faber and Piper over the length of the guides. Elsewhere in the letter he says, "I find the cutting down on pages, when there is fine material, and the general uncertainty quite intolerable. A guide should be as long – within reason – as it seems to the editors it ought to be".[3] What may have been going on was a degree of positioning by Piper since he was in effect laying claim to the new, longer, more in-depth form of the guides whereas Betjeman's correspondence at this time was often about editorial freedom. Betjeman was taking on the sponsor while Piper was struggling with the publisher. In hindsight it seems that Piper won these arguments with Faber and kept Shell on-side, since right up until 1984 the guides consistently got longer and more illustrated and the early Betjeman–Piper style of the guides to 1951 completely disappeared.

The sixties also saw the introduction of a new type of author to the guides. Prior to Scarfe's *Suffolk*, Betjeman's influence is clear in the selection of guide writers like Harrod, Verey and Lees-Milne who were kindred spirits with similar religious or architectural concerns as Betjeman, and were often his friends. The new authors of the sixties were subtly different. The best of them, like Norman Scarfe (*Suffolk*, *Essex* and *Cambridgeshire*), W.G. Hoskins (*Rutland* and *Leicestershire*) and in particular Henry Thorold (*Lincolnshire*, *Derbyshire*, *Staffordshire*, *Nottinghamshire* and *Durham*), were also friends of Betjeman, but they were sympathetic to the increasing

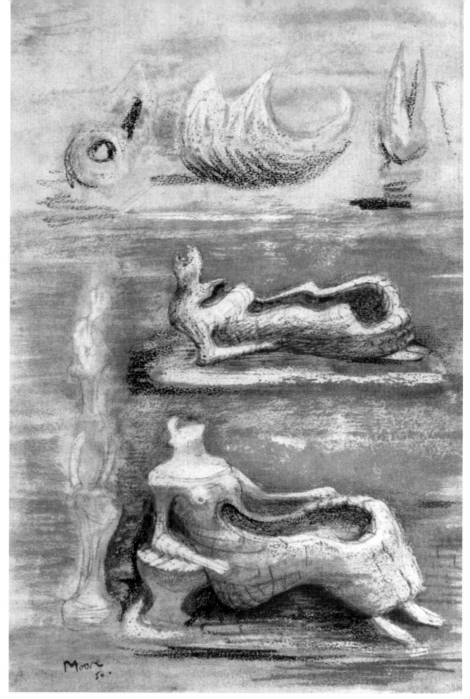

'His lines follow Life back into the stone' by Henry Moore, dated 1950, frontispiece of Jacquetta Hawkes' A Land

seriousness with which Piper viewed the guides – and in fact, ended up working far more closely with Piper, in Thorold's case to the end of the series, his *Nottingham* being its last hurrah.

Significantly Hoskins and Scarfe were part of a new movement in academic history, pioneered by Hoskins and Leicester University,

Jacquetta Hawkes' *A Land* was typical of books that reflected the general interest in the national identity in the late forties and fifties and which combined Romanticism and apparent rigour to make the arcane sexy to the general reader.

where Scarfe was a colleague. This was termed local history. In fact its roots lay in the application of archaeological techniques to the study of settlement and land rather than simply ancient sites, making it a sort of etymology of places. This was different from the local history of earlier periods which sought to relate places to the great movements of monarchy, religion and war in British history. Hoskins described himself as a landscape historian not a local historian. This approach to history, which also had adherents in archaeology like the cartographer O.G.S. Crawford[4] and the archaeologists Christopher and Jacquetta Hawkes, touched a nerve with the British intelligentsia in the thirties and during the war, and became a subject of publication for the 'general reader'. This continued after the war, history becoming widely appreciated by a new and enlarged generation of educated middle class through evangelising books like Hawke's *A Land* (1951) and Hoskins' seminal *The Making of the English Landscape* (1955). Hoskins' own career began as an amateur local historian in the thirties while he was a lecturer in commerce at Leicester. By the end of the decade he was a lecturer in local history and eventually founded the first department of local history in the UK, at Leicester. His book (of 1955) was made into a popular TV series in the mid sixties.

The trajectory of local history from parochial hobby to new academic subject and favourite of the 'general reader' found a huge ally and proselytiser in Piper and the Shell Guides, as it extended two fields that Piper had always been interested in since childhood: topography and antiquarianism. Moreover, it fed his equal if later enthusiasm for the ancient England hidden beneath the landscape in the neglected fields and ruinous buildings that frame so many of the entries and observations in *Oxon*. It is important to emphasise Piper's role here because, even before Betjeman and the Shell Guides parted company, Piper was making an increasing mark on the series. Appointed assistant editor in 1959, Piper steered the guides beyond Betjeman's original brief which focussed so clearly on reappropriating Georgian, Regency, Victorian and, later, Edwardian architecture as the proper concern of architectural guides, toward a more comprehensive appreciation of the relation between land, settlement and architecture that could accommodate any period or subject felt to contribute to the aesthetic of a place. This was an insidious process. Though Betjeman often found authors, his editorial hand became if more liberal also more distant whereas Piper was increasingly involved in the photography and layout of the guides, and as involved in the text as Betjeman. Slowly, through his editorial control, Piper really began to create in the guides a mirror of his view of each county, seen through the lens of the guides' authors. One effect of this close working relationship between this generation of guide authors and Piper was the development of long working relationships that were developed over a series of guides and had the effect of creating a more consistent and coherent set of guides than

LIDDINGTON

TIXOVER: in the background the only factory chimney in Rutland

STOKE DRY RESERVOIR looking towards Leicestershire

VALE OF CATMOSE with Oakham spire, the central jewel of the Vale

Liddington, Tixover, Stoke Dry Reservoir, Vale of Catmose, Rutland, 1963, p.1

Left: One new feature of the series that created a sense of rural place was the inclusion, at the beginning of guides, of panoramas of typical county landscapes like these of Rutland which emphasise Piper's love of the spectacular in the ordinary – here through the use of limitless openness; big views with big skies.

Below: This aerial shot shows the relation between the present and the ancient in a way invisible to the motorist. It is an attempt to encourage the reader to interpret landscapes speculatively, to look for evidence of the past rather than accept the landscape as timeless.

Aerial shot of Brooke, Rutland, 1963, p.50

had hitherto existed through a constant honing of the format.

The first guide of this new type was *Suffolk*. Norman Scarfe first proposed writing this guide in 1954 to John Betjeman at dinner at Farringdon House, the home of the deceased Lord Berners. At the time, he was a lecturer at Leicester and wanted a chance to use their new academic discipline to do a study of his home county[5] and a Shell Guide offered an opportunity to achieve this. Equally with the publication of Hoskins' *The Making of the English Landscape* the following year, it must have seemed to Betjeman, Piper, Faber and Shell that the new discipline might offer a way of bettering Pevsner's guides through a broader and more symptomatic reading of the landscape and rural built environment. Local history and the sub-specialism of landscape history that was Scarfe's and Hoskins' interest was also something that might offer a new, more profound analysis of the interstices between settlements than the 'appreciations' of landscapes that featured in the guides to date – something concrete, as well as beautiful to appreciate through the window of a passing car. Landscape also offered new possibilities for photography, which had until then in the main formed the backdrop to buildings in the guides.

Though Scarfe was the first Shell Guide local historian, Hoskins had already produced guides to Leicestershire and Rutland for Leicester City Council in the 1940s during the boom in 'know your country' publications; so his Shell Guide to Rutland published in 1963 is a good place to start looking at the influence of these new authors on the guides, not least because Hoskins' guide combined eccentricity with a fresh view of a county that was both familiar and new to the Shell Guides' readers. He is a transitional figure and it is a transitional guide.

Rutland was written during 1961 at a time when the county was, as Hoskins states at the beginning of his introduction, "fighting for its independence against the urban theorists who seem to dominate the world of planning today".[6] The dominant image of the cover, virtually repeated as a header to the gazetteer, is a sign added below the old-fashioned county border sign so that together they read, "RUTLAND FIGHTS TO KEEP LOCAL GOVERNMENT LOCAL".[7]

Hoskins' introduction asserts that, "Rather than being exterminated in favour of a larger unit with no historic meaning, [Rutland] should be set aside at once as England's first Human Conservancy".[8] He goes on:

> Rutland is still largely untouched (except for the short stretch of the Great North Road that belts across its eastern fringe), still a picture of a human, peaceful and slow-moving, pre-industrial England, with seemly villages, handsome churches, great arable fields and barns. One would like to think that one day soon at each entrance to this little county, beside a glancing willow-fringed stream, there will stand a notice saying, *Human Conservancy: Abandon the Rat-Race at This Point.*[9]

Cover, Rutland, 1963

On the following page though a snake is introduced into this Eden:

> The worst blot on the landscape is not indeed buildings at all, but the hideous poles and wires of the electricity board. Few villages have not been crucified in this needless way, and few counties have suffered more than Rutland from the New Barbarians. Mercifully the human eye rejects these horrors after a while and sees only the beauties of the past. When one looks steadily into a camera, in some otherwise perfect street, one sees what a crime has been committed.[10]

Hoskins' *Rutland* is really the first guide to adopt the contemporary attitude toward rural England, a thorough-going rejection of all things modern in favour of the conservation of a perceived authentic and necessarily pre-industrial England. And *Rutland* was the first Shell

This cover marks the entry of the Shell Guides into the politics of conservation and popular anti modernism.

Guide since the thirties to be political – political in the sense that it rejects the modern as inimical to the rural and proposes the rural as a sort of reservoir of authentic Englishness. Except for a few instances, this position was to remain an underlying assumption of all subsequent guides right up to R.M. Healey's *Hertfordshire*, which finds the real county amongst the ruins of the twentieth century.

For Hoskins, the main charm of *Rutland* is that it survives as a testament to the period of England's development from the Conquest to the enclosures. One of the maddest yet most charming sections of the book is a gazetteer of 'The lost villages of Rutland'. This describes the absent remains of villages that disappeared predominantly as a result of the Plague of 1349 optimistically illustrated by a very O.G.S. Crawford or Time Team aerial photo of the sub-surface shadows of the lost village and priory of Brooke. Romantic and elegiac though it is, *Rutland* is also the first guide that attempts to describe why the county is as it is, drawing the reader to consider the implications of enclosure on the forms of roads, the etymology of place names and even encouraging us to recognise the "predominantly Georgian landscape of the fields surrounding Whissendine". In all it is a very Quixotic guide, proposing the reader engage in a search for the county even where it may not exist. Its final entry is for the lost village of Witchley and begins, "The evidence for a 'lost village' of Witchley Warren is at present very slight"[11] but continues tantalisingly, "A field here was called Town Close in the early seventeenth century, an almost infallible clue to a buried village. The site is 1.5 miles north-west of Ketton".[12] *Rutland* is also a very modern guide in that it tells the reader how to consume the county, how to observe it at leisure; but Hoskins' method is provocatively and self-consciously arcane even for 1963, and wonderfully eccentric in the best tradition of the early Shell Guides. It is the only guide to give specific advice as to how to eat, drink and drive around its county.

According to Hoskins, Rutland is some kind of Shangri-La even for the motorist – "Motoring in Rutland is still a pleasure as it was thirty or forty years ago"[13] – and he introduces a category of driver that seems almost mythical today: "Now that the 'slow' motorist is under attack from all sides, even officially".[14] What he means by slow is that, "Road traffic is so light that one can slow down to enjoy the wide, watercoloured landscapes, or even stop altogether without creating confusion in all directions".[15] What then follows is a delightful if alarming description of how to enjoy a roadside picnic in Rutland which, as he says, is practically a French experience and recalls the advice in Murray's guides for Victorian travellers more than any motorists' guide. "So one does as in France: buy bread and cheese, fruit, and a bottle of wine in the town before setting out for the day (no hotel 'packed lunches' which are usually grisly and not worth half the money charged for them)." He goes on:

True the wine is more expensive than in France but it is also better in quality if one takes a little trouble in the buying… and a bottle should last husband and wife for two days unless one intends to fall asleep after lunch. Red wines are better than white for this form of travel as white wines tend to become tepid in a car and therefore rather horrid. An excellent way of getting over this difficulty, if one can do it, is to buy a bottle of white or rose wine, chill it for an hour or so in a refrigerator and transfer it to a vacuum flask before departure. If one can do this it is the ideal treatment for a luncheon wine as red wines in summer, especially at mid-day, tend to be highly soporific. Not that this really matters on a warm day in Rutland…[16]

After describing the gentle progress of such a day toward "a good well-cooked English dinner", he concludes with the almost Edwardian remark, "A week of this treatment in Rutland sends one back ready to fight politicians and jacks-in-the-office with one hand tied behind one's back".[17]

Rutland is the most wonderful and Ruritanian of all the Shell Guides for its enthusiasm for, by its own admission, the most "hard to place"[18] of English counties and its otherworldly travel recommendations; but behind this lies a much broader approach to a county than was common previously. Hoskins is effortlessly able to tie things and places and events into a comprehensible historical context that is often disguised by his eccentricity, as can be seen in this detail for the entry for Burley:

Professor Pevsner attributes the design to John Lumley, but another authority considers that Finch was his own architect. If so, this was a worse risk financially than employing a professional architect: but the result is a house that is "one of the most sweeping compositions of its kind in England which can only be compared to such houses as Chatsworth or Petworth… Many a ruler of a minor state in Germany would have been proud of such a place". (Pevsner) The interior is not so exciting, and in any event is not at present shown to the public.[19]

The rest of the entry goes on veering from quotation to personal aside as if Hoskins were there beside us and this is surely all one could want from a guide: a broad, attractive, enticing authoritative description peppered with personal qualifications. *Rutland* is still a popular guide and my copy cost me £35 in Stamford's Oxfam Shop, a testimony to its continuing local value. Hoskins' second guide, *Leicestershire*, followed in 1970, though this was a book based on work going back to the war. However, where Rutland seems to have been an unalloyed joy to Hoskins, Leicestershire was not and his honesty in this is what makes this guide weaker, despite valiant efforts in the design and imagery of the book. What traveller would wish to visit a county of which, in the second paragraph of the introduction, their guide's author writes, "The western side of the county I never came to like, though I am frequently told this merely shows a lack of such detailed knowledge as I have of the east"?[20] Or where of its county town Leicester he lukewarmly concludes, "At any rate, Leicester, which makes so unfavourable a first impression, deserves a couple of days exploration on foot. Gastronomically, though an important element in strenuous exploration in a busy town, I have found it quite depressing, it has moments, but they are sadly few".

If with Hoskins, as with many of the Shell Guides' other authors, expertise was no guarantee of a good guidebook the same cannot be said of his colleague at Leicester University, Norman Scarfe. Though sharing many of Hoskins' views, Scarfe nonetheless managed to write three very qualified but positive and detailed guides to what in two cases, Essex and Cambridgeshire, may appear to be very tough counties to sell to the motoring holidaymaker. But in truth by the sixties the guides were changing in their intention, even if this was not apparent to the publisher or sponsor. What is clear from the ever longer, more idiosyncratically illustrated and oddly anodyne designs of the guides that emerged as the decade wore on and Piper became their chief dramaturg was that they were no longer seen as simply an encouragement to motoring for pleasure. Rather, they took on the mantle of the reference book, a sort of subjective Pevsner, and it is at this sort of guide that Scarfe excelled. In fact a comparison between Norfolk and Scarfe's Suffolk is instructive since, though only three-years apart, where Norfolk[21] doesn't cover every parish and is full of padding with sections on the Norwich School, Norfolk Churches, Broadland and Rivers and then more churches in a reprint of some of Cotman's 'Specimens of the architectural antiquities of Norfolk' (1815), Suffolk needs only an introduction and a gazetteer to cover all 500 parishes in the county. Where the former harks back to the compilation style of the guides in the thirties the later is straightforwardly a reference book, albeit self-declaredly a subjective one, and this comparison really marks the difference between the guides as they developed under Betjeman and those that developed under the closer scrutiny of Piper.

With the exception of Norfolk, the unwritten Huntingdonshire and Juliet Smith's Northampton and the Soke of Peterborough, Norman Scarfe is responsible for representing East Anglia in the Shell Guides. His first, Suffolk, originally out in 1960, reprinted two-years later, revised in 1966, revised in 1976 and published as a paperback in 1982, was by any standards a success. It is unsurprising that Piper asked him to produce a second guide, Essex, published in 1968. This was reprinted with corrections in 1975 and published as a paperback in 1982. Soon after, in 1983, his Cambridge was published, one of the last Shell Guides. Scarfe's guides are exemplary of the new direction the series took after 1960. The format was pared down to a preface and introduction followed by a gazetteer and greater attention was given to providing large images including representative landscapes often juxtaposed in panoramic strips of

three, arranged vertically. Bigger images were accompanied by longer gazetteer entries and by introductions that described the history of the county, its land, building materials and architecture. Like the gazetteer entries, the introductions became longer, Suffolk doubling in length and Essex running to 36 pages. There was also an expectation that the new guides would cover all of the county in as much detail as needed. By the time Piper took over the editorship in 1967 the new guides coming through to be published, like Essex, were double the length of those published in the early sixties.

Scarfe's Essex is exemplary of these new guides, representing a new level of accurate historical detail whilst retaining the personal voice of the Shell Guide brand. But Scarfe is not simply a writer of detailed guides; he is also one of the few Shell Guide authors to attempt to make explicit his ideas of what defines a good village or town and also to address the problem of the modernisation of the counties in a way which elucidates in detail the problems whilst remaining open to the modern as a positive force particularly in architecture (though less so in planning). In this he differs absolutely from the ostrich-like tendencies of many of the Shell authors not least his colleague Hoskins – to whom, incidentally, he dedicated his Cambridgeshire.

While Scarfe is at pains to be impartial, he gives the impression that below the surface is a desire for the new to be as good as the old, optimism, and an anger at the stupidities of the age. His frustrations are most clearly seen in small photographs that appear in the gazetteer with titles like 'Dereliction: Airfield at Metfield' or the wonderfully laconic shot of a caravan park simply titled 'East Mersea' and, above it, the image of an entrance to a similar site framed by the words 'Happy Days', grimly reminiscent of other camps and titled 'regretfully at Maldon'. Elsewhere more punningly there is an illustration of a bugbear he shared with Betjeman, Hoskins and Piper titled 'GOOD EASTER bad polescape'. In the later guide, Cambridgeshire, there is a more subtle essay on the same subject. Concluding the gazetteer, three pictures of farm landscapes are juxtaposed: arable land (bordered by woods) being harrowed, an orchard in winter and a wheat field in summer dominated by 11 high-tension power pylons.

Scarfe's re-write of Suffolk in 1965 gave him the opportunity of adding to the end of the gazetteer a 'Postscript, Suffolk in the 60s', in which he describes in detail the pressures on the county to expand its population and build new houses. This is indeed a sorry tale of mad post-war expansion into an area it made no sense to develop at that rate; but Scarfe uses the section to propose that if there must be expansion it should at least be good and to give examples of good local architects and their modern architecture. The images of a school and old people's accommodation are interesting in that they show, as he notes, that the local architects favoured a style that anticipated the general vernacular revival of

Right: Norman Scarfe's guides were militant in their critique of the modernised landscape and are an unequivocal summary of the subtext of most of the post-war guides. The Shell Guides represented the reservations of the middle class about the future; they weren't so much anti modern as opposed to the ugly accretions of the unthoughtful changes that were fast building up in the country.

'Dereliction: Airfield at Metfield', Suffolk, 1966, p.87

'GOOD EASTER bad polescape', Essex, 1982, p.94

Three pictures of farm landscapes, Cambridgeshire, 1983, pp.218–19

'East Mersea', Essex,
1982, p.133

'Regretfully at Maldon',
Essex, 1982, p.133

Gusford Primary School, IPSWICH, designed by Johns, Slater and Haward

Cottages in Church Street LAVENHAM, September 1954

The same cottages at LAVENHAM in September 1965

Old people's neighbourhood, Church Green, LOWESTOFT, designed by Tayler and Green

School and old people's accommodation, Suffolk, 1966, p.116

Terrace at Lavenham, 1954 and 1965, Suffolk, 1966

Scarfe was really against thoughtless change, as seen here in his attack on the unthinking revealing of beams in East Anglian timber-framed houses; this is balanced by his support for the early Neo Vernacular style that emerged under the influence of Raymond Erith in the early sixties.

the late sixties and early seventies – which, he points out, was described as postmodern by "Dr Pevsner".[22] Not only is Scarfe prepared to like modern public architecture, he also criticises what we would now call 'heritage'. On the following page are two images of the same terrace at Lavenham shot in 1954 and 1965. In the second, the buildings have been stripped of their plastering to reveal their wooden frames of which Scarfe comments, "The whole town is in danger of looking like a great sprawling half-timbered Trust House [a chain of 'olde worlde' detailed hotels owned by Charles Forte]. Happily, almost miraculously, a well-designed council estate has gone up near the railway station".[23]

Essex is Scarfe's most thorough guide, with its exhaustive historical and topographical introduction and very detailed gazetteer. It runs to 211 pages and deals with everything from suburbia to moated farmhouses in equal detail. Leaving aside his penchant for

villages with distinct edges (Stebbing) and towns that have country views from their centres (Saffron Walden) and his dislike for caravan sites (and of course, electricity poles and pylons), *Essex* is a most optimistic guide.

In its second edition, of 1975, it celebrates an Essex "being more clearly understood and more affectionately fostered, as I believe it is".[24] This was because of the 1973 *Essex County Council Design Guide for Residential Areas* that enshrined as policy[25] the sort of vernacular modernism Scarfe had admired in his second edition of *Suffolk*. In the gazetteer he enthusiastically endorses the new towns of Basildon and Harlow. Basildon is complemented thus:

Enter from the W. the so-called Town Square, the best new central piazza in England. Success depends on the impressive breadth of the paved deck area between flanks of shops N. and S.: sense of leisure

'Stebbing: a proper village-edge', Essex, 1982, p.167

College buildings of the '60s:
left: Queens' Erasmus building
below: Caius' Harvey Court by Leslie
Martin and Colin St J. Wilson
opposite: Corpus' Leckhampton
House

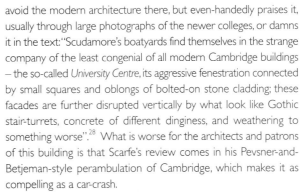

'College buildings of the 60s', Cambridgeshire, 1983, pp.78–9

created without reducing bustle at shop doorways: dignity and grace are added by 14 storeys of flats, *Brooke House*, perfectly conceived and placed (Anthony B. Davies with Sir Basil Spence). Human scale is restored immediately by playful figures in a fountain that sends up the right amount of spray to catch the breeze perpetual near tall buildings.[26]

Harlow's endorsement is even more enthusiastic:

The first feeling we have is of wonder: we have reached this town centre without quite grasping that we have driven 'through' the town, parked the car easily in the open at ground level, and walked straight into a centre free from traffic nuisance, yet full of bustle. The market is delightful, like Norwich or Leicester's, but on a more agreeable scale with gay awnings, and modern bronze sculpture…[27]

Though decades of anti modernism make this sort of enthusiasm seem inappropriate now, this heart-on-the-sleeve opinion is what is great about Scarfe and the guides in general. Scarfe in particular is an enthusiast for both the past and the future but not one of the mediocre and this makes his *Cambridgeshire* a better guide than most to the City of Cambridge. Unlike most guides, Scarfe's doesn't

avoid the modern architecture there, but even-handedly praises it, usually through large photographs of the newer colleges, or damns it in the text: "Scudamore's boatyards find themselves in the strange company of the least congenial of all modern Cambridge buildings – the so-called *University Centre*, its aggressive fenestration connected by small squares and oblongs of bolted-on stone cladding; these facades are further disrupted vertically by what look like Gothic stair-turrets, concrete of different dinginess, and weathering to something worse".[28] What is worse for the architects and patrons of this building is that Scarfe's review comes in his Pevsner-and-Betjeman-style perambulation of Cambridge, which makes it as compelling as a car-crash.

Along with *Cornwall* – and being an Essex dweller – I read Scarfe's guides most and to me they are preferable to any Pevsner, particularly the newer ones; but of the new sixties generation of Shell Guide authors, Henry Thorold stands out as the most adventurous and productive not least for his successful efforts to make *Lincolnshire*, *Staffordshire* and *Nottinghamshire* seem great places to take a touring holiday. It was Betjeman who inveigled Thorold into writing a guide with Jack Yates, as Candida Lycett Green explains in a footnote to a letter from Betjeman to Thorold reprinted in her *John Betjeman, Letters, Volume Two*.

Left: Scarfe had what could be called proto-ecological views about the rural as shown here in his insistence that villages should have clear edges and not simply straggle off into ribbon suburbs, as many began to do as a result of the increased pace of building in the UK in the sixties.

Above: Scarfe was unusual among Shell Guide authors for being pro conservation, anti development and pro contemporary architecture. His criticisms of architecture were not anti new but against the self-centred insensitivity of some new buildings to their surroundings.

First published in 1980
by Faber and Faber Limited
3 Queen Square London WC1N 3AU
Set, printed and bound in Great Britain by
Fakenham Press Limited
Fakenham, Norfolk
All rights reserved

© Copyright Shell U.K. Ltd 1980

Although sponsoring this book, Shell U.K. Ltd would
point out that the author is expressing his own views.

Replica of Locomotion No. 1 at Beamish

British Library Cataloguing in Publication Data

Thorold, Henry
County Durham. – (A Shell guide).
1. Durham, Eng. (County) – Description and
travel – Guide-books
I. Title   II. Series
914.28'6'04857   DA670.D9
ISBN 0–571–11640–X

*Waterfall at High Force, Teesdale (title pages), replica of
Locomotion No. 1 replica at Beamish Open Air Museum
(imprint page), County Durham, 1980*

*Stained-glass fragments of woman and a man at
Fledborough (illustration credits), Nottinghamshire, 1984*

Fourteenth-century fragments . . .   **Fledborough**

*Figure from a Jesse Tree in fourteenth-century glass at Gedney (frontispiece), big
wheel and helter-skelter at Skegness (title page), Lincolnshire, 1965*

A Shell Guide

Derbyshire

by Henry Thorold

Faber & Faber 3 Queen Square London

Venus at Bolsover (frontispiece), recumbent statue of Bess of Hardwick, Derby Cathedral (title page), Derbyshire, 1972

Henry Thorold's guides had a subtle, subversive and slightly ribald humour that was a little invisible beneath the very straight modern designs Piper began to use after 1967.

Abbots Bromley Horn Dance (title page), sculpture of St George and the Dragon by Thomas Wright, 1958, at Darlaston (imprint page), Staffordshire, 1978

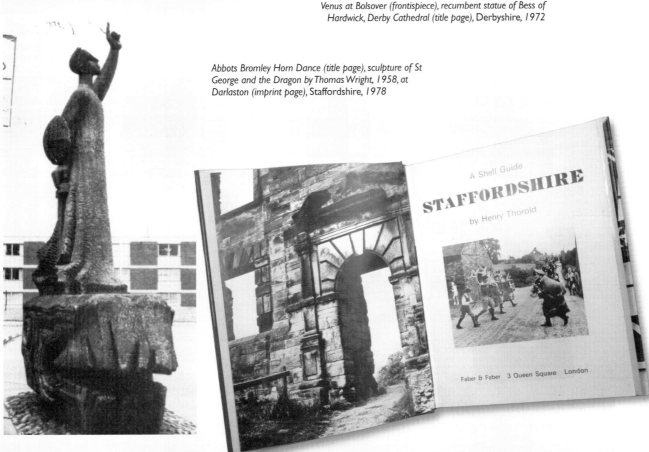

A Shell Guide

STAFFORDSHIRE

by Henry Thorold

Faber & Faber 3 Queen Square London

Fishtoft, Lincolnshire, 1965, p.59

Fishtoft's images combine the remote and ghostly church, sinister in an M.R. James-ish way, with the more modern chill of the warning sign post. *Lincolnshire* is full of a jolly foreboding that makes the county as attractive as a Hammer Horror.

'*At Fishtoft*', Lincolnshire, 1965

HT recalls that after Jack Yates had suffered a coronary JB said "I say, dear boy, I think our own dear friend Jack is rather sad having to give up his bookshop and he gets a bit bored sitting on his bum in Westgate. I think you and he should do a *Shell Guide* together. He'll do all the work, of course, but you and he can have some expeditions together in the school holidays." JB then went to see Jack and said, "I say, dear boy, I think you and Henry ought to do a *Shell Guide* together. He'll do all the work, of course…"[29]

This happened in 1960.[30] *Lincolnshire* was published in 1965. The following year Betjeman asked Thorold to re-do *Derbyshire* and this was published in 1972. Piper then asked him to do *Staffordshire* (published 1978), and as he was completing this in 1974 Piper asked him to re-do *County Durham* after Thorold had "enthused about maligned counties".[31] Then, again in 1977, as he was writing *County Durham*, Piper said to him, "'There are a few counties still unallotted, what would you like to do?' I asked if I could do *Nottinghamshire*. 'Of course' he replied, 'I don't think anyone else wants to do it'."[32] Thorold notes in his acknowledgements that, "As I write these lines news comes to me of the death of Sir John Betjeman, founder of the *Shell Guides*. It was those spiral-backed volumes that first thrilled me in the 1930s; it was he who invited me to write my first Shell Guide in 1960. My final tribute – of gratitude and affection – must be to him".[33] *Nottinghamshire* was the last Shell Guide to be published and won the Thomas Cook prize for best guidebook that year, 1984.

Lincolnshire was an instant hit, at least with Piper and Betjeman. The latter wrote to Piper in April 1966 saying, "it is far the best of the Shell Guides so far and the text is really good too. We have got Pevsner on the run".[34] Betjeman's favourite bits were the entries for Fishtoft, Harlaxton and Norton Disney, the entry for which he described as "the funniest entry I know".[35] In the same letter he says that *Lincolnshire* read "as though it were a thriller… it is funnier and more succinct than any *Shell Guide*".

Actually, though it is funny, it is with a sort of gallows humour and reading the introduction reveals a strong elegiac element; it is funny but poignant, like a county at the end of the pier. The introduction concludes: "There is a goneness about Lincolnshire that is difficult to capture in words. Old families expire, and nobody ever comes to live here. The majority of houses still belong to the descendants of their original builders. More than in most counties the old pattern still goes on: there are many treasures still undiscovered and unspoiled".[36] This sets the tone for what follows, a mixture of neglect and revelation and an innovative succinct imagination with a sense of the surreal behind it all – a Shell Guide's Shell Guide. The title page has a surreal humour that continued in the next guides he wrote. In *Lincolnshire*, a stained-glass window is juxtaposed with a big wheel and a helter-skelter, seen at night as outlines formed of points of light from the bulbs that decorate their structures, the one

Harlaxton Manor, Lincolnshire, 1965, p.79

image somehow the antithesis of the other and yet the same. For *Derbyshire* the juxtaposition is of a climbing and disrobing Venus at Bolsover, full of intent, and a devoutly praying, recumbent and much-married Bess of Hardwick in Derby Cathedral. Thereafter the humour is more subtly displayed: for *Staffordshire*, a boy with a tiny bow and arrow menaces the deer and hobby horse of the Abbots Bromley Horn Dance on the title page, while on the imprint page a preachy and wimpish contemporary sculpture of St George at Darlaston recalls the boy of the previous page. For *County Durham*, the title page is a double spread of the immense rush of the waterfall at High Force in Teesdale, while on the following imprint page the other side of Durham, industry, is represented by a vignetted photograph of a puny Locomotion No.1 replica steaming timidly across the outdoor museum at Beamish. Finally, at the top of the double spread of illustration credits in *Nottinghamshire* are images of stained-glass fragments of a chubby smiling woman (possibly) leering at a rather worried-looking man. Together the editors and Thorold

Harlaxton is for Piper the gem of Lincolnshire, its Hafod. In the later guides to 'lesser-known' counties, Piper liked to present the viewer with a stunning surprise almost as a validation of the idea of guides to the less touristic counties.

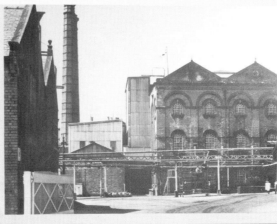

The great achievement of the later Shell Guides is to give industrial landscapes like these at Burton-on-Trent or Bolsover the same value as the tourist destinations of the Cotswolds and the West Country.

Burton-on-Trent, Staffordshire, *1978, pp. 70–1*

Bolsover, Derbyshire, *1972, pp. 44–5*

had a lot of fun matching up images and text: their surreal humour is gentle and a bit obscure but this style was by then part and parcel of their very British charm.

Betjeman's appreciation of the Fishtoft entry was partly due to the layout designed by Piper's son. As John Piper took on more of the editorial weight of the guides, Edward Piper began to work on their graphic design which became notably more modern – particularly after 1967 with his father's assumption of full editorial control of the series. What Betjeman liked in the layout was the not-quite-double-page spread that allowed a picture of the remote village of Fishtoft to dominate its diminutive entry: "A vegetable village in the fens near Boston, near the seabank of the wash. A tree-surrounded rectory, and a distant scatter of farmhouses. The smooth stone church has plain west tower and some clear-glassed windows to the aisles: others are drearily glazed. Spacious, but scraped with dark pointing. But as a landscape feature, among elms and fields, it is proper medieval, marshland architecture".[37] The entry recalls the final words of the introduction but also has something of Wilkie Collins or M.R. James. This effect is intensified by John Piper's extremely black-and-white image of the church and its elms, the two together as irresistible and real in atmosphere as any ghost story could hope to be. Over the page is another image captioned 'At Fishtoft' showing an old fingerpost in a winter landscape near a cheerless prefab post-war bus stop. The sign reads 'CUT SCALP END'. It is hard to imagine that this combination of Gothick signifiers was anything but deliberate and they certainly radically alter one's idea of Lincolnshire. What Betjeman found revelatory at Harlaxton comes not from the entry, which has a bare-bones description of an early-Victorian Jacobean revival house by Salvin and Burn, Harlaxton Manor, now owned by Stanford University. The revelation comes from the brooding Gothic images of the semi-derelict estate taken by John Piper that run over five pages, which are as romantic and eerie as his earlier imagery of Hafod in Wales (see next chapter). The feeling is of a lost country discovered: perhaps this is what Betjeman meant when he compared *Lincolnshire* to a thriller. Norton Disney's entry shows another side to Thorold, an eye for detail that can transform a minor village into a gem of an entry. The entry is very traditional guidebook stuff: "There are later monuments to the family of Admiral Lord St Vincent (Glorious 1st of June), who held the manor and lived at the hall, an early 19th century house deep in the woods. Early 19th century vicarage".[38] What makes it a great entry is the research that makes it possible to say, "Lost in the willows of the Brant, and surrounded by woods, this romantic village

Thorold's guides to the unfashionable counties manage far better than most of the earlier Shell Guides to celebrate the wonders of the Victorian – Betjeman's original intention for the series – as here in this five-page photo essay on Burton.

Burton, Staffordshire, 1978, p.72

was once dominated by the castle of the Disney family, whose name lives on in the creator of Mickey Mouse". What makes it funnier is the relaxed punch-line, "a descendant of a junior branch".[39]

What Thorold and Yates achieved with *Lincolnshire* was to take a county that by their own admission few visited and transform it into somewhere that seemed unexplored and inviting – through a good mixture of gifted writing, an eye for dark humour and the Gothick possibilities of the remote, brooding and, apparently, deserted.

Yates, a university friend of Betjeman's, died soon after; but for Thorold it was the start of a new phase in his life since completing *Lincolnshire* and starting on *Derbyshire* shortly preceded his retirement as a housemaster at Lancing school in 1968.[40] *Derbyshire* was another labour of love which he specifically asked to do since Hobhouse's *Derbyshire* of 1935 was his first Shell Guide, bought while still at Eton. *Derbyshire* should be considered with *Staffordshire*, his subsequent guide, for together they encompass the Peak National Park. In fact, with the exception of *County Durham*, Thorold's guides cover a contiguous region from the east coast across to Staffordshire, which with the exception of the Peak District continues to be barely known outside its borders. Equally, with the exception of the city of Durham, or more accurately its cathedral, *County Durham* is a rather unknown area sitting between its big brothers North Yorkshire, Cumbria and Northumbria. Thorold's importance for the Shell Guides is that he, more than any of the other authors, moved the guides away from the natural stamping grounds of the traditional tourist guide to cover areas that were largely unknown, even to their own populations. His guides with those of Scarfe moved the ambitions of the Shell Guides forward from being inducements to tour to being a new kind of reference book for the counties, supplanting works like Arthur Mee's series The King's England and offering a more subjective but no less rigorous account of the counties than Pevsner's guides. Moreover, they were more modern than either in their understanding that images were crucial in a guide to an unfamiliar place and that erudition needs to be balanced with entertainment to sustain the interest of the general reader who increasingly gained information from other media – the television, radio and the much-improved print media of the 1960s.

Scarfe gave great depth to his accounts of the superficially obvious prettiness of East Anglia, bringing the depth of culture to the surface of Cambridge Pink, flint walls and thatching. In contrast, Thorold's great vision was to take counties that had once been rural but by the sixties had become better known for their industry – in the case of *Lincolnshire* this might be taken to include agribusiness – and hence perceived ugliness, and recover the same fascination with place that we all take to areas like the Cotswolds or Cornwall. He achieved this primarily because he was interested in everything and could make a reader see the value in anywhere. Achieving this in his

home county emboldened him to take on *Derbyshire*, which Hobhouse in the thirties had edited down to be in essence (what would later become) the Peak National Park – he virtually ignored the rest of the county, as we do today, except for his lengthy account of Bess of Hardwick and the Cavendishes. Thorold's *Derbyshire* covers all of the county and wither the text goes so do the images: Thorold was encouraged by Piper to make long lists of possible images that could later be photographed but he also often took the photographer Peter Burton with him on his peregrinations. As with the other Shell Guides, the images draw in the reader; but Thorold's great achievement was to see that, if photographed and described in the right way, Burton-on-Trent was as fascinating as Bath.

Equally, he revelled in the conjunction of the industrial and the architecturally aristocratic. At Bolsover, John Piper's intensely black-and-white panoramic shot gives equal weight to the castle and the colliery, the former very white and the latter correspondingly black. Somehow it draws the reader back to the previous page, where a more conventional 'Ministry of Public Works' image by Patrick Rossmore sits under Thorold's entry. This is at its best and most thrilled when describing the view *from* Bolsover Castle, rather than the view of it:

> The town of Bolsover is of little consequence, but the position of the Castle looking over the great, open, blackened vale of Scarsdale is memorable indeed. From the terrace it is possible to see the towers of Hardwick to the SW, the gaunt ruin of Sutton Scarsdale to the W – and everywhere the collieries, with their smoke, railway sidings, miners' cottages and now, the M1.[41]

Both Piper's photograph and Thorold's entry have the same kind of sublime Romanticism and thrill that, in the eighteenth century, Joseph Wright and De Loutherburg brought to their images of the dawning industrial revolution.

As Thorold says, "Except to the initiated, [Staffordshire] remains a mystery".[42] "Is it all potteries? Or is it the Black Country? Or are they the same thing? Is there much to see?"[43] The folly of these rhetorical questions is by then evident for surrounding them are images of the Staffordshire moorlands that make up its little-known section of the Peak National Park, as wild as any part of the Yorkshire Dales.

But the best thing about the guide is the depth it finds in places like Burton-on-Trent, the entry for which begins quite unbelievably: "From the by-pass Burton looks splendid".[44] This is perhaps the particular talent of the guide author, like the poet or the surrealist, to make the familiar unfamiliar, which in Thorold is taken to an extreme. He continues: "From the road there is a view across towers and churches and chimneys and breweries and streets and houses to the country beyond. The mammoth power station of Drakelowe is on the far side of the river, in Derbyshire."[45] His task here then is to convince us that all this industrial stuff is attractive, so what follows immediately are two pages of images of Maltings and Marston's Brewery photographed with an emphasis on their pared-down functional classicism and then the Gothic town hall shot at an angle to make the most of its spiky tower, skyline of gables and chimneys, and its buttressing. It is only then that the entry really starts. This is what differentiates Thorold's *Staffordshire* from Pevsner's – the effort to sell you the idea, not simply represent the place.

What follows is, to begin with, an essay on brewing at Burton which tells us that, "Catherine the Great is said to have been 'immoderately fond' of Burton Beer"[46] and that in the nineteenth century there were 40 breweries "all over the town and maltings all over the suburbs, and an elaborate network of railway lines between them crossed the streets in all directions".[47] In effect there are two entries in the gazetteer: the introduction, a drive-by view with some imaginatively attractive details, which is then thoroughly surpassed by his long perambulation around the town. This treats Burton with a seriousness elsewhere accorded to towns like Oxford and Cambridge. Snippets stand out: "Alas, this view down Lichfield Street is now ruined by the monstrous new telephone Exchange, which rises, an enormous and aggressive lump, behind it. Shame on our Planners!"[48] Thorold, more than other Shell Guide authors, took industrial town architecture as genuinely seriously as any other and with pleasure – a gift still unusual in writers on architecture. Even the front endpapers of *Staffordshire* show the solid mid-nineteenth-century facades of Burton's brewery offices.

What distinguishes the last Shell Guide from Thorold's others is that its subject, Nottinghamshire, is seemingly less well known than Staffordshire and even more dull than Lincolnshire, possibly combining the demerits of both. Thorold's great entry on Nottingham itself begins "The Queen of the Midlands"[49] and concludes, some pages later, with the self-confidence of Baedeker on Florence: "This is about the extent that even the most energetic walker will wish to explore on foot: for the suburbs a car will be necessary, and these may be best classified alphabetically".[50] However, the real value of this guide even now lies in its coverage of the villages of the county, which gives the impression of a cornucopia of undiscovered atmospheric gems, and good weather, through entries that grab you immediately – which, after all, is the purpose of any good guide.

Flintham begins by describing how "The casual unsuspecting visitor may be astonished, when driving through the village, to espy at the end of the street what appears to be part of the Crystal Palace".[51] At Langold, though, it begins "The colliery village on the main road (A60) is unpromising, but…" and soon the reader finds, "The words 'Langold farm' on the map… do not prepare one for the buildings which were erected here… and which, indeed, still stand here used as a farm: great brick walls enclosing the kitchen garden; magnifical

Staffordshire, 1978, front endpapers

stables looking like buildings in a Piranesi print; and a little garden pavilion with pedimented front and spreading roof a la James Paine".[52] This type of entry is as good or maybe better than either Betjeman or Piper, though it has the qualities of both – the vivre of Betjeman and the quest for the undiscovered in Piper. In Thorold the reader has a very versatile, omnivorous cicerone as good at revitalising the well known as revealing the unknown. His entry for Eastwood manages to deal with D.H. Lawrence, who was born there, by describing why he loved the place (in his own words), our preconceptions and finally the village, doing so tactfully and informatively so that other important facts are not missed:

John Piper's edit of Edward Piper's photographs recreates the sense of a High Victorian streetscape so that the endpapers become a leitmotif for the most surprising elements of Thorold's *Staffordshire*.

Eastwood, Nottinghamshire, *1984, p.64*

Langold Stables, Nottinghamshire, *1984, p.94*

Flintham, Nottinghamshire, *1984, p.75*

Nottinghamshire picks up and develops the themes of surprise and discovery Thorold employed in *Lincolnshire* at 'Harlaxton' by using photographs to celebrate the fallen grandeur of redundant luxury. By contrast, Eastwood is left largely to the imagination as its entry is centred round D.H. Lawrence's description of an Eastwood long gone. The lack of pictures forces the reader to see through Lawrence's eyes – all that is shown is a very bucolic and un-Lawrentian lock and lock keeper's cottage, thus making the point that Eastwood is semi-rural.

"To me it seemed, and still seems, an extremely beautiful countryside, just between the red sandstone and the oak trees of Nottingham, and the cold limestone, the ash trees, the stone fences of Derbyshire... Go to Walker Street and stand in front of the third house – and look across at Crich on the left, Underwood in front – High Park Woods and Annesley on the right. I lived in that house from the age of 6 to 16, and I know that view better than any in the world... that is the country of my heart". The local scenes moulded Lawrence: it was about these that he wrote. Many of the landmarks in his novels may be recognized here... It was at Haggs Farm, home of his friend Jessie Cambers, a little N of the Moorgreen Reservoir, where he first conceived his idea of writing: "a tiny farm on the edge of the wood. That was Miriam's farm, where I got my incentive to write"... it was Eastwood that inspired and coloured all his writing. Another holy place, but this time for train lovers, is the *Sun Inn*, at the crossroads beyond Victoria Street – known as the birthplace of the Midland railway...[53]

It goes on to mention the Hall, the church and the Plumptre family, which though conventional rather alters our view of Lawrence's birthplace, normalising it. The photograph of Eastwood is of the Erewash canal and shows a lock and small lock-keeper's cottage, again dragging the imagination away from a pit village and back to a solid Midlands scene of rural–industrial calm that, surprisingly, happens to be the birthplace of both Lawrence and the Midland Railway.

The use of photography to add to the gazetteer entries rather than merely illustrate an aspect of them, as is the case with the photos in a Pevsner, had by *Nottinghamshire* become a discreet hallmark of the guides. But the apparent subservience of the photographs to the voice of the author was, like the increasingly modest design and layout of the guides under Piper's editorship, an illusion. Together design and image managed soto voce to construct a self-effacing but dominant discourse about the Englishness of England that was completely in the control of John, and to some extent Edward, Piper. One has the impression that as the layout became more subtle and quieter, the photographs took on a more subversive role and their discourse – the way they spoke in subject, composition and tone – powerfully directed the way the Shell Guide audience was supposed to see England. The authors had their say, but the image of England remained in Piper's control regardless of whether he used his own, his son's or someone else's imagery; for Piper was clear and ruthless in his cropping of his own and others' work, its narrative meaning being far more important to him than the sanctity of the taken image. Really to understand the England and Wales of the guides after the late fifties, it is vital to understand Piper's photographic language. Although it was secondary to each author in each particular guide, when considered in total, it is an essay on the Nation in itself.

NOTES

1 Including eight pages of padding from Piper in the form of reproductions of Cotman's Specimens of the Architectural Antiquities of Norfolk.
2 Lycett Green, 1995, p.256
3 Lycett Green, 1995
4 The Pipers read Crawford's journal, *Antiquity*.
5 He was also on the county planning committee for East Suffolk, which by his own account significantly informed his point of view when writing his Shell Guides.
6 *Rutland*, 1963, p.7
7 *Rutland*, 1963, cover and p.19, image by Reece Winstone
8 *Rutland*, 1963, p.7
9 *Rutland*, 1963, p.7
10 *Rutland*, 1963, p.8
11 *Rutland*, 1963, p.52
12 *Rutland*, 1963
13 *Rutland*, 1963, p.15
14 *Rutland*, 1963
15 *Rutland*, 1963
16 *Rutland*, 1963, p.16
17 *Rutland*, 1963
18 *Rutland*, 1963, p.7
19 *Rutland*, 1963, p.25
20 *Leicestershire*, 1970, p.9
21 Prior to the 1982 edition, which is in the format of Scarfe's *Suffolk*.
22 *Suffolk*, 1966, p.117
23 *Suffolk*, 1966, p.119
24 *Essex*, 1975, p.7
25 Later across the entire south and midlands
26 *Essex*, 1975, p.49
27 *Essex*, 1975, p.112
28 *Cambridgeshire*, 1983, p.83
29 Lycett Green, 1995, p.572, footnote to letter to Henry Thorold of 22 September 1981
30 *Nottinghamshire*, 1984, p.5
31 *County Durham*, 1980, p.5
32 *Nottinghamshire*, 1984, p.5
33 *Nottinghamshire*, 1984
34 Lycett Green, 1995, p.303, letter to John Piper, April 1966
35 Lycett Green, 1995, p.572, footnote to letter to Henry Thorold 22 September 1981
36 *Lincolnshire*, 1965, p.23
37 *Lincolnshire*, 1965, p.59
38 *Lincolnshire*, 1965, p.107
39 *Lincolnshire*, 1965
40 Piper had also known Thorold through his friend Kenna, who had introduced them. Thorold had also been Edward Piper's housemaster at Lancing.
41 *Derbyshire*, 1972, p.43
42 *Staffordshire*, 1978, p.9
43 *Staffordshire*, 1978
44 *Staffordshire*, 1978, p.69
45 *Staffordshire*, 1978
46 *Staffordshire*, 1978, p.73
47 *Staffordshire*, 1978
48 *Staffordshire*, 1978
49 *Nottinghamshire*, 1984, p.119
50 *Nottinghamshire*, 1984, p.124
51 *Nottinghamshire*, 1984, p.73
52 *Nottinghamshire*, 1984, p.96
53 *Nottinghamshire*, 1984, pp.63–5

COMPONENTS OF THE SCENE

We in our haste can only see the small components of the scene
We only watch, and indicate and make our scribbled pencil notes.

'Components of the Scene', Donald Bain[1]

FROM THE OUTSET IT WAS understood by Betjeman that the Shell County Guides' appeal would depend as much on their photography, illustration, typography and layout as on the quality of their writing. In this understanding they were on the side of the new media age that in the thirties was represented by the illustrated magazine – like Hubert De Cronin Hastings' revamped *Architectural Review* but even more by titles like *Vogue* and later *Picture Post*. In recognising the power of photographic illustration, Betjeman was embracing the shallow inattention of the modern world. Because of their apparent triviality the Shell Guides have suffered from cultural snobbery in the same way as television, which in part developed out of illustrated magazines and which Betjeman also embraced. This has meant that the Shell Guides are treated as marginalia in the work of Betjeman and Piper – and incidentally, in the inventory of British Culture. But, also like television, the perceived facile qualities of guides in general provided Betjeman and Piper with opportunities to construct a discourse about what Britain is that was implicitly sought for by the reader. This discourse could be carefully constructed below the radar of the reader through the apparently transparently 'informative' images and their arrangement around the text that was so conscientiously read.

Though Betjeman rather ruefully understood the power of images, he, being a writer, dealt with them as examples, ways of making things in the text visible and therefore as things essentially given meaning by the text. Betjeman's Shell Guide illustrations were collections of images gathered from existing sources and assembled to illustrate his view of the world like a scrapbook. If he wanted to talk about neglected Georgian terraces there had to be a photograph that would illustrate his point; if he wanted to make an ironic comment about holidays he could do so with a captioned illustration about picnics.[2] Later, if there was something to be said about industrial archaeology or Victorian popular culture there would be a picture of a shop front or an iron bridge.[3] The longer this process of illustration went on, the better Betjeman understood the importance of scale and layout when dealing with images and the better he understood the value of a good photograph. In his adoption of the gazetteer as the main structural element in the text of the guides, Betjeman recognised that texts laid out in small unrelated sections are a very forgiving medium for dull writing compared to conventional book narrative structures like chapters. In a gazetteer, a bad entry is easily overlooked for a better one nearby; it can be left unread without subverting the whole. However, a gazetteer on its own is a bit undirected, there is no motor, no

Cornwall, 1934, p.59

This jolly picture with its nannying message is an appeal to a nostalgia of the recently experienced, a chance for youth to recover childhood in the holiday. The viewer is both the child and the adult who remembers to bring the can of petrol – which is, in essence, the mood of the Shell Guides.

Shropshire, 1951, p.32

Ironbridge in 1951 was a forgotten backwater not associated with tourism but this and other picturesque representations of its iron bridge in *Shropshire* helped make it into a tourist destination by emphasising its actual beauty as well as its 'heritage' significance.

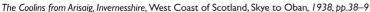

The Coolins from Arisaig, Invernesshire, West Coast of Scotland, Skye to Oban, 1938, pp.38–9

St Catherine's Chapel, Abbotsbury, Dorset, 1936, p.22

direction to the narrative. The most significant innovation in the design of the guides under Betjeman's editorship was the use of illustration to drive the reader through the gazetteer: by placing an image for a place appearing under T in the middle of the section R, the reader is invited to flick forward or even backward quickly rather than proceeding dutifully from A to Z. The reader will always flick through a guidebook but this use of illustration encourages it.

In the Betjeman-edited guides there was always a clear understanding of the guide's need to tell the reader how to see; but this was always textual and usually laid out in a section describing how to see, in which the images illustrate the place and not 'how to see'. In the pre-war guides compiled by writers there is a palpable separation between the intention of the image and the text, the image playing a subordinate exemplary or illuminating role that can only by accident go beyond the text. The most striking example of this is John Rayner's *Hampshire* where the images lie around, overwhelmed by a lively text.

The Shell Guides produced by artists are a bit different. In these guides the images are given some equality with the text: they are more likely to be pregnant with meaning beyond acting as a full stop for a description. In Bone's *West Coast of Scotland,* the beauty of Scotland, its long open views and big skies are shown in the images as counterpoint to the extended political essay of the text – as a reminder of why one should go there. In Nash's *Dorset,* photographs not only suggest the presence of an ancient subcutaneous Britain under the grass but, through their concern with revealing underlying form, make further links between the Primitive forgotten and Nash's modern sensibility that is apparent in an image but virtually inexpressible in words.

Betjeman certainly saw this. In Piper, he found someone who could make the image equal to the text in the way that Betjeman encapsulated in the notion of "the seeing eye" – the idea that someone like Piper could reveal the potential for extra meaning in things seen. In his article 'The Seeing Eye',[4] Betjeman placed himself (and the reader) in the position of recipient of Piper's aesthetic, allowing him "To Like Everything", to suspend the excluding eye that often passes for knowledge. Piper gave Betjeman a new way of seeing, and the very strategic Betjeman saw Piper's editorial potential for the Shell Guides.

The Shell Guides came to Piper at a time when he was putting aside his earlier desire to be a modern artist in the European mould and reconnecting, as were others like Paul Nash, with his earlier self in the hope of creating art informed by modernism, but particular to the British Isles. The guides were a chance for Piper to express his view of Britain and at the same time create the framework for that expression.

In his early work for the series before he was made assistant editor, Piper used the idea of the sketchbook as a basis for his approach to the compilation and layout of his guides. In the second edition of his *Oxfordshire*[5] he says, "I like a guide book to be to some extent a diary, with a diary's prejudices and superficialities. And perhaps some of its vividness".[6] But actually its form, and that of the earlier *Shropshire* and the later *Mid-Wales,* is closer to his sketchbooks.[7] In common with many artists' sketchbooks, these are made up of drawings, found objects, brief diaristic entries, notes of colours and lists of things or places. This format worked well with Betjeman's own tastes for the inclusion of found illustrations and referential photographs around the gazetteer entries, a good

Top left: This landscape by Stephen Bone's father, Muirhead Bone, shows the scope of the artist's eye, which is more detailed in both information and narrative than was possible in a photograph or the kind of brief description possible in a guide. Betjeman was quick to see the possibilities of the artist's eye for the guidebook form.

Top right: Nash's photograph of this well-known beauty spot declines to emphasise the picturesque in favour of suggesting that the chapel lies on an ancient *man-made* landscape, all-too-often represented as an apparently natural hill.

113

example of the style being *Mid-Wales* edited by Piper.[8] But after 1960 and more pronouncedly after 1967 when he became editor of the Shell Guides, Piper began to rely solely on carefully edited photographs and ever more restrained modern layouts (modern in the sense of the neutralism of Swiss typography). Once John Piper had assumed the role of editor the layouts became more neutral and the photographs became much more loaded with Piper's aesthetic; and yet their increasing personal content was to a large degree masked by their monochromy and the blandness of their context, thus making them very effective pedagogic tools.

Piper's new approach to the design of the guides is most easily seen in his revisions of *Norfolk*. In 1969 he had the cover of *Norfolk* simplified into the standard design created for him by Berthold Wolpe of Faber and Faber. This used a large photographic image in black and white laid between a header, in white with a coloured title in a hard-edged display face typical of Wolpe's work as a typographer, and a footer with the author's name reversed out against a background coloured the same as the title. The Shell logo appeared below next to the suffix 'A SHELL GUIDE' in black upper-case letters. Inside, the guide remained as it had been laid out in 1957 with a large number of small images, many gleaned from commercial sources, and a facsimile section of etchings of churches by Cotman printed on different stock. In 1982, *Norfolk* appeared in a completely revised form, longer and with the Cotman etchings used as endpapers. The chief difference in the guide is that there are around 100 more images and even the smallest of them is much larger than those in the earlier editions. In addition all the images were produced by Edward and John Piper, Peter Burton and Christopher Dalton. The cover was a colour photograph and the titles were in a new softer serif face in black laid onto the cover image, with Faber's 'ff' logo reversed out bottom right.

Piper was a keen photographer from the age of ten onward. Thousands of the images in the Shell Guides series were taken by him, latterly often the majority in any guide. Later, after he became editor, he was joined by his son Edward who acted as photographer and, increasingly, as graphic designer particularly in the last editions of the guides. As well as being de facto staff photographer for the guides, John Piper also began to use photographers that had an individual style that was 'artistic', in contrast to the Maurice Beck type of photographer used by Beddington and Betjeman in the thirties. Photographers like Beck were modern and stylish but, as Piper would have thought, 'commercial'. His abiding dislike of this concept pervaded all his judgements and led him to trust plain craftsmanship rather than commercial style – a good example being his use of A.F. Kersting's work. Generally, though, Piper liked a photograph with personality; but he was no respecter of the photographer's rights of authorship, even with his own work. He was an instinctive editor. Seeing the final design as more important

These images taken together demonstrate the difference between an imagery of information and sketchbook imagery which highlights incident. At Coalport, Piper's interest was the vertical elements of the skyline seen against the hill behind the town. At Dolau he picks up the interplay between the wintry stick-ness of the site of the chapel and the strange relation this makes with the angel with upraised arms and the bough shadows on the church wall – an image of narrative atmosphere rather than description. In the last image it is clear that Piper's layout of this page from *Shropshire* mixes disparate elements of image and text to create a sense of energy in the page that has close similarities to the feel of a sketchbook. A good deal of this energy comes from the sense of the hand moving to make the image and the odd features different graphic techniques reveal, like the swastikas on the priest's vestment.

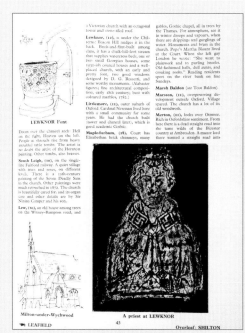

Lewknor font, Milton-Under-Wychwood church, and 'a priest at Lewknor', Oxfordshire, 1953, p.43

A chapel at Dolau, Mid Wales, 1960, p.44

Coalport, Shropshire, p.26

than any contributory part, he would usually ruthlessly crop images to extract only that component of the scene he was interested in. This often meant that a fraction of an image was blown up to fit the place in the layout with the result that the printed image was very grainy and soft.[9]

The effect Piper was searching for in his use of photography was more rhetorical than descriptive, and this implied an opposition to the conventions of commerciality and the cliché. Through his work as an editor and photographer of the guides, Piper achieved far more than simply placing nice photographs in a tidy layout. His very particular eye transformed the guides into essays on how to experience the counties; Piper, as it were, made his own Claudian lens and applied it to Britain. His work was so coherent and right-seeming that, by the series' demise in 1984, the Shell Guide view of Britain was the starting point for all commentaries on the nation, whether utopic or dystopic. The effect of this is most strangely felt in the dystopic views of Britain where Shell Guide villages are invaded by aliens (see *Village of the Damned*, MGM, 1960) and the jolly fertility rights of Maypoles are carried to their sacrificial conclusions (*The Wicker Man*, British Lion, 1973).

Piper didn't have one constant view but rather, over a long career, amassed a number of ways of seeing that together define a coherent approach to looking at the country. Inevitably the photographs that Piper took, and his choice for the guides of those taken by others, changed and modified over time according to his changing attitudes to the country, tourism, architecture and photography. Because these changes developed over a very long period, Piper's photographs and his use of photographs in the guides are a subtle and comprehensive presentation of the nation, one that often seems objective but is actually a preferred view of the country. Though this view has often been challenged by more contemporary, documentary images of Britain, the 'eye' of the Shell Guides – since 1959 increasingly Piper's eye – has become the established view against which any new position must define itself. It became established for the reason that the Shell Guides occupied a similar 'reference book' position in the national bibliographic imagination as Pevsner. This was in part due to the lack of topographical and popular architectural content in Pevsner, but more because there are so few images in Pevsner and so many in the Shell Guides – leaving aside the challenge to the 'general reader' that Pevsner poses in contrast to the accessibility of the Shell Guides.

To understand fully the evolution of Piper's or, latterly, John and Edward Piper's view of Britain one has to look at images in the guides, for their view only exists in the final layout after the photographs have been taken, printed and edited. In fact, their power as creators of an authoritative view of Britain is that they *are* intended to be definitive as printed. Rather than the more usual story of heartless editing and filleting authorial intentions, we can be

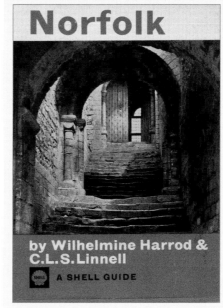
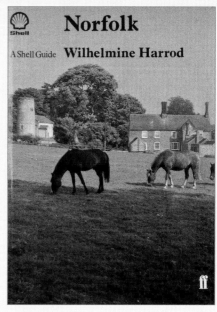

Cover of Norfolk, 1969

Cover of Norfolk, 1982

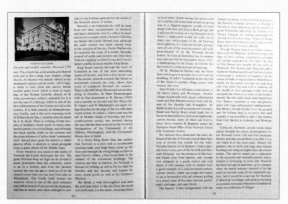

Norfolk, 1969, pp.62–3

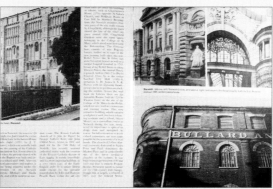

Norfolk, 1982, pp.118–19

Above: Piper's new, simpler and modern layout for the guides made good typography more significant. Here the relationship between each letter in the word 'Norfolk' can be seen to have been individually judged, particularly the relation between the R and the F. Together with the choice of typeface, this has the effect of emphasising the separation and join between the word's two syllables. In the last *Norfolk* cover, the graphic design is very minimal and a bit dull, though the FF publisher's logo is well placed, in favour of foregrounding a very picturesque image of essential Norfolkness.

The internal layout of the early editions of *Norfolk* was often very dull, something only rectified in the last edition (1982) which brought it in line with the graphic vitality usual in the guides.

115

sure that for the most part guides edited by John Piper are as near his intended vision as is practicably possible.

From here in the digital age of photography it is apparent that the Shell Guides occupied a period of photography that is now passed but nonetheless can be characterised as modern. Modern in the sense that the cameras, films, lenses and photography developed in this period still define photography today, as the new digital media struggle to set out what makes them different from their analogue predecessors. Piper began photographing in the early part of the last century but quickly adapted to and exploited all the advances in photography up to the mid-nineteen-eighties, just prior to the digital age of photography.

His first camera, bought when he was ten, was a Box Brownie of which he said, "I didn't use it for taking people as personalities…. I used to photograph churches with my Two Brownie."[10] At fifteen he moved on to an Ideal with a rising front and a Zeiss lens. The job of a rising front is to allow the lens to be moved in the vertical plane to counter the distorting effects of lenses on verticals when taking close shots of tall objects like buildings.[11] The Ideal was an unusually specific camera for a teenager and was a carefully thought out choice. This approach to his equipment continued throughout Piper's career, and as equipment improved he took up new and better tools. He liked the medium format of the Ideal better than the 35mm Leica, but when Hasselblads became available in the late 1950s he bought one because they were highly regarded for their wide-angle lens and extreme reliability. Equally at about the same time the Nikon F became available and he bought one of these because, though it was a 35mm camera, it had a through-the-lens viewfinder and a range of high-quality lenses – including a telephoto lens which, like the wide-angle, offered him an extension to the limitations of the photograph. His approach to film was equally based on an appreciation of innovation. He first used Ferrania black-and-white film partly because of how it looked and partly because it could be used on the camera in packs of 12 rather than as individual plates. Later he moved to Ilford film because it was a fast black-and-white film that was very black and white.[12] Equally, he was not a really technically obsessed photographer: he used the Ideal camera long after he'd borrowed a more up-to-date Leica to photograph the still-burning Coventry Cathedral[13] (because "one couldn't possibly use a camera or a sketchbook [as] people would immediately think you were cashing in on the misery",[14] whereas he could use a Leica discreetly by pulling it out of his hip pocket and shooting, "just like that"[15]).

Piper said of the Ideal, "I used it almost entirely for architecture in those days because I wasn't interested in using photography for landscape purposes. I used it really as a recording instrument".[16] However, in the same interview he also said, "I was, in those days, very interested in archaeology… and I did a lot of landscapes in

Wiltshire – barrows – right up to the war, when I was a war artist I did several pictures of land use, too when they were ploughing up land that had never been ploughed up since Doomsday".[17] Reading between the lines it seems Piper felt archeologically interesting landscapes were more like 'architecture' than 'landscape' to his romantic imagination. It was the photography of the humanised landscape that dominated all Piper's photography from the age of ten onwards. He liked to see human agency at work in the land.

Piper felt his approach to photography changed first when he began his relationship with Myfanwy, his second wife. As he says, "I really didn't start doing anything that I regard as worth doing until I met Myfanwy. One of our first activities, before we had children, was to constantly go around England photographing what archaeologists still call Golliwogs, you know, corbels and fonts and things".[18] It is not so much what he photographed but how he began to take photographs. A sense of what he means can be understood from what he says about working with Myfanwy and a little later with J.M. Richards: "Myfanwy held the lamp and moved it about a bit so that there wasn't too hard a shadow round the back of a lot of fonts that had never been photographed before".[19] (A good example, from Nash's *Dorset*, of one of these images is reproduced in Chapter 5 and shows the font at Toller Fratrum.) "Jim Richards and I went around photographing Buoys and Bollards – single objects – and then you really had to look at those things, knowing that you were trying to illustrate something positive, in the best light you could find".[20] This refers to Piper's article 'The Nautical Style' that appeared in the *Architectural Review* in January 1938, which in contrast to his

Piper, through his work at the *A.R.*, was able to write about and photograph subjects with which he was fascinated; and in the process, he found a way of imbuing the ordinary with the greater cultural significance that he believed it possessed.

Piper, 1948, p.21

images of fonts is shot in the harsh clear light of the seaside. What these brief views into Piper's method have in common is his desire to show things often ignored in such a way as to make them meaningful – to transform them from things and into representations of a culture.

Looking back on his early photography, this sense of the reclamation of the forgotten is often found in Piper's work of the late 1930s. His scarecrow pictures, featured by Anthony West in his monograph on Piper,[21] are good examples of this, as are his inclusions of Myfanwy's essay 'Deserted Places' and Katherine Esdaile's 'Monuments' in his first Shell Guide, *Oxon*. Most of these images are quite neutral in their *mise en scène*, Piper relying on the object itself to speak; but this changed quickly in the 1940s as he began to analyse English Romanticism[22] and fall under the spell of Samuel Palmer and William Blake. Their view darkened his and his pictures began to take on the drama of Romantic chiaroscuro that is so clearly demonstrated in his article 'Decrepit Glory: A Tour of Hafod' for the *Architectural Review* of June 1940. In the photographs for this piece the contrast is so exaggerated that the building appears ghostly white and pierced with apertures revealing only a black interior, the whole set against an equally black forest of which he says, "the drooping woods close in on the carcase of a house… The Hafod valley is a rent in this tumbled table land that has been decorated artificially, but so exquisitely that its beauty is as great in decay as it was in youth."[23]

At Hafod Piper stage-managed his photographic images in a way that is evident later in his Shell Guides; and equally, his love of contrasty photographs is more apparent than in his earlier *Oxon*. The Romanticism of his eye is matched by the mannered darkness of the photographs – a darkness that he would have seen in documentary photographers at the time like Bill Brandt. From the 1940s right through to 1984, dark, contrasty images were an increasing feature of the Shell Guides.

For Piper, all the possibilities of photography simply expanded the way that he could express his vision of the nation. But his photographic vision was inextricably bound up with his artistic vision, which defined his photographic aesthetics. He was primarily an artist who used all available media to express one vision of the world. That said, Piper was concerned not so much with transcendent art but rather an art that illustrated the transcendence of the real. Looking at the development of his artistic sensibility and then at the development of the kinds of photographs he used in the Shell Guides it is possible to coalesce his coherent view of Britain from the disparate sources he drew on and the vast range of imagery he took, edited and laid out in the Shell Guides.

Inexplicably, since he contributed hundreds of photographs to the Shell Guide series and is credited with editing "at least fifteen Shell Guides",[24] Piper is not often regarded as a photographer. In fact,

John Piper's 'Decrepit Glory: A Tour of Hafod', A.R., June 1940 (reprinted in Piper, 1948, pp.46–7)

in an interview for the *British Journal of Photography*, Paul Joyce, his interviewer, summed him up thus: "His photographic output might be compared to the journal or letters of a great novelist…. At best the results are splendid accidents (and in fact he often treats them as just this, messing about with them, cutting them up, walking on them with his fingers, so to speak) and at worst merely ordinary."[25] Piper in the same interview says of himself, "I've never really regarded myself as a professional photographer at all. The camera is a very useful and serviceable object."[26] This remark may give the clue to his attitude to photography in suggesting that he is an artist and the camera *a* tool, not *the* tool. Earlier he says, "I always saw the landscape as I thought it would look in the camera. And then looked to see if it did, and usually it didn't…. At the moment, you see, I still don't ever see things complete; I don't see it as a picture. I sometimes dream a picture, but I never see it. Once a year probably, probably, and it's pretty wonderful to be able to do it, I dream there's a great area of yellow with some black lines going into it, and some red, or something – but quite clearly. I never see that in terms of the camera."[27]

Piper is quite clear about his process of image making: the camera image in the viewfinder is rarely what he wants and pictures rarely come to him fully fledged. He must work things through until

Piper's mature style evolved over a period of around three years and combined the subject matter of British Romanticism and the technical innovations of European modernism. Hafod, a house in Wales, provided Piper with a sort of aesthetic epiphany and this image shows both a subject type and treatment that was to be reproduced in variations over the coming decades. The very conventional full-frontal view has been pushed in various ways to de-nature it so that the house is almost glowing with light while its surroundings silhouette its outline. This deepening of the dark tones is repeated in the fenestration so that the contrast is balanced throughout; the foreground and the clouds are given a more naturalistic treatment which disguises the extent of the Gothick exaggeration, with the effect of naturalising the intensely Romantic centre of the image.

they are as he wants. From his remarks, and evidently in his work, it is in editing and placing photographs in context, in an article or a book, that Piper makes 'the picture'; the image with meaning. Back in the eighties this may have seemed odd to readers of the *British Journal of Photography* and in the profession where the image recorded and processed was considered to be the photograph; but in the digital age where post production has assumed a new artistic importance, Piper's scant regard for the photograph's 'integrity' seems entirely normal — as does the idea that the image as it appears in the book or article or wherever it finally ends up *is* the actual final work.

A good example of Piper's approach to the photographic is his treatment of Stonehenge and Avebury in his *Wiltshire* of 1968. Piper had been interested in the antiquities of Wiltshire since he had joined the Wiltshire Archaeological Society as a teenager at the end of the First World War. He had sketched and photographed them at that time and they had set off his interest in topography, ancient sites and architecture. It is not surprising then that in *Wiltshire* he devotes pages to monuments that in other guides might merit one good image. The front endpapers show a very grainy, cropped image of the stones seen through a telephoto lens. The foreground and background have become muted grey patterns while the stones themselves are bathed in light and somehow this has all but disintegrated any signs of the fence that surrounds the site. The effect of the image is at once to recall the usual way that most people first see Stonehenge, from a distance coming down the A303 from the east or west, toward the junction with the Devizes road in the fork of which Stonehenge sits; it is a fleeting drive-by view. But

Piper had been fascinated with Wiltshire for many years before he worked on its Shell Guide. His fascination with its chief archaeological remains, Stonehenge and Avebury, is reflected in the extensive photographic treatment he gives the sites; but these images really come down to two things: an attempt firstly to convey the spiritual architecture of the whole; and secondly to elaborate the mystical qualities of the sites by treating the individual stones in the manner of Nash's *object personages*.

Wiltshire, 1968, front endpapers

Wiltshire, 1968, pp.60–1

Wiltshire, 1968, pp.160–1

Wiltshire, 1968, p.59

Wiltshire, 1968, p.40

Wiltshire, 1968, p.163

intertwined with this is another way of seeing the stones. Out on the open plain in strong light that gives them bright faces and strong dark backs, they look more like a Greek temple of great antiquity caught in harsh Mediterranean light. The image gives Stonehenge a sense of status as a human rather than a particularly British culture.

The images in the gazetteer, one wide-angle close up and the other two long focus, each provide a different aspect of this complex building. The square wide-angle, probably shot with his specialist architectural camera that corrected curved verticals in a wide image like this, presents the stones as architecture, as a temple, but focussing on the standing stones, composing them in such a way as to suggest a complete structure. The loose stones are lost in shadow on the ground. Immediately below, a long, thin, cropped image of the stones with people serves to emphasise their scale, lost in the image above. The two images act like a mini lecture on the form of the henge and its site. The last image of Stonehenge, cropped but probably a standard focus shot, shows the stones seen from the same place as in the previous long shot, but in the gloaming against a setting sun; it is a spiritual image, reminding the viewer of the intentions of the builders and how effective they were.

Piper's images of Avebury are more surreal, in the sense that they transform the cruder standing stones of this site into Moore-like individuals, almost as if they were walking or standing around at a cricket match. This is achieved through the use of composition, shooting them against the village, or with strong contrast and in a line as if walking away. Such subjective responses to these sites are one of their enduring pleasures. The double-page, low, wide-angle shot, on the other hand, shows them as a henge surrounded by an earthwork, as if to remind us of the fantasy element in the previous images.

Piper's guides contain themes in his choice and use of images which occur again and again; but there are also new types of image which appear in his work and new approaches, so that even in the last guides of the 1980s Piper would find some new way of giving meaning to the mute objectivity of a building or a landscape.

One place to start would be a theme that underlies all the Shell Guides, particularly after 1960: the attitude to tourism. Piper and Betjeman, in common with the majority of their class, had a dislike of the 'tourist' and all things pertaining thereto. This dislike enabled them to understand and present a preferred Britain to their largely middle-class readership who like them wanted an authentic experience of their country – for whatever else may be said of the tourist, the industry that caters for them has managed to parody and render bogus the very authenticity it is often physically based within. Whilst this irresistible drift toward self-parody began at the seaside, it has extended even to the heritage that people like Betjeman and Piper sought to protect.

Piper had a very developed sense of the encroaching

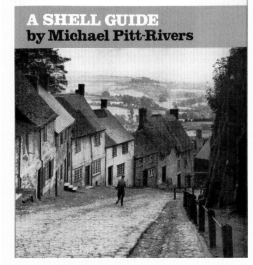

Dorset, 1966, *cover*

Devon, 1974, *cover*

inauthentic, to the degree that he was very suspicious of things that others had 'discovered' and much preferred to discover something similar himself. This desire for the authentic lay behind his love of the neglected, for dereliction guaranteed authenticity. From *Oxon* onwards Piper was careful to praise the dishevelled and the ruin and to deprecate the restored. A good illustration of this is a comparison between the cover of the second edition of *Dorset* (1966) by Michael Pitt-Rivers and the cover of Ann Jellicoe and Roger Mayne's *Devon* (1974). Piper disliked the former, which he felt to be too obvious.[28] The latter shows a remote farmstead under a lowering sky[29] and, whilst perhaps a perverse choice for a guidebook cover, represents all the ideals of cottage life that Piper had pursued since he and Myfanwy took on their own ruinous cottage at Fawley Bottom in the 1930s.

In fact, the Pipers revelled in the unkempt, like Pevsner, for holidays at least. Francis Spalding relates that at their first house in Wales, at Nant Ffrancon, "after one downpour, water poured in at the back of the house and out the front door".[30] This Spartan aesthetic is a common feature of the middle-class metropolitan cottage holiday where familiar central heating is replaced by arcane water heaters and reluctant fires. Their appeal has something to do with *nostalgie de la boue*[31] and with regaining childhood, especially childhood holidays. The cottage is part of a romantic fantasy that, like the American Dream, is simultaneously understood as fantasy yet

This image of Gold Hill at Shaftesbury was disliked by Piper who didn't want it to be used as a cover for *Dorset* because it was of a well-known tourist viewpoint, even though Smith's treatment of the view is actually a bit dour. Piper favoured images which suggested the unknown aspects of a county or counter-tourist views like the grim cover for *Devon* by Roger Mayne.

longed for – a thing that replaces the compromises of urban adulthood with an ambition to find an optimistic place of childlike simplicity. The British dream, among the middle class at least, is inherently old fashioned, recalling a simpler less-affluent youth, chilly opened-up new–old rooms and secret places discovered. Piper more than Betjeman understood this; and if not quite every guide contains its remote, romantic, rainy hideaway, certainly almost every guide that Piper edited showed as many modest and tidy double-fronted farms, shot squarely from the front, as stately homes.

Piper understood the ambitions of his readership to discover ruinous stately homes and to lust after not-too-small cottages. Furthermore Piper understood that the task of the Shell Guide was not simply to describe the great places, or even to re-establish the reputation of the Georgian (which by the sixties was assured anyway) but to show the reader the detailed charm of the vernacular. So with the cottages come photographs of back doors, paths through vegetable gardens, old walls and espaliered fruit trees.

Piper was concerned to bring life to his gazetteers and this led to one of the most striking photographic tropes of the guides: their treatment of churches. Piper was less churchy than Betjeman and both knew how dead these buildings can seem; but Piper, following the example of Katherine Esdaile, was very interested in parish church funerary sculpture, which she had suggested was the repository of the British sculptural tradition. He used these sculptures in graveyards and naves up and down the counties as a way of repopulating the church with a sense of historic community in the most direct and humorous way, by using photographs that, through suitable point of view and lighting, made the figurative sculpture seem alive. Piper's guides are full of quizzical recumbent Jacobeans, vocative Georgian baronets and their beautiful virtuous wives, not to mention dutiful victims of public service and underdressed regency ladies.

Betjeman wanted to go beyond the great buildings, people and events school of guides; but Piper, seeing this battle won, went further and used photography to revive the interest in the everyday and the small-scale products of industrialisation that had first been revived by surrealists in the twenties and thirties and – less ironically – by the *Architectural Review*. To be more exact, Betjeman and authors like Robert Byron were sensitive to the beauty of items of popular culture like trade plates: Betjeman freely quoted from these in the ironic title pages of his first Shell Guides and Byron even had one reproduced for his *Wiltshire*. Piper's use of popular cultural material was different, coming not from a penchant for the camp vulgarity of Victoriana but rather modern art's fascination with the *objet trouvé*. Before Piper's rift with Modern European Art just prior to his involvement in the *A.R.* and Shell Guides, his work frequently used *objets trouvés*, such as arcane tobacco labels, inserted into his paintings. This practice continued in his photography and bled into

This view sums up a sort of ideal Englishness for Piper, grand and plain: the caption reads, "a stone and stucco late Georgian building of character in a sweeping landscape of open fields and small copses".

Marshwood House, Dinton, Wiltshire, 1968, p.93

Banded ironstone walling at Caldecott, Rutland, 1963, p.9

In Betjeman's picture editing you might get flowers as details but in Piper there are usually details of vernacular architecture and horticultural references to the back-door areas of farms and cottages. Though the caption for this image says "Banded ironstone walling at Caldecott" this is just a fig leaf: it is really about a rough and ready horticultural beauty that was part of Piper's own vision of an idealised built environment.

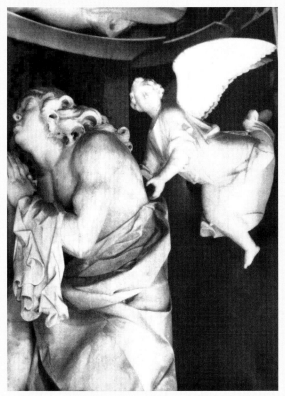

Piper was very influenced by Katherine Esdaile's idea that the history of British sculpture lay in its parish churches and every Shell Guide he was involved with had this type of image where the photographer tries to play Pygmalion and bring the dead stone to life.

Pierrepoint Monument, West Dean, Wiltshire, 1968, p.177   *Sir Edward Lewys Monument, Edington, Wiltshire, 1968, p.99*

his appreciation of architecture so that commercial and information graphic design and layouts, chosen for their counterpoint aesthetic only rather than their ironic value. Thus with the cottages and living sculptures come old cast iron, flights of locks and railways, as well as the kitchen gardens of stately homes and streetscapes of old shops or lost regency terraces in tiny Spa Towns.

The recurrent imagery of Piper's counties is of the middle-class heritage of the nation, which the new affluent 'endless middle' of the sixties and seventies and the heritage-conscious eighties yuppies could take as their imagined past – free of the implied genuflection of the stately home tour or, later, the patronising package of the heritage experience.

Piper's photos give the reader the kind of places needed to recover a past that we hope is still there when we escape from our compromised present. Even though we know this is a lie, the very ordinariness of the text and the dour photos reassure us that we are not expecting too much and that what is shown is real – or at least as real as Dylan's Llareggub.

All the photographs in the later Shell Guides are primarily poetic evocations and are only nominally real, but this is particularly true of the landscapes. With these, Piper's editing and choice of image were freer than the grudging respect for actuality he showed toward images of buildings and sculpture. Many of the Shell Guide landscapes represent agricultural counties and few are of the sublime since few mountainous or vertiginous regions feature in the guides. To represent the charms of these landscapes meant celebrating trees, fields, ditches and hedges over and over again. Piper evolved a twofold approach to this problem that was both formulaic and beautiful. He treated all these landscapes with their regular features as patterns, which he showed in different lights and seasons through the distorting points of view of the telephoto and the wide-angle lens. The effect of wide-angle shots, especially when combined with grainy, contrasty printing, was to render hedges, grass and ploughed land as a series of layers of rich and abstract texture that is more art than reportage. Conversely, telephoto shots across wide Midland vales could be given almost the reverse treatment. By cropping out the foreground and mildly overexposing the whole, or by burning in a big cloudy sky, the landscape could be made to seem bathed in an evanescent glow that gives a sublime endlessness

Cast iron things, Shropshire, 1951, p.9

Ironbridge, Shropshire, 1951, p.31

SHROPSHIRE CAST-IRON

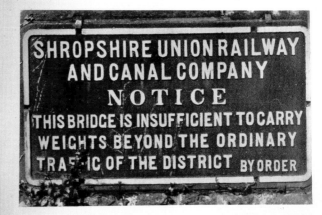

Above: Iron Tombstones at MADELEY.

Below: Notice on a Shropshire Union Canal Bridge.

SHROPSHIRE UNION RAILWAY
AND CANAL COMPANY
NOTICE
THIS BRIDGE IS INSUFFICIENT TO CARRY
WEIGHTS BEYOND THE ORDINARY
TRAFFIC OF THE DISTRICT BY ORDER

9   B

Opposite : One kind of Shropshire scenery. CARDING MILL VALLEY, CHURCH STRETTON.

Bucknell Station, Shropshire, 1951

Delicate Victorian shop fronts below an early eighteenth-century façade in Gloucester, Gloucestershire, 1952, p.39

Streetscape of old shops, Shrewsbury, Shropshire, 1951, p.51

Lift Bridge, Shropshire, 1951, cover

Shropshire

by Michael Moulder
A SHELL GUIDE

Piper, more than Betjeman, was interested in what Gordon Cullen named townscape, which is really a way of looking at the total built environment down, rather than either pure country or pure architecture, as a source of aesthetic pleasure. The townscape idea favoured the accidental beauty of the functional or the gaudy or the popular, allowing the most ordinary object to become the equivalent of the artist's *objet trouvé*.

Church Stretton, Shropshire, 1951

Pillar Box Great Malvern, Worcestershire, 1964

123

to hedges punctuated by hedgerow trees. This treatment was also applied to industrial landscapes of mills or coal workings and, as much as his wide-angle landscapes are rooted in abstraction, his long-focus landscapes are rooted in English Romantic painting. This abstraction and Romanticism have the effect of sensitising the viewer to their own sense of the aesthetic and the intellectual because the images – being so clearly enhanced visions of the real – invite analysis. Strangely, they make the viewer feel clever when they appreciate them, and this sense that Piper's images flatter the sensibilities of the reader is the very thing that Betjeman recognised in Piper's "seeing eye".

As well as having an eye for the Romantic and the surreal, Piper also retained a strong sense of abstraction and texture which enabled him to articulate the pleasures of open landscapes and distant views. He presents these as if they were abstract images only made of form and texture, even if the abstract image is in reality of an only-too-tangible colliery village.

Warsop Vale, Nottinghamshire, 1984, p.29

Near Royston, Cambridgeshire, 1983, p.15

Rutland, 1963, rear endpapers

One area of photography that Piper had difficulty with was colour. "But not colour, never colour! I never took a colour picture at all until well after the war. I don't suppose there was much colour film until after the war, anyway".[32] There was colour, of course: Kodachrome had been invented and the Autochrome process had been around since before the First World War; but Piper did not like colour in photographs, though in other media he loved it. Piper's problems with colour photography may have come from what colour was used for by others and how it looked. At one level, colour photography existed as the perfect medium for post-war holidays and by the early sixties colour imagery was something that the market made a point of. The fly-sheet blurb of Arthur Raistrick's *Yorkshire and the North East*[33] begins "The magnificent colour photographs which form the basis for this book have been selected from many thousands" and even postcards were keen to embrace colour photography (as opposed to colour printing): Valentine's cards made much of their "VALCHROME" series which were "REPRODUCED FROM A COLOUR PHOTOGRAPH". However, colour did not always make a good photograph as it needed lots of light and often ended up simply offering a tinted view of an essentially monochrome scene. Alternatively the combination of photographs taken specifically because they were coloured and the printing process could produce a wildly exaggerated view of reality that could only disappoint when seen for real, as in the case of the image of Runswick Bay.

Equally, colour had been used not for its inherent glamour but for its extra realism, as can be seen in Collins' New Naturalist series where colour is crucial for the veracity of the images. As the general description of the series states on the frontispiece, "The plants and animals are described in relation to their homes and habitats and are portrayed in the full beauty of their natural colours, by the latest methods of colour photography and reproduction". This concern for realism extended to all the subjects covered by the series, sometimes to surreal effect as in Gordon Manley's *Climate and the British Scene*.

The strange thing about one of the images is its caption, "Princes street, Edinburgh; early May. Springtime: almost calm, slight haze, very light air from S.E. Cautious retention of coats by older Scotsmen." It

Right and next two pages: As an artist, Piper was very interested in colour; but as a photographer and editor he was highly suspicious of its connotations of tourism, through its use for postcards, and of scientific accuracy (colour in the post war period being used to add veracity to evidential imagery).

Princes Street, Edinburgh, from the chapter 'The English Spring and Early Summer', Manley, 1952, p.111, photo by Cyril Newberry, courtesy of Collins Rights

Raistrick, 1963, p.57

Postcard of Black Rocks, Criccieth (Valentines of Dundee)

Lecture slide, possibly 1947, Cambridge, from the collection of the author, 5x8 autochrome slide mounted in glass

is oblivious to most of the content of the picture, a city street busy with cars and people, or the possibility that it may be a bad reproduction or a bad photograph and thus seems to assume, as the reader must, that the image is 'true' or 'real'. This use of colour in the New Naturalist series seems to have its origin in academic lectures, as shown by a lantern slide autochrome image of a man in a duffle coat pushing a bicycle along the banks of the river Cam near the Fen Causeway. It is the literalness of these early colour images that Piper rejected as much as the unreality of the postcard. For Piper, colour was something to be used carefully and creatively, so colour photography as it was practised after the war and into the sixties

had little appeal for him. It seemed either literal or, the reverse, artificial and unpredictable – and probably too popular and touristy.

That said, in the mid sixties, Piper did begin to use colour in the frontispieces of the guides. These were either in the form of reproductions of colour prints, as in the case of Snaffles' wonderful 'Finest view in Europe' (1924; looking across Spratton Vale to Brixworth) used in Juliet Smith's *Northamptonshire*, or in reproductions of stained-glass windows such as, for example, those in *Kent* (1965), showing "Martyrdom in the 13th-century stained glass in Canterbury Cathedral", and in *Suffolk* (1966), showing a crucifix of lilies at Long Melford. Piper loved stained glass and found

127

Colour images had been used in the Shell Guides since the mid fifties to illustrate something that couldn't be photographed – in this case, the idea of the Midlands shires as the best foxhunting country in England.

Northamptonshire and the Soke of Peterborough, *1968, frontispiece*

its representation in colour acceptable because of the extreme separation and purity of colour and the strange darkness of stained glass. He did experiment more with colour in the guides and was successful when he could find images that 'fitted' with his aesthetic – as in the frontispiece to *Mid Western Wales* (1971), which shows a cottage with a red door in a wood, an image that could have been executed in stained glass such is the separation and abstraction of reds, greens and whites. But there were some failures too, as in the case of the frontispiece for *Leicestershire* (1970) showing the west end of Stapleford church. Here Piper clearly liked the pastel Gothick walls but, unfortunately, the timber gallery in front is so brown it kills the delicate colours behind.

Piper was no doubt being pushed to use colour by his sponsors and publishers and after he became editor it was increasingly employed, eventually becoming standard for the covers. Here there were disasters too, as in the cover of *East Sussex* (1978), the first guide with a colour cover. It showed a small seafront-sitting pavilion at Hove. It is surreal and bleak and not an inducement to visit the county. *Staffordshire* was published in the same year and its cover is a great success, a backlit image of ruins at Croxden Abbey seen through trees.

It uses monochrome effects of browns through to golds with black to create a very un-Staffordshire-like image of Gothick mystery. The success of this image lay in its closeness to Piper's artistic aesthetic, being a photo version of many of his Romantic paintings of ruins from the forties onwards. With this use of colour Piper had hit his stride, finding images that were in the same territory as his paintings. He produced really imaginative and evocative covers

Right and next page: Piper loved stained glass from an early age and later in life became a stained-glass artist. Almost the only colour images he used regularly were details of stained glass. Where he did use colour images elsewhere, they often looked like stained glass as in the case of this cottage in *Mid Western Wales*. Sometimes Piper showed poor judgement in his use of colour, unlike his use of black and white.

Crucifix of lilies, Long Melford, Suffolk, 1966

Mid Western Wales, *1971*

Leicestershire, *1970*

Staffordshire, *1978, cover*

East Sussex, *1978, cover*

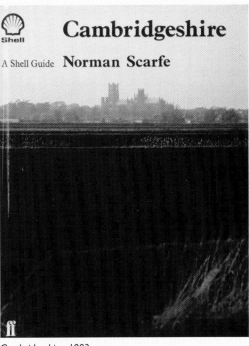

Cambridgeshire, *1983, cover*

for the new edition of *Essex* (1982), a photograph of Brightlingsea mud flats by Norman Scarfe, and *Cambridgeshire* (1982), a wonderfully and subtly balanced tonal image of Ely Cathedral floating above the fen by Edward Piper. But against these successes there were others less successful: *Durham* (1980), *Hertfordshire* (1982) and *Nottinghamshire* (1984). These are so different from John Piper's usual choice of image, whether black and white or colour, as to lead one to think that they were attempts to make the guides more popular, edited by Edward Piper, coming as they did at the end of the guides' long run.

By the end of the series in 1984, the covers had become weaker; yet in comparison even to recent guides the interiors were as distinctive as ever and, whilst probably being the result of Edward's editing, very much in the style of John Piper.

In fact, the strength and power of the later guides is entirely due to John Piper's format, which Edward very skilfully managed. The

essence of this was really a series of slowly evolved image conventions whose purpose was to represent counties as places to be found, not sequences of must-sees to be ticked off. In doing this, Piper created a formula for the guides that, when large numbers of them are compared together, is obviously repetitive; but this did not matter since no-one reads series of guides coincidently. To evolve such a set of formulae, Piper needed to have a clear perception of his audience and what they wanted. It was Piper's charm in his art, much as it was Betjeman's in his poetry, to represent in his own taste and aspirations those of an entire and growing class of people before they were aware they had them – and over details they did not yet know were significant. Each revealed the transcendent in the ordinary; but while Betjeman latterly expressed himself in various public media, Piper's widest address but most discreet authorship was his work on the Shell Guides.

Over time Piper adapted his black-and-white sensibility to the problem of colour by treating it as if it were black and white: his use of colour moved from being about separating colours toward being about the relationship of tones and hues.

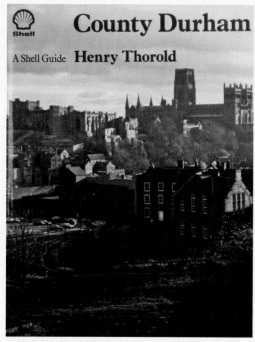

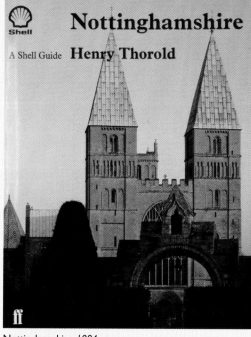

County Durham, *1980, cover*

Hertfordshire, *1982, cover*

Nottinghamshire, *1984, cover*

THE END

Nottinghamshire was the last Shell Guide. It was published in 1984, the year of Betjeman's death and the miner's strike that marked the end of so much that had characterised the previous forty years. In 1985 it won the Thomas Cook Award and one can't help but feel this was some kind of Pyrrhic 'lifetime achievement' recognition. Shell and Faber had long before indicated that neither was happy with the guides. In 1987 the series was revived under a different publisher and editor by Shell, who thought that they might succeed in a more commercial, consumerist form: they ceased publishing the series after a year. The truth was that the Shell Guides had had their day and that contemporary tastes had moved on. The age of British holidays was over: roads were congested, hotels and cottages were expensive, pubs didn't admit children and beach cafes served unfashionable heart-clogging food; but most of all it was cheaper to

fly to Spain, Italy or Greece, where it was warmer and the food was good. Faber and Faber had seen this and in 1978 published Laurence Durrell's guide *The Greek Islands* in the same format as the Shell Guides, and in 1989 Peter Mayle's *A Year in Provence* came out. I remember at that time sitting in a pub in Thixendale in the Yorkshire Wolds listening to two farmers. One asked the other about his summer holiday plans and he replied, "We were thinking we'd try the Seychelles".

But now things are different again. Britain is a destination for the British and, in truth, if you look at the guides in the bookstores today, none have the sense of discovery, the depth of knowledge, the simple comprehensible layout, or the gorgeous, enticing pictures of the Shell Guides. But that is hardly surprising since they haven't been thoughtfully written by a *Who's Who* of characters from the *Dictionary of National Biography* or made and remade over 50 years by a poet and an artist – let alone by a Betjeman or a Piper.

The very late covers of the Shell Guides were sometimes bland and touristic. This may have been because of the influence of Edward Piper on the design of the guides; but more likely it was due to pressure over sales from Faber and/or Shell.

Nottinghamshire, *1984*

Cambridgeshire, *1983*

County Durham, *1980*

While the late covers were sometimes uncharacteristically bland, the same cannot be said of the title pages which were as innovative as ever and kept up with the aesthetics of British photography – which by the mid eighties was still fascinated with strong chiaroscuro effects that had become a British photographic tradition.

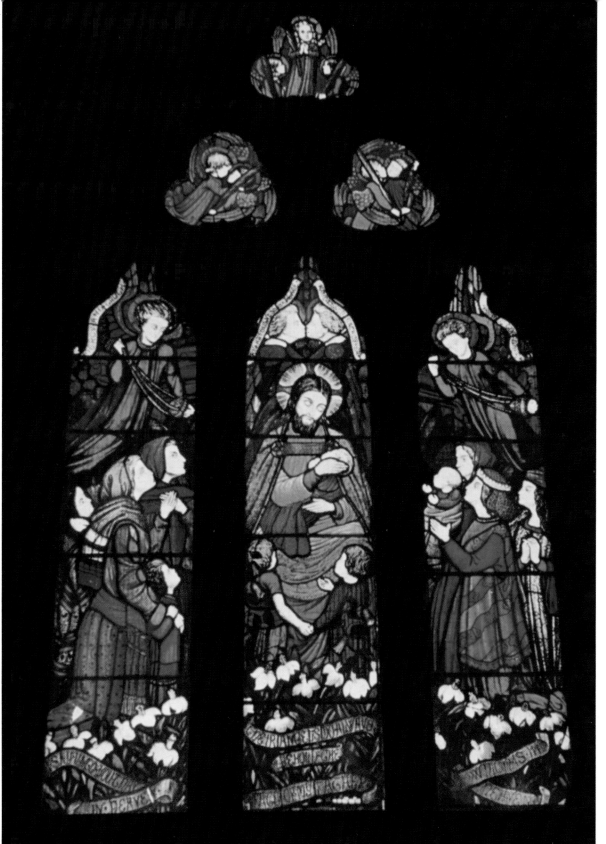

Piper was very suspicious of
colour but where he did use
colour images in later Shell
Guides they were often
paraphrases of this image by Percy
Hennell, who produced a number
of colour-photograph-illustrated
books in the war.

*Our Lord Blessing Children, Ford Madox
Ford at Brightwalton, image 147,*
Murray's Berkshire Architectural
Guide, 1949, p.97

EPILOGUE

The Shell Guides were published from 1934 to 1984, roughly marking the period from the beginnings of general car ownership and paid holidays to the birth of cheap, fast and universal international holiday travel. The Shell Guides ostensibly were created to encourage people to take motoring holidays in Britain, but in fact they were a discreet art installation built by a couple of generations of artists, poets, writers and photographers interested in revealing an unknown Britain to the 80 per cent of people who lived in the nation's metropolises. Paid for by a multinational oil company and a bourgeois publisher, they promoted a view of the nation predicated on the ideas of discovery and pleasure in landscape and an inclusive history of hitherto uncelebrated aspects of national life. Only rarely did they mention food or drink or accommodation; they offered nothing consumable beyond pleasure in discovering the country. They were, are, a success and in their day sat as reference texts alongside Pevsner's Buildings of England series in public libraries.

In my own life I have met the generations who did and did not know the Shell Guides. My father-in-law was really of the pre Shell Guide era and to him, though an early motorist, a drive beyond the confines of his home, the Vale of York, seemed unnecessary; for him a car simply replaced the bicycle. When I first moved to York from London he had a cleaner, Mrs Goddard, who coming from a poorer background never left York except for two trips, decades apart, to "the Lakes". Even in the early 1990s while walking in Rosedale with the dog we met a man who asked us where we were from. "York", we said. "I've been there a couple of times" was his reply and he meant two. By contrast my father, born eighteen years later than my father-in-law, was a keen traveller in Britain, and I remember as a boy his library copy of the Shell Guide to Cornwall by Betjeman; but more than that I remember the Toad of Toad Hall enthusiasm which he and others like him – and one suspects Betjeman – shared. Driving to North Wales with my mother and two sisters in a Mini I remember my father cheering as we managed to top a hill in third gear and muttering darkly under his breath about the coming of 'the Midland link' as we sat in a traffic jam in Cannock Chase. Travelling to Cornwall I remember his trying to engage me in a debate about the relative cultural merits of taking the A272 to join the A303 or the conventional A30–A303–A30 route. Even more vivid is the memory of leaving south-east London at half six in the morning and heading west. We reached Stonehenge, a sight I still love, by nine, but due to 'tootling', my father's term for going from 'place of interest' to 'place of interest', we arrived in Boscastle, North Cornwall at half-past-nine at night. Tootling, which in the end gave me some kind of education, was the condition of using a Shell Guide. It belongs to an era now past. The aim of this book is to celebrate these books that remain the best guides to a Britain which still, bar its industry, exists – though it is slowly being forgotten county by county as we retreat into a nation who know the world better than where we live.

NOTES

1 Bain, 1966, p.8
2 As used at the back of the original Shell Guide, *Cornwall*.
3 As in *Devon* of 1935, *Gloucester*, 1939, and *Shropshire*, 1951
4 Betjeman, November 1939
5 Previously titled *Oxon*
6 *Oxfordshire*, 1953, p.5
7 Held in the Piper Archive at the Tate Britain Gallery.
8 And in respect of which he was made assistant editor, though he had been de facto joint editor for some time.
9 This is evident in many of the images chosen for the third edition of *Wiltshire* (1968) which he edited, photographed and co wrote with J.H. Cheetham.
10 Joyce and Piper, 25 November 1983, p.1,240
11 The verticals cease to be straight and become bowed.
12 His photographs on the Ideal using Ferrania film often involved two-minute exposures.
13 As he had been instructed to do as a War Artist.
14 Joyce and Piper, 25 November 1983, p.1,241
15 Joyce and Piper, 25 November 1983, p.1,241
16 Joyce and Piper, 25 November 1983, p.1,240
17 Joyce and Piper, 25 November 1983, p.1,241
18 Joyce and Piper, 25 November 1983, p.1,242
19 Joyce and Piper, 25 November 1983, p.1,242
20 Joyce and Piper, 25 November 1983, p.1,243
21 West, 1979, p.48
22 His book *British Romantic Artists* was published in 1942.
23 Piper, 1948, p.42
24 Joyce and Piper, 25 November 1983, p.1,239
25 Joyce and Piper, 25 November 1983, p.1,240
26 Joyce and Piper, 25 November 1983, p.1,243
27 Joyce and Piper, 25 November 1983, p.1,243
28 It was later used as the basis for a long-running Hovis advert.
29 Peter Burton relates that Ann Jellicoe was approached as author for the third *Devon* and that she agreed to do it on the proviso that Roger Mayne, who was very depressed at the time, would do the photography.
30 Spalding, 2009, p.269
31 Nostalgia for dirt
32 Joyce and Piper, 25 November 1983, p.1,243
33 Raistrick, 1963

BIBLIOGRAPHY

SHELL GUIDES

John Nash, *Bucks*, London: B.T. Batsford, 1937

Norman Scarfe, *Cambridgeshire*, London: Faber and Faber, 1983

John Betjeman, *Cornwall*, *Illustrated in a Series of Views, of Castles, Seats of the Nobility, Mines, Picturesque Scenery, Towns, Public Buildings, Churches, Antiquities &c.*, London: Architectural Press, 1934

John Betjeman, *Cornwall*, London: Faber and Faber, 1964

Henry Thorold, *County Durham*, London: Faber and Faber, 1980

Christopher Hobhouse, *A Shell Guide to Derbyshire*, *a Series of Views, of Castles, Seats of the Nobility, Mines, Picturesque Scenery, Towns, Public Buildings, Churches, Antiquities &c.*, London: Architectural Press, 1935

Henry Thorold, *Derbyshire*, London: Faber and Faber, 1972

John Betjeman, *Devon*, London: Architectural Press, 1935

Brian Watson, *Devon*, *Shell Guide, Compiled with many illustrations and information of every sort by Brian Watson*, London: Faber and Faber, 1955

Paul Nash, *Dorset*, London: Architectural Press, 1936

W.S. Mitchell, *East Sussex*, London: Faber and Faber, 1978

Norman Scarfe, *Essex*, London: Faber and Faber, 1968

Norman Scarfe, *Essex*, 2nd ed., London: Faber and Faber, 1975

Norman Scarfe, *Essex*, 3rd ed., London: Faber and Faber, 1982

Anthony West, *Gloucestershire*, *A Shell Guide by Anthony West*, London: Faber and Faber, 1939

Anthony West, revised by David Verey, *Gloucestershire*, London: Faber and Faber, 1952

John Rayner, *Towards a Dictionary of the County of Southampton, Commonly Hampshire or Hants by John Rayner, Shell Guide*, London: Batsford, 1937

David Verey, *Herefordshire*, London: Faber and Faber, 1955

R.M. Healey, *Hertfordshire*, London: Faber and Faber, 1982

Lord Clonmore, *Kent*, *a Series of Views, of Castles, Seats of the Nobility, Mines, Picturesque Scenery, Towns, Public Buildings, Churches, Antiquities &c.*, London: Architectural Press, 1935

W.G. Hoskins, *Leicestershire*, London: Faber and Faber, 1970

Henry Thorold, *Lincolnshire*, London: Faber and Faber, 1965

David Verey, *A Shell Guide to Mid-Wales: The Counties of Brecon, Radnor and Montgomery*, London: Faber and Faber, 1960

Vyvyan Rees, *Mid-Western Wales*, London: Faber and Faber, 1971

Wilhelmine Harrod and C.L.S. Linnell, *Norfolk*, London: Faber and Faber, 1957; reprint of 3rd edition, 1969; 4th edition, 1982

Juliet Smith, *Northamptonshire and the Soke of Peterborough*, London: Faber and Faber, 1968

Thomas Sharp, *Northumberland and Durham*, London: B.T. Batsford, 1937

Henry Thorold, *Nottinghamshire*, London: Faber and Faber, 1984

John Piper, *Oxon*, London: B.T. Batsford, 1938

John Piper, *Oxfordshire*, *not including the City of Oxford*, London: Faber and Faber, 1953

W.G. Hoskins, *Rutland*, London: Faber and Faber, 1963

John Piper and John Betjeman, *Shropshire*, London: Faber and Faber, 1951

C.H.B. Quennell and Peter Quennell, *Somerset*, London: Architectural Press, 1936

Henry Thorold, *Staffordshire*, London: Faber and Faber, 1978

Norman Scarfe, *Suffolk*, 2nd ed., London: Faber and Faber, 1966

Stephen Bone, *West Coast of Scotland, Skye to Oban*, London: B.T. Batsford, 1938

Robert Byron, *Wiltshire*, *a Series of Views of Castles, Seats of the Nobility, Mines, Picturesque Scenery, Towns, Public Buildings, Churches, Antiquities, &c.*, London: Architectural Press, 1935

J.H. Cheetham and John Piper, *Wiltshire*, London: Faber and Faber, 1968

J. Lees-Milne, *Worcestershire*, London: Faber and Faber, 1964

GENERAL

Amory, M. (1998) *Lord Berners: The Last Eccentric*, London: Chatto & Windus

Anonymous (1899) *A Handbook for Residents and Travellers in Wilts and Dorset*, Fifth Edition with Maps and Plans, London: John Murray

Anonymous (1927) *A Pictorial and Descriptive Guide to Warwick, Royal Leamington Spa, Kenilworth, Stratford upon Avon, Coventry & the George Eliot Country*, London: Ward Lock & Co.

Artmonsky, R. (2006) *Jack Beddington: The Footnote Man*, London: Artmonsky Arts, 2006

Bain, D. (1966) *Components of the Scene: Stories, Poems, and Essays of the Second World War*, ed. R. Blythe, London: Penguin

Baring-Gould, S. (1925) *Devon*, New York: Robert M. McBride and Co.

Betjeman, J. (1937) *Continual Dew*, London: Murray

Betjeman, J. (1938) *An Oxford University Chest*, London: John Miles

Betjeman, J. (November 1939) 'The Seeing Eye: or How to like Everything', *Architectural Review* 86, pp.201–4

Betjeman, J. (1960) *Summoned by Bells*, London: Murray

Betjeman, J. and J. Piper (eds) (1948) *Murray's Buckinghamshire Guide*, London: Murray

Betjeman, J. and J. Piper (eds) (1949) *Murray's Berkshire Architectural Guide*, London: Murray

Betjeman, J. and L. Russell Muirhead (1951) *The English Scene: A Reader's Guide*, Cambridge: CUP for National Book League

Bland, D., J. Shand and H. Williamson (1954) *Exhibition of British Book Design 1954, an exhibition of books published in 1953 chosen for the National Book League by David Bland, James Shand and Hugh Williamson*, Catalogue 1954, London: National Book League

Bone, G. and S. Bone (1925) *Of the Western Isles*, London: T.N. Foulis

Lord Clonmore (September 1933) 'London, Morecambe and Elsewhere', *Architectural Review*, pp.93–9

Denton, P. (2002) *Seaside Surrealism: Paul Nash in Swanage*, Peveril Press: Swanage

Harrison, C. (1981) *English Art and Modernism 1900–1939*, London: Yale

Hauser, K. (2008) *Bloody Old Britain: O.G.S. Crawford and the Archaeology of Modern Life*, London: Granta

Hillier, B. (1988) *Young Betjeman*, London: Murray

Hoskins, W.G. (1948) *Touring Leicestershire*, Leicester: City of Leicester

Ingrams, R. and J. Piper (1983) *Piper's Places: John Piper in England and Wales*, London: Chatto and Windus

Joyce, P. and J. Piper (25 November 1983) 'The Arbitrary Eye: A Photographic Discourse between John Piper and Paul Joyce', *British Journal of Photography*

Kirkham, N. (1947) Vision of England, *Derbyshire*, illustrated by Malvina Cheek, London: Paul Elek

Knox, J. (2003) *A Biography of Robert Byron*, London: John Murray

Lambert, B. (31 October 1993) 'Peter Quennell, a Man of Letters and Man About Town, Dies at 88', *The Times*

Lycett Green, C. (ed.) (1994) *John Betjeman Letters Volume 1, 1926–1951*, London: Methuen

Lycett Green, C. (ed.) (1995) *John Betjeman Letters Volume 2, 1951–1984*, London: Methuen

Manley, G. (1952) *Climate and the British Scene*, New Naturalist series, London: Collins

Sir J.A.R. Marriot (1941) *Modern England 1885–1939*, London: Methuen

Nash, P. (1949) *Outline: An Autobiography*, London: Faber and Faber

Nash, P. (1951) *Fertile Image*, ed. by M. Nash, introduction by J. Laver, London: Faber and Faber

Peterson, W.S. (2006) *John Betjeman: A Bibliography*, Oxford: Clarendon Press

Pevsner, N. (1960) Buildings of England, *Buckinghamshire*, London: Penguin

Piper, J. (1942) *British Romantic Artists*, Britain in Pictures, London: Collins

Piper, J. (1948) *Buildings and Prospects*, London: Architectural Press

Raistrick, A. (1963) *Yorkshire and the North East*, Edinburgh and London: Oliver and Boyd

Richards, J.M. (November 1938) 'Black and White – An Introductory Study of a National Design Idiom', *Architectural Review*

Richards, J.M. and E. Ravilious (illustrator) (1938) 'High Street', *Country Life*

Salmon, A.L. (1903) *The Little Guide: Cornwall*, London: Methuen & Co.

Scott-Giles, C.W. (ed.) (1946) *The Road Goes On: A Literary Account of the Highways, Byways and Bridges of Great Britain*, London: Epworth Press

Spalding, F. (2009) *John Piper, Myfanwy Piper; Lives in Art*, Oxford: OUP

Steers, J.A. (1953) *The Sea Coast*, New Naturalist series, London: Collins

Ward, C.S. (1904) *North Devon (Including West Somerset) and North Cornwall From Exmoor to the Scilly Isles with Description of the Various Approaches*, Thorough Guide Series, London: Dulau & Co.

Ward, C.S. and M.J.B. Baddeley (1885) *South Devon and South Cornwall Including Dartmoor and the Scilly Isles*, Thorough Guide Series, London: Dulau & Co.

West, Anthony (1979) *John Piper*, London: Secker and Warburg

INDEX